Advance Praise for
CONSERVATIVE

"DeMint and Bovard have defined Conservatism in simple, common-sense terms. This book is a much-needed force to unite Americans with positive ideas."
—Mark R. Levin, National Radio and Television Host and Bestselling Author

"Conservative is the most comprehensive exposé on Conservatism in our generation!"
—U.S. Senator Mike Lee (Utah)

"Jim DeMint is the Dean of the Conservative Movement. Rachel Bovard is the Valedictorian. Conservative is their graduate thesis!"
—Charlie Kirk, founder and president of Turning Point USA

"Jim DeMint, one of the most trusted names in Conservatism, teams up with Rachel Bovard, one of the Movement's young, new faces. Together, they skillfully explain why Conservatism is more relevant than ever in this complex, modern moment."
—U.S. Congressman Mark Meadows (North Carolina)

"It is easy to call ourselves 'conservative,' but what does that mean? What exactly are we trying to conserve? The conservative movement is lost without an answer to that question. Conservative provides the answer—concisely and clearly. This book is more urgently needed than ever."
—Matt Walsh, writer and host at *The Daily Wire*

CONSERVATIVE

KNOWING WHAT TO KEEP

JIM DEMINT & RACHEL BOVARD

FIDELIS
BOOKS

A FIDELIS BOOKS BOOK

An Imprint of Post Hill Press

Conservative:
Knowing What to Keep
© 2019 by Jim DeMint and Rachel Bovard
All Rights Reserved

ISBN: 978-1-64293-223-2
ISBN (eBook): 978-1-64293-224-9

Cover Design by Ryan Truso
Author photos by Ed Corrigan

Post Hill Press
New York • Nashville
posthillpress.com

Published in the United States of America

To the patriots at the Conservative Partnership Institute and all our fellow Americans working to build a strong, unified, and effective Conservative Movement.

CONTENTS

FOREWORD

By Congressman Jim Jordan

I try to avoid associating myself with political labels—principally because everyone seems to have a different definition of what they all mean. My job is to do what's best for the people I serve and the country I love. This requires knowing what works and what doesn't. Sounds simple, but nothing is simple in Washington, D.C.

I consider myself a Conservative in a broad sense because I define the term as common sense. If it works, if it makes people's lives better, let's keep it—let's "conserve it." But I'm aware there are many people today who define "Conservative" in very negative ways, such has hateful, bigoted, racists—you probably know the many descriptions of Conservatives used by those on the Left. But real Conservatism has nothing to with these negative pathologies. Quite the opposite. Conservatives want to keep all the positive ideas and policies that made America great in the first place.

Americans need to recapture a philosophy, a worldview, and a belief system to guide us. How can we hold our country together if we have no shared values or common beliefs to unify us? Conservatism is knowing and keeping the principles and practices that have united Americans in the past and learning how to apply proven ideas to the challenges of the future. Conservatism is a discipline that is always building on the things that work.

My high school wrestling coach talked about "discipline" every day. We had to know the basics, practice the basics, and never think we were too good to use the basics in every situation. What are the basics for America today? I believe they are wrapped up in a package we call Conservatism.

And all of us in public service, as well as every American citizen, must have the discipline to draw from the basics with every challenge we face.

This discipline is desperately needed in America today. Many forces are trying to use our diversity to divide us. Like it or not, diversity is who we are. America is the most diverse nation in history. We are, in effect, *the world* because people from all around the world have come here for generations. How do we the "many" become "one"? How does this "E Pluribus Unum" (Out of Many, One) really work?

CONSERVATIVE reminds us of the many good things from the past that can hold all this diversity together in the future—the things we must keep so we can live together in harmony as Americans. I enthusiastically recommend this book to you. It will make you think, even if you don't agree with everything in it.

CONSERVATIVE is unlike any book related to politics I have read recently. It doesn't ignite the reader with indignation by describing all the terrible things being done by the bogeymen on the other side of the political spectrum. It actually fills most of its pages with what is good about America, what made America great in the first place, and what we must do to create a better future for everyone. This book is focused on the science of Conservatism: discovering what has worked in the past and figuring out how to apply those proven principles to today's challenges.

Conservatism is knowing what to throw away and knowing what to keep.

I wholeheartedly call myself a Conservative. And I think you will too after reading this book. Not that we will all agree on every political issue, but we might all see ourselves as a "community of souls" working toward the same goals as described by Russell Kirk.

Kirk, the author of *The Conservative Mind* published in 1953, is arguably the father of modern American Conservatism. This book, *CONSERVATIVE: Knowing What to Keep*, translates Kirk's ideas into a language we can all understand today. I hope it will start a national conversation about how we can actually identify and keep the things that really matter.

The authors of *CONSERVATIVE* are two of the most credible Conservatives I've known. They have both served in the arena we call the "Swamp" and survived unscathed—they still have their integrity.

Jim DeMint was a businessman for twenty-five years before running for Congress. He is, in today's vernacular, an "old white guy." He has a wife of forty-five years, four children, five grandchildren, and he came up the hard way. He earned success in the business world before joining the political fray at forty-seven years old. He served fourteen years in the U.S. House and Senate before founding the Conservative Partnership Institute with Rachel Bovard and other Conservative leaders, and he demonstrated how Conservatives could stand and fight for principles in a constructive and civil way. He has been tested under fire and did not wilt.

Most of DeMint's experience is in what we call "civil society." He understands the things that make America great do not come from the political arena. He knows "government that governs best governs least" (Thomas Jefferson). In other words, Conservatives should work to get the government out of our lives, not think of more ways the government can control us.

Rachel Bovard is a wonderful prototype of a knowledgeable, articulate, and principled millennial Conservative. She is still in her thirties, a prolific writer, and spokesperson for common sense ideas. She also served in the U.S. House and Senate as a staff leader and now trains other young staffers as part of her role at the Conservative Partnership.

The DeMint / Bovard duo provide a good representation of a modern version of Russell Kirk's Conservatism. Their simple focus on the good things we should keep takes the idea of Conservatism far above the political fray, but also provides important political applications of Kirk's Conservative "thought." Importantly, DeMint and Bovard give us insights into the motivation, goals, and organization of the opponents of Conservatism—the Progressive Left.

The battle in America today—just as it has always been—is for freedom. Living in freedom should be the birthright of every American. But there are many on the Left who are fighting against freedom. The policies of Liberals and Progressives are all motivated by one thing: control. *CONSERVATIVE* will help you understand this motivation in terms of all the issues we are debating today. I hope every American will take the time to know what to keep, what to throw away, and how we can fix what's broken. Enjoy!

INTRODUCTION

[...] to conserve the spiritual and intellectual and political tradition of our civilization; and if we are to rescue the modern mind, we must do it very soon [...]. If we are to make that approaching era a time of enlightened Conservatism, rather than an era of stagnant repression, we need to move with decision. The struggle will be decided in the minds of the rising generation—and within that generation, substantially by the minority who have the gift of reason. I do not think we need much fear the decaying "Liberalism" of the retiring generation; as Disraeli said, "Prevailing opinions are generally the opinions of the generation that is passing." But we need to state some certitudes for the benefit of the groping new masters of society.[1]

—Russell Kirk, *The Conservative Mind*

Americans hunger for something real to believe in—honorable leaders and ideas that actually work to make their lives better. The current political system is not satisfying this hunger and people are rebelling. Polished, experienced candidates in both the Democrat and Republican Parties are facing stiff competition from radical but more authentic candidates.

Except for some backroom party sabotage, avowed Socialist Bernie Sanders might have been the Democrat nominee for president in 2016. The same phenomenon played out on the Republican side where Donald Trump—an unconventional candidate dismissed and ridiculed by political pundits—not only became the Republican nominee, but won the presidency.

This unconventional, seemingly spasmodic reaction in our politics speaks to something deeper at work in the American electorate. A pervasive sense of rootlessness and an acute sense of loss imbues our culture and our discourse.

Modern America is unmoored, set adrift by an indifference to history and a powerful sense that our society is infected with something fraudulent and incomprehensible. Our politics have become increasingly hyperbolic and vitriolic—designed by all sides to incite fear and discontent—with our elections defined by unachievable promises, simplistic slogans, and almost no constructive debate or search for common ground. We are at record levels of distrust in our institutions. Attendance at traditional churches is plummeting. Overall, research suggests Americans "are in greater pain than citizens of other countries" and have been growing steadily more miserable for the last several decades.[2]

> According to the *Morbidity and Mortality Weekly Report* of the Centers for Disease Control, the number of suicides in the United States has now surpassed the number of deaths from car accidents. In 2010, there were almost 34,000 deaths from collisions, and 38,000 suicides. Even more alarmingly, the suicide rate for Americans *in mid-life,* ages 35–64, increased between 1999 and 2010 by nearly 30 per cent. This is huge.[3]

Despite being told we have more power than ever before in history, the daily American experience seems to be one of powerlessness. Love of country has declined significantly.

> There's been a sharp decline in American patriotism. Today, only 52 percent of Americans are "extremely proud" of their country, a historical low. Among those 18 to 29, only 34 percent are extremely proud. Americans know less about their history and creed and are less likely to be fervent believers in it.[4]

The obvious question is: why? How is it that, at this peak of technological achievement, prosperity, and opportunity, Americans feel their country is so fundamentally debased?

The answer to this question is far more nuanced than a political solution—though that is, indeed, a component. Rather, Americans are turning inward in search of meaning. The recognition of and desire for community, family, and authenticity is growing, swelling over the tides of a superficial culture that defines self-worth through Facebook likes and self-actualization through triumphing in reality television.

A February 21, 2015 article in *The Washington Post*[5] delved into the questions of why more than a million teenagers were leaving Facebook every year. The article included some insightful comments from one teenager:

> People don't have to hang out with their friends, they can just see what they're doing. [...]. I prefer actually talking to people. I would rather get their number than be friends on Facebook, where you have a 100 friends you never talk to. It's a meaningless friendship [...]. I feel like friend is becoming very vague [...]. It's like the word love[...]. You say love to a lot of people and things you don't actually love. It's more of a compliment now. I know you and I'll talk to you. It's like saying, "We can converse." It's kind of like being polite.

The same teenager continued,

> If you want a girlfriend, go get Facebook. You can get one real fast. You can say whatever you want without real emotion. You can say, "You're attractive. I would like to get to know you." In real life, you'll get all nervous. But there's a drawback to living your social life online—it means you're less likely to be present to the one in front of you.

Americans are becoming dissatisfied with shallow relationships, endless critiques, and negative political narratives unhinged from reality. But they are not sure where to look for real meaning. More of us are beginning to realize the human journey is ultimately the search for what is permanent, for what is immovable and immutable in the midst of the maelstrom. In other words, Americans are searching for what to let go of and what to keep.

While it may shock many—particularly on the Left—this search for authenticity and a concern for the social order is the very essence of Conservatism. The movement of Conservative ideas, though expressed in many ways politically, has a far broader reach in its fundamental concern with the roots of ordered freedom, the virtuous life, and things of permanent worth.

Contrary to the Left, which seeks to elevate the state to the status of the primary object of human loyalty, Conservatism insists that the church, family, and community play leading roles in political life. The very social bonds that are necessary to preserve the social order are nurtured not by the state but at the dinner table, at the local parish or temple, and in community relationships.

This is why Thanksgiving is the heaviest travel time of the year. A Pew Research study confirms why people endure traffic jams and airport lines to get home: Family is America's number one source of meaning, fulfillment, and satisfaction in their lives.

> The Pew survey, conducted in two waves in 2017, found clear and consistent answers among all demographic groups, as nearly 70 percent of Americans mention their family as a source of meaning and fulfillment […] (and) a fifth of Americans said religion is the most meaningful aspect of their lives […] And among those who do find a great deal of meaning in their religious faith, more than half say it is the single most important source of meaning in their lives […] If you then follow up and ask which of these is the most important source of meaning, religion is a clear second (after family).[6]

While our hearts may try to lead us back to the only things that can give real meaning to our lives, almost everything around us screams for us to look somewhere else—to find meaning in some unnatural identity or association. And, as traditional families, religious faith, and the sense of community continue to decline, more Americans are following the loudest messages in our culture. This has led many Americans down a dead-end street. Alienation and social disintegration are rising as we increasingly define ourselves as a class, ethnic group, race, or other disaffected group instead of individuals created by God to serve others in mutual pursuit of genuine happiness.

After several generations of ignoring our history, traditions, and our hearts, the American polis now finds itself deeply divided, alienated, impoverished, and reactionary.

But, in This Chasm, There Is Opportunity

As Russell Kirk was fond of saying, we must "rear up a new generation of protectors of the Permanent Things." Later, he underscored his comment with urgency: "if we are to rescue the modern mind, we must do it very soon."

Filling the current void of values and vision in America can only be accomplished by appeal to the long and well-established ideas that have withstood the ravages of time. Indeed, the early Conservative luminary Willmoore Kendall identified a healthy American culture as one that was kept "alive within itself" with its citizenry steeped in "historical memory, i.e., knowledge of their own traditions—lest in ignorance of them, they forget, like madmen, what and who they are."

The traditions Kirk and Kendall referred to are identified today in the broad terms of Western values or Judeo-Christian beliefs, and, more specifically, to the United States, the principles that shaped Americanism and American exceptionalism. But the definitions of these terms are far more specific, thoughtful, and nuanced than this modern age would have one believe, and are blurred by years of educational neglect and misrepresentation by civil and political leaders. Even the term "traditional" is anathema to many who are disgusted with the status quo.

That modern Conservatism is thought of as intellectually bereft speaks to the power of the American Left, which, in the ultimate Faustian bargain, has traded allegiance to transcendent principles for present gain.

They are aided by the lack of consensus in the modern Conservative movement, which frequently seems unclear about what traditions we are trying to conserve. Without consensus among Conservatives, the void in America's soul will continue to be filled by the empty promises of ambitious elitists who thrive on government power and control—the antithesis of Conservatism. The "presentism" of the Left—defined by Allen Tate as an effort to begin each day as if there were no yesterday—has robbed Americans of their history, and, therefore, our identity as a moral agent.

In this book, we humbly submit ourselves to Kirk's exhortation to restate Conservatism for our current moment. It is incumbent upon Conservatives to state clearly and unambiguously what we are trying to conserve and why it matters.

Americans have tired of the Left's broken promises. And, despite having almost complete dominance for decades over young minds with their charismatic political, media, academic, and entertainment industry advocates, the Left's policies have not delivered results. These visible and undeniable failures have been noticed even by Americans who have been inundated for years by the constant deluge of irrational utopian gibberish. Conservatives offer a positive, reasoned alternative.

Most of us know what works, but the Left has made it politically incorrect to even talk about the policies and practices proven to make life better for everyone. If we are to save America and restore its greatness, we must lead a national discussion about the ideas that made America successful in the first place. That is the goal of this book. We need to rediscover the value of traditions and relearn the art of using proven ideas from the past as building blocks for a better future. This vital connection between the past and the future is foundational to understanding Conservatism.

The Promise and Evolution of Conservatism

The promise of Conservatism is enduring. It is a tradition handed down through the generations, preserving the ancient moral traditions of humanity so that all Americans will have the opportunity to shape the course of their own lives and achieve the things they value.

CONSERVATIVE translates the intellectual precepts of Kirk's *Conservative Mind* into a plain-language, modern-day guide for Conservatives in America and around the world.

Ideas are no small things in politics. Armed with the knowledge contained in *The Conservative Mind* and shaped by the worldview it offered, Conservatives helped win the Cold War, take over the Republican Party, and end decades of Democratic control of Congress. In doing so, they redefined how Americans thought about the federal government and spurred unrivaled growth and prosperity. No less significant, Conservatives reshaped an entire branch of the federal government by refocusing the judiciary on the importance of an originalist understanding of the Constitution.

Yet, despite its victories, it is hard to escape the feeling that Conservatism today is in danger of being routed by the money and rhetorical appeal of the Left. Our foundational societal framework of family, faith, and civility have been dramatically altered. The economic and political traditions of American exceptionalism are being replaced with arbitrary Socialist populism. But these recent setbacks stem more from a misguided understanding of what it actually means to be a Conservative than a defect in its underlying intellectual foundation.

Today's Conservatism hardly resembles the traditions Kirk first identified in 1953. Instead of appealing to proven principles that unite and strengthen our national fabric, politicians calling themselves Conservatives have abandoned its intellectual foundations and redefined Conservativism in terms of their preferred policies. Conservatism has been reduced to arguments about how much the government should spend or not spend on particular programs. There is no consensus definition of Conservatism in America today, and "Conservative" is often used as a term of derision and division.

Liberalism and Progressivism have failed, and Conservatism is ill-defined, maligned, and misunderstood. There is a wide void in our nation's belief system. America needs more than a new political philosophy or label. America needs to restore within itself a worldview that unites and inspires our citizens. Now is the time to fill this void with the principles, practices, policies, and promises of Conservatism. We must act quickly, because there is much damage to repair.

Americans are widely reported to be deeply divided along political, generational, racial, ethnic, economic, and philosophical lines. You've heard the narrative. Baby Boomers can't understand millennials. Whites are bigoted against blacks. Liberals hate Conservatives. Men discriminate against women. The rich take advantage of the poor. Business owners mistreat their employees. If you believe the politicians and the media, America has become a conglomeration of disparate groups who serve themselves at the expense of people in other groups.

Critics would have us believe Americans have little in common to unite us as a nation. This is far from the truth. Most of the divisions in America are caused by people in positions of influence who secure their power by separating people into competing groups and fomenting mistrust. The truth is that most people want the same thing: the opportunity to pursue a life they value. Americans have much more in common than the popular narrative would have us believe.

While you may not currently think of yourself as *a Conservative*, you are probably *conservative*. That's only natural. The disposition to conserve is in our DNA. It is pervasive throughout our culture. From Russell Kirk to iconic country music star Kenny Rogers, we all know that, to survive and thrive, we must know what to throw away and what to keep.

That's why we wrote *CONSERVATIVE*. We want Americans to better understand what it means to be a Conservative on Kirk's intellectual level, as well as on the everyday level where most of us live. And, as a national band of brothers and sisters fighting together to save America, Conservatives need our fellow citizens to have the necessary confidence in our ideas to reassert control over their lives and government.

Government should serve the people, but, currently in America, it does not. Government primarily serves itself and the special interests that support the status quo. This will be difficult to change. But the course of history, especially American history, has been shaped by ordinary individuals doing extraordinary things. As Martin Luther King wrote from a Birmingham jail in 1963, "Human progress never rolls in on wheels of inevitability."[7] No. Progress only happens "through the tireless efforts of men willing to be coworkers with God."[8]

That's why we haven't lost hope. Indeed, we are hopeful because Conservatism, at its core, is more a desire to preserve the good than destroy the bad. Unlike the Left, which seeks to mount a total revolution in every generation, Conservatives look to hold up the good, and point it out to successive generations.

As Richard John Neuhaus put it in his book, *American Babylon*:

> We seek to be faithful in a time not of our choosing but of our testing. We resist the hubris of presuming that it is the definitive time and place of historical promise or tragedy, but it is our time and place. It is a time of many times: a time for dancing, even if to songs of Zion in a foreign land; a time for walking tougher, unintimidated when we seem to be a small and beleaguered band; a time for rejoicing in momentary triumphs, and for defiance in momentary defeats; a time for persistence in reasoned argument, never tiring in proposing to the world a more excellent way.[9]

We wrote this book to enlist as many people as possible to join us in this "tireless effort:" to love the good more than we hate the bad; to improve rather than to dismiss; to build on what works instead of tearing everything down.

It won't be easy. True progress never is. It is our hope by highlighting the eternal truths that have been instrumental to human progress in the past, we will identify the essential ingredients to building a better future—the things we all collectively want to keep. And, by building on the best of the past, we are confident Americans will achieve the fullness of the Conservative promise in the future.

PART I

KNOWING
WHAT TO KEEP

Overview of Chapters 1–6

What Are Conservatism and Progressivism?

As a working premise [...] one can observe here that the essence of social Conservatism is preservation of the ancient moral traditions of humanity. Conservatives respect the wisdom of their ancestors [...] they are dubious of wholesale alteration. They think society is a spiritual reality, possessing an eternal life but a delicate constitution: it cannot be scrapped and recast as if it were a machine. "What is Conservatism?" Abraham Lincoln inquired once. "Is it not adherence to the old and tried, against the new and untried?" It is that, but it is more.

—RUSSELL KIRK

One of the primary goals of this book is to connect with young Americans who have been taught that Conservatism means bigoted, hateful, selfish, racist, white supremacist, and many other pejoratives. The young are most vulnerable to the false promises and propaganda of the Left because they don't have the benefit of observing outcomes over time. We will help them see the future through the clear lens of the past. But this book is not just for the young. All Americans need to know what we should keep from the past and understand why it matters.

We are especially concerned about America's youth, because polling reveals even the basic concept of liberty has become an abstraction. Similarly, America's founding principles and the miracle of economic capitalism, as well as most of the foundational principles that made America great, are misunderstood and held in low esteem by many of America's youth. Without an understanding of the importance of individual liberty and the principles that created the most successful nation in history, young people will continue to be mesmerized and duped by the utopian ideas and empty promises of the Left.

Kirk's use of words such as "ancient," "ancestors," "traditions," and "old" should not discourage our younger readers. These words are simply Kirk's way of saying we need to know what to keep from the past to build a better future. Businesses and organizations refer to this concept as "making the best even better" or continuously improving on "best practices."

Conservativism is not resistant to change. It simply advocates orderly change guided by proven ideas and principles. This is the only way to achieve real and lasting progress. Everything we consider modern that works—especially the technology running the worldwide web and the myriad of digital devices working with it—was developed using a continuous improvement process fueled by generations of "best practices."

Change is inevitable, and the pace of change in America will continue to accelerate exponentially. Conservatism serves as the restraint, the brakes, and the counterbalance when special interests, intellectuals, and politicians attempt to use change as an opportunity to reshape society to fit their worldview. The thoughtful pause of Conservatism allows the "cool and deliberate" sense of community and history to guide change toward real and lasting progress, rather than allowing the country to be carried away by the winds of the faction du jour.

Conservatism as a political movement is not monolithic. It includes social, cultural, economic, and foreign policy Conservatives. There are many varieties of Conservatives—real and imagined. The religious Right, the fusionist movement, libertarians, and neo-cons are just a few of the labels. But, at its root, Conservatism is one overarching and simple concept: the continuous quest to identify, understand, and apply the best ideas of the past to build a better future. In other words, Conservatism is knowing what to keep. Our hope with this book is to unify Americans by helping everyone, especially the young, understand being a Conservative is just common sense.

Most Americans associate the term "Conservative" with politics, but, as we consider and define Conservatism, we will remind our readers it is much more than a political movement or philosophy. Conservatism is: a way of living and looking at the world; the appreciation and value of those who came before; the knowledge of what has been tried, what has succeeded and failed; and the wisdom to know history frequently repeats itself—leading us to focus on what has worked, rather than repeat the mistakes of the past simply because a novel approach sounds exciting or comes in a shiny new rhetorical package.

In other words, Conservatism is an approach to life, not just a shallow political movement.

The primary purpose of Conservatism is to conserve liberty as well as the traditions and institutions that protect and preserve individual liberty.

The clearest examples of how Conservatism works come not from government, but from private sector businesses and organizations. Free-market competition forces businesses and civil institutions to continuously improve products and services. This is why consumers in America are treated to a constant parade of new digital networks, cell phones, tablets, automobiles, on-demand and online entertainment, and churches with casual clothes and live bands. Much of what is offered by the private sector is marketed as "new and improved," even when the products and services may be only 1 percent new and 99 percent old. But 1 percent improvement every year will eventually lead to more advanced and higher quality products based on accumulated improvements over many years. The Wright brothers built the first airplane in 1903. By 1969, we'd built on their technology enough to use rockets to send men to the moon.

Unfortunately, politics and government services often escape the same positive incentives and accountability of free markets. The slow-developing and long-term impact of bad public policies make it difficult for voters to know who to blame. Politicians, therefore, are rarely accountable for the poor results of their promises and policies. This is a serious problem for America because we are on an unsustainable course and voters don't know who to trust for solutions.

America's federal government has acquired virtual monopoly power over vast swaths of public and private life. This has resulted in unsustainable debt, high costs, corruption, inefficiencies, and waste. More importantly, the government's power over education, healthcare, and many private-sector industries has reduced consumer choices, increased prices, lowered quality, and impeded the ability of individuals to make their own decisions about many areas of their lives.

Common sense suggests the continuous improvement approach of the private sector—which is reflective of Conservative principles—should be employed with as many products and services as possible. Federal government monopoly power should be limited to areas such as national defense that cannot be provided by the states or the private sector. But common sense is not common in politics.

Liberals and Progressives—the people and organizations of the Left—seek to concentrate power in the hands of government, despite abundant evidence that government programs often hurt the people they are intended to help. Conservatives—those who want to continuously improve outcomes by building on proven ideas and principles—believe limiting the scope of government and optimizing individual and societal liberty is the most effective way to make life better for everyone.

In addition to their insistence on government control, the Left has demonstrated a tendency toward radical experimentation unmoored from proven principles and policies. Whether it is the redefinition of marriage and the family, abandoning the concepts of character and virtue, denigrating the capitalist economic system, eliminating fossil fuels, diminishing incentives to work, opening our borders to undocumented immigrants, or hollowing out America's military, the Left consistently attempts to replace proven ideas and principles with untested theories and experiments.

This was the approach of Liberals in Kirk's time and continues to be the approach of Progressives today. Kirk described adherents of Liberal philosophies as radicals and revolutionaries, using words such as novelty, impulsive, experimental, superficial, unreasoning, centralization, and secularism to describe their philosophies. Today's Progressives are even more dangerous to free societies than Kirk's Liberals because they are more disdainful of traditions and less willing to employ evidence-based decision-making or to be held accountable for unsuccessful outcomes.

These fundamental differences in approaches—continuous improvement built on proven principles leading to liberty versus continuous experimentation and reinvention of methods leading to poor results and government control—represent the major points of departure between Conservatives and Progressives. These differences are not distinctly represented by the two major political parties in America. Many Democrats understand the value of conservation and many Republicans who claim to be Conservatives are, on some issues, more Progressive than the Democrats. Most politicians are driven less by genuinely held philosophical beliefs than their quests for power and position.

Who will win the battle between Progressives and Conservatives? Kirk, more than thirty years after the first edition of *The Conservative Mind*, says the outcome depends on the commitment of Conservatives.

> Both the impulse to improve and the impulse to conserve are necessary to the healthy functioning of any society. Whether we join our energies to the party of progress or to the party of permanence must depend upon the circumstances of the time. Of rapid change, healthy or unhealthy, we seem sure to experience more than enough in the concluding years of this century. Whether the Conservative impulse with modern society can suffice to prevent the disintegration of the moral order and the civil order by the vertiginous speed of alteration—why, that may hang upon how well today's Conservatives apprehend their patrimony.[1]

Conservatives cannot understand their role in shaping the future until we have a clear definition of what it means to be a Conservative. It is no longer enough to simply repeat Conservative platitudes; we need to re-animate, illustrate, and remake the case for how Conservatism makes life better for everyone. The chapters in Part I of *CONSERVATIVE* will define Conservatism as well as Progressivism by translating Kirk's definitions into today's vernacular. We will also use examples of specific public policies and civil society practices to show how these two philosophies produce totally different results.

Defining the Right: What Is Conservatism?

The Left has exerted more effort defining Conservatism than Conservatives. John Stuart Mill referred to Conservatives as "The Stupid Party." Lionel Trilling wrote that Conservative ideas were "irritable mental gestures which seem to resemble ideas." And today's education establishment, media, and entertainment industry regularly denigrate Conservatives with words and accusations so harsh many Conservatives are afraid to even associate themselves with the label.

Contemporary definitions of Conservatism are shallow and confusing. For example, the definition offered by the online encyclopedia Wikipedia overlooks critical truths. Wikipedia's definition of Conservatism implies the philosophy is opposed to change and supportive of monarchies, which are irrelevant to the American system of government.

> Conservatism is a political and social philosophy promoting traditional social institutions in the context of culture and civilization. The central tenets of Conservatism include tradition, human imperfection, organic society, hierarchy and authority and property rights. Conservatives seek to preserve a range of institutions such as monarchy, religion, parliamentary government and property rights with the aim of emphasizing social stability and continuity while the more extreme elements called reactionaries oppose modernism and seek a return to "the way things were."[2]

The definition above misses the whole point of Conservatism: preserving the ideas and institutions of the past for the purpose of guiding constructive change in the future. Russell Kirk helps us understand Conservatism at a deeper level.

In *The Conservative Mind*, Kirk defines Conservatism using six "canons" of Conservative thought. We have organized Kirk's six "canons" into four principles or tenets of Conservatism. These are the principles we believe America should understand and keep because they have been proven to create liberty, security, and prosperity for individuals and societies.

What Does Liberty Have to Do with Submission to Authority?

First Principle of Conservatism—Submission to God, Law, and External Authority

Russell Kirk summarized his first cannon of Conservative thought as "the belief in a transcendent order." This "thought" likely triggers alarms for many Americans who have been taught religion and spirituality have no place in government or public affairs. But "transcendent order" encompasses much more than religion, and this "thought" exposes one of the fundamental disagreements between Conservatives and Progressives: the true nature of humanity.

Arthur Milikh, in his essay "Civility and Rebarbarization," concludes the Progressive approach (he uses the "fashionable approach"),

> fails to grasp the underlying preconditions for civilized self-government, the means by which human passions are formed toward civility, and the nature of its alternative—barbarism. Having been neglected for so long by our intellectual authorities, civility and barbarism are thought to be merely synonymous with politeness and coarseness. In truth, however, they describe two distinct and opposing organizations of the human character. By rediscovering this distinction, we can revive our understanding of the prerequisites for establishing constitutional republics and clarify how we can preserve our own. [3]

Milikh's article is an exposé on some of John Adams's most profound writings about civilization. Adams, according to Milikh, believes "civility is a condition in which man has been made governable by laws." This can only happen if people are willing "to submit to an authority outside of himself." This training in submission and civility, according to Adams, begins with a willingness to submit to parents, God, and, subsequently, the laws authorized by civil authorities. As Milikh writes, "This 'third person' is an authority outside of oneself to whom one defers and submits, such as law, courts, or God." This is Kirk's "transcendent order."

Within this first principle of Conservatism lies the great irony of liberty. As Ben Franklin said, "only virtuous people are capable of freedom."

Conservatives understand "natural laws," "inalienable rights," and "all men are created equal"—all concepts embedded in America's founding documents—are based on the presumption of the providential guidance of an eternal deity. The "Belief in a Transcendent Order" is the first and most critical foundational principle of Conservative thought. We guarantee the discussion will be provocative and controversial.

How Can Diversity Create Unity?

Second Principle of Conservatism—Celebrate and Preserve the Diversity of the Human Experience

We combine Kirk's second and third canons of Conservative thought into our second principle. Kirk believes Conservatives should respect, celebrate, and enjoy the intrinsic differences in all people. Progressives believe forcing uniformity promotes equality. But the goal of uniformity ignores reality. Everyone is different. People have different aptitudes and interests. We have different learning styles and gifts. Forcing uniformity is repressive, and, ultimately, results in tyranny. We all want different things, which means free societies must accommodate and celebrate human differences. Kirk explains in his second canon:

> "[Conservatives have an] Affection for the proliferating variety and mystery of human existence, as opposed to the narrowing uniformity, egalitarianism, and utilitarian aims of most radical [Progressive] systems."

Kirk's third canon applies human differences to society. Conservatives, Kirk says, have the conviction that civilized society requires orders and classes, as against the notion of a "classless society."

Progressives will squeal bloody murder at this politically incorrect statement because they don't understand it. Kirk is not suggesting societies should be organized by class; he is saying the natural result of diversity is a variety of societal stations. The inherent differences in ages, interests, abilities, skills, and values will naturally result in many different social classes, economic levels, and a wide variety of civic associations—from bowling leagues and Bible studies to exclusive country clubs.

But, in a free society, these different stations should be voluntary and temporary. Liberty requires the opportunity to change one's station in life, the freedom to succeed or fail. Conservatives insist on class mobility—specifically, upward mobility. In a free society, people can be born in poverty (lower class), but, through education, work, and persistence, rise to wealth and prestige (upper class). One person may occupy many different stations and classes during his or her life.

Progressives view the natural differences in conditions and classes as inequality. They seek to remedy this perceived inequality by using the power of government to force class leveling and society uniformity. Kirk offers a more balanced perspective:

"Ultimate equality in the judgment of God and equality before courts of law, are recognized by Conservatives; but equality of condition, they think, means equality in servitude and boredom."

Why Is Owning Property Relevant to Freedom?

Third Principle of Conservatism—Property Rights Are Essential to Liberty

Kirk's fourth canon of Conservative thought highlights the importance of having the freedom to own personal property. He views personal property as the antidote to government tyranny: "[…] separate property from private possession, and Leviathan becomes master of all."[4]

The concept of ownership is inseparable from the reality of liberty. The critical importance of ownership extends far beyond the issue of real property (land, homes, and money). The rights to real property are emblematic of the principles guarding the rights to acquire, possess, and control personal beliefs, opinions, speech, weapons as well as real property. These protections are the purpose of America's Bill of Rights.

Socialist and Communist governments limit individual ownership of property. Inevitably, these governments also limit freedom of religion, speech, gun ownership, and geographic and economic mobility. Progressives in America generally prefer government ownership and control of schools, parks, utilities, public transportation, hospitals, digital networks, and low-income housing. While local or state government ownership may be appropriate in some cases, the tendency of politicians—particularly at the federal level—to prefer government ownership or control over private ownership is a constant threat to liberty. Kirk quotes Paul Elmer More in the excerpt below.

> "Security of property is the first and all-essential duty of a civilized community." Life is a primitive thing; we share it with the beasts; but property is the mark of man alone, the means of civilization; there, says More in a bold phrase which has infuriated his humanitarian opponents, "To the civilized man the rights of property are more important than the right to life."[5]

Why Are Old Ideas Relevant to the Present and the Future?

Fourth Principle of Conservatism—Traditions Are the "Quality Control" for Real and Lasting Progress

Kirk's fifth and six canons are combined into our fourth principle. In his fifth canon, Kirk concludes tradition ("custom, convention, and old prescription") is the best prevention of societal chaos ("man's anarchic impulse and upon the innovator's lust for power").

In canon six, Kirk reminds us of the importance of continuous change in society but warns that good politicians (statesman) are guided by God (Providence) and wisdom (prudence).

"Society must alter, for prudent change is the means of social preservation; but a statesman must take Providence into his calculations, and a statesman's chief virtue, according to Plato and Burke, is prudence."

Traditions are essentially the "best practices" from the past. There is a natural connection between the successes from the past (traditions) and the process of creating a more successful future. Quality control in business means comparing new products to established standards. Traditions are the established standards for society.

Conservatives recognize there have been bad and destructive traditions in America. This is why Conservatives continuously assess what to throw away and what to keep (the "science" of Conservatism). There have been traditions that encouraged unfairness, inequality, and unjust discrimination. But these traditions have been inconsistent with America's founding principles and values. And this is why, over time, those who sought to conserve American values have led the fight against slavery, for civil rights, and for women's rights. The American tradition of equality under the law eventually overcomes the temporal and unjust traditions of inequality.

Defining the Left: What is Progressivism?

Contemporary definitions of Progressivism fail to capture the corrosive nature of this philosophy. Wikipedia's definition of Progressivism sounds reasonable ("advocacy of improvement of society by reform") but omits its history of aggressively seeking change unhinged from proven principles and successful outcomes.

"Progressivism is the support for or advocacy of improvement of society by reform. As a philosophy, it is based on the Idea of Progress, which asserts that advancements in science, technology, economic development, and social organization are vital to the improvement of the human condition."[6]

Who could disagree with Progressivism as defined above? We all want progress and believe "science, technology, economic development, and social organization are vital to the improvement of the human condition." The problem is that this is not how Progressivism works.

Russell Kirk says the principles of Conservatism have remained generally consistent within the six canons of Conservative thought for two centuries, but he finds it more difficult to define the "radical thought" of what we now call Progressives. By nature, Progressives are constantly reinventing their ideas and labels, so it is challenging to identify consistent defining principles.

Kirk explains the "opponents" of Conservatism:

> To catalogue the principles of their opponents is more difficult. At least five major schools of radical thought have competed for public favor since Burke entered politics: the rationalism of the "philosophes," the romantic emancipation of Rousseau and his allies, the utilitarianism of the Benthamites, the positivism of Comte's school, and the collectivistic materialism of Marx and other socialists. This list leaves out of account those scientific doctrines, Darwinism chief among them, which have done so much to undermine the first principles of a Conservative order.

Kirk does find four common denominators of leftist or Progressive (radical) thought but cautions that organizing the tenets of radicalism "probably is presumptuous."

> All the same, in a hastily generalizing fashion one may say that radicalism since 1790 has tended to attack the prescriptive arrangement of society on the following grounds:
> (1) The perfectibility of man and the illimitable progress of society: meliorism. Radicals believe that education, positive legislation, and alteration of environment can produce men like gods; they deny that humanity has a natural proclivity toward violence and sin.
> (2) Contempt for tradition. Reason, impulse, and materialistic determinism are severally preferred as guides to social welfare, trustier than the wisdom of our ancestors. Formal religion is rejected and various ideologies are presented as substitutes.
> (3) Political levelling. Order and privilege are condemned; total democracy, as direct as practicable, is the professed radical ideal. Allied with this spirit, generally, is a dislike of old parliamentary arrangements and an eagerness for centralization and consolidation.
> (4) Economic levelling. The ancient rights of property, especially property in land, are suspect to almost all radicals; and collectivistic reformers hack at the institution of private property root and branch.

"As a fifth point, one might try to define a common radical view of the state's function; but here the chasm of opinion between the chief schools of innovation is too deep for any satisfactory generalization. One can only remark that radicals unite in detesting Burke's description of the state as ordained of God, and his concept of society as joined in perpetuity by a moral bond among the dead, the living, and those yet to be born—the community of souls."[7]

We believe Kirk's fifth point—the Left's view of the role of government—is especially pertinent to today's sharp divisions in political opinions. We have combined Kirk's five points into four principles defining the key elements of Progressive thought.

Aren't All People Basically Good?

First Principle of Progressivism—People Are Perfectible Under the Right Conditions

The Left's view of human nature creates a distorted view of the role of civil society and government. If people are basically good, then all crimes, violence, and human failures are caused by the inequality of conditions. Instead of trying to train and restrain the innate flaws of human nature, the Left is constantly trying to manipulate conditions to create equality and sameness—the same schools, the same healthcare, the same neighborhoods, the same or comparable incomes, the same beliefs, and so forth. Freedom will never create the same conditions for everyone—primarily because people don't want the same conditions. Freedom is the enemy of the Left. Big, controlling government is the only way to achieve their goals.

Aren't Traditions the Cause of Racism, Bigotry and Discrimination?

Second Principle of Progressivism—Traditions Are the Source of Inequality and Injustice

Progressives are constantly maligning America's values and history in an attempt to discredit the ideas that created the greatest nation in the world. They believe American values have created the inequality of conditions that have caused societal pathologies of poverty, crime, and injustice. For the Left, traditions are all about bigotry, racism, inequality, and injustice. You know, the Bad Old Days.

Eric Holder, formerly Attorney General under President Obama, has become a vocal spokesman for the Left's criticism of America's history. He mocked the idea America was ever great in an interview on MSNBC in 2019:

> "When I hear these things about 'Let's make America great again,' I think to myself: 'Exactly when did you think America was great?'"[8]

Most religious traditions insist on hard work, morality, marriage, the sinful nature of mankind, the need for discipline and punishment, and the need for grace and redemption. These ideas are anathema to the Left because they place responsibility for problems on the individual, not society. The traditions derived from the belief in the "transcendent order," as Kirk described it, are the most essential traditions to a free society. Conservatives fight to keep them. This is why the Left is so insistent on destroying any traditions based on Biblical or other traditional religious principles.

Why Shouldn't Government Take from the "Haves" and Give to the "Have Nots"?

Third Progressive Principle—Government Should "Level" Social and Economic Disparities

For the Left, it stands to reason that, if external conditions cause social and economic disparities, then government should forcibly equalize conditions. This means imposing higher taxes on high-income earners and creating welfare programs for the poor. It means forcing young people from different socioeconomic levels into the same schools. It means government housing for the poor. It means everyone has access to the same healthcare. And everyone has the same retirement program. These are traditional Liberal ideas that should be debated with civility.

Russell Kirk's Liberals believed in social welfare and the redistribution of income. Today's Progressives, however, have gone much further. They vilify capitalism and promote socialism. They demean hard work and success, coining disparaging terms such as "white privilege." They persecute Christians and Jews. And they glorify those who protest America.

The Left's answer to historical injustice is for government to destroy the ideas and institutions they believe made America unjust. Despite overwhelming evidence their approach is unraveling the fabric of society, Progressives continue to insist on deconstructing American traditions to achieve their misguided and unachievable worldview.

Isn't Government Control the Only Way to Achieve Fairness?

Fourth Progressive Principle—Government Control Is Necessary to Achieve Equality and Justice

The result of the Left's distorted view of human nature and tradition is their insistence on government ownership, planning, and control—ideas anathema to Conservative thought. From the Left's perspective, only a central power can achieve equality and level socioeconomic conditions for everyone. This is why Progressives push for government programs to address virtually every problem facing America. And this is why the federal government has become a big, blundering dysfunctional behemoth that is corrupt and trillions of dollars in debt.

The following chapters in Part I will focus on the unique and proven Conservative ideas we want to keep. These ideas will be presented in the context of the differences between Conservative and Progressive philosophies and will provide numerous examples of policy differences. Part II of *CONSERVATIVE* will discuss how Progressive policies have failed, how Conservative policies will work to make life better, and how Conservatives can win the battle for the hearts and minds of Americans—and save the country we love.

CHAPTER 1

Keeping Our Covenants

Covenant was the binding together in one body politic of persons who assumed through unlimited promise, responsibility to and for each other, and for the common laws, under God. It was government of the people, by the people, for the people, but always under God, and it was not natural birth into natural society that made one a complete member of the people, but always the moral act of taking upon oneself, through promise, the responsibility of a citizenship that bound itself in the very act of exercising its freedom. For in the covenant conception the essence of freedom does not lie in the liberty of choice among goods, but in the ability to commit oneself for the future to a cause and in the terrible liberty of being able to become a breaker of promise, a traitor to the cause.[1]

—RICHARD NIEBUHR

To be an individual in the 21st century is to be confronted with more options for how to live than anyone else in the history of the world. Today, we can live almost anywhere, in whatever community we decide. We connect across continents with a click on a trackpad or post pictures on Instagram in the middle of the jungle. We define our own gender and personal pronouns. We buy throw pillows with slogans on them telling us to "pursue our own truth"—while selecting from a menu of options about what, exactly, that truth will be.

We have never had this much individual freedom to define who we are and how we will live.

This license has certainly given us more choice. But it is arguable whether these choices have made us freer, our relationships richer, our lives more meaningful, or our society better off. Rather, it seems the option to choose—rather than the substance, the weight, and the contemplation of the choice itself—has become the highest good. (One recalls the plaintive wail of *Sex and the City*'s Charlotte York, "I choose my choice! I choose my choice!") In pursuing our hyper-individualist, choice-saturated lives, we seem to have lost something fundamental.

To paraphrase Conservative scholar Yuval Levin, pursuing society's highest hope—our individual freedom to work, play, and live as we choose—has come at a cost. As society has sprung individuals free from oppressive social constraints—rightly, in many cases—we have diminished the bonds of family, community, work, and faith. In accepting a profusion of options in every part of our lives to meet every conceivable want, we have unraveled society's foundational faith in institutions. In loosening or outright rejecting cultural conformity and national identity, we have deeply fractured our mutual trust—in society, and in one another.

The consequences of this are real and must be acknowledged. A sense of general anxiety, "unrootedness," loneliness, and anomie have begun to define our age. *New York Times* columnist David Brooks diagnosed it more specifically:

> Alienated young men join ISIS so they can have a sense of belonging. Isolated teenagers shoot up schools. Many people grow up in fragmented, disorganized neighborhoods. Political polarization grows because people often don't interact with those on the other side. Racial animosity stubbornly persists.[2]

This is the particular paradox of modernity—individual liberation was supposed to lead to mass empowerment. Instead, it's led to a malaise in our politics and a pervasive sense of powerlessness in our society—a lonely, anxious dysfunction characteristic of our age.

The obvious question is: why? Why are people living in the most successful Liberal democracy on Earth so discontented? Why has the prosperity generated by one of the world's strongest economies not brought a proud sense of accomplishment rather than a general ethos of vague dissatisfaction and self-loathing? "Why," as author Paul Rahe asks, "is there such fury, such disdain for the authorities whose traditions and discipline produced the luxury of such emotion in the first place?"

In other words, why do we rage so hard against the machine when the machine has brought us the means to live as freely as possible?

The "exhaustion of Modernism," so voluminously described by sociologist Daniel Bell, has its roots not in the structural system of our government, but in the means by which we pursue societal happiness.

Even Bell, once a committed Socialist, somewhat reluctantly concluded "the system"—in his case, capitalism—was not ultimately to be blamed for the growing national miasma. That is because the system has less to do with how we live in relation to one another. Rather, citizenship, patriotism, "American-ness," has far more to do with the choices we make than the wealth or abilities we have.

"We are moving into problems of modernity where public policy is not obviously relevant," wrote Charles Murray as he sought to define the pursuit of modern happiness. The modern life has brought us material wealth, but also a need for a new understanding of how the world works—"a historical phenomenon on a grand scale for which Congress presumably has no quick fixes."

That is because of the nature of our relationship to one another, which patterns the relationship we have between ourselves and our government. It's relational, not structural.

As it turns out, people are most effective in pursuing their individual goals and identities when they are grounded in something larger than themselves—community, religion, family, or work, to name a few.

The challenge of our current era is to preserve, as one academic put it, "separability amid situatedness."[3] In other words, how do we maintain the individualism which our freedom cherishes with the social fabric that makes it possible? How do we go off and create and explore and revel in the independence required to push boundaries while maintaining the strong communities and robust cultural infrastructure that gives rise to these values and goals in the first place?

Later chapters will seek to answer this question more specifically. But we propose before those ideas can even be discussed, an even more foundational concept must be reclaimed. And that is the idea of covenant.

What Is a Covenant?

Many Americans, at least those with a decent civics teacher, are likely familiar with the Lockean notion of a social contract. The idea is, as a citizenry, we give the government detailed authorities in exchange for certain services. When the government fails to uphold its end of the bargain, it is the right of the people to withdraw their consent. Contracts are temporary, temporal, and mutable.

A covenant is something entirely different. It is "a relationship of reciprocal concern, the commitment by each to give for the flourishing of the other, generously, not quid pro quo."[4] Put another way, "covenants have three interrelated concepts: permanence (even extending beyond the lives of the promising parties), unconditional love, and involvement (or witness) of God, or, at minimum, the larger community."[5]

In other words, a covenant involves choosing to join in long-term, mutual commitment, pursuits, responsibilities, and concern for the other. It is a commitment based upon principle rather than conditions and is carried out by a way of living rather than an execution of terms.

Couples who marry in a church make a covenant to one another and to God. Babies are baptized or dedicated in a covenant relationship with Christ, their parents, and the church congregation. Neighborhood covenants are formed when people living in community get together to form voluntary agreements to guide how they will live together.

In a national sense, covenants occur when individual citizens make commitments to their fellow citizens, their government, or to a greater, more sacred cause. As Brooks writes, "Out of love of country, soldiers offer the gift of their service. Out of love of their craft, teachers offer students the gift of their attention."

It is this freely given commitment, this care for our country, our family, and our neighbors, that forms the basis of our social fabric. Covenants are not compelled by the government. They arise out of a sense of love, commitment, patriotism, religious duty, or the simple, profound desire to live in community and care for one's neighbor.

This foundational idea of living in thousands of tiny covenants has its roots in the goals of America's founding. Our Constitution is nothing more than a "covenant of covenants," defining the nature of our government as a relationship between equals rather than a hierarchy of the ruling and the ruled.

In that sense, covenants are more about responsibilities than rights— responsibility for ourselves and our fellow citizens. It is about stewardship of our communities, states, and nation. In short, it is about being a citizen bound in covenant with other citizens to build a stronger nation and create a better life for everyone. The preamble to the Constitution sums up the purpose of this covenant:

> We the People of the United States, in Order to form a more perfect Union, establish Justice, insure domestic Tranquility, provide for the common defence, promote the general Welfare, and secure the Blessings of Liberty to ourselves and our Posterity, do ordain and establish this Constitution for the United States of America.

The writers and signers of our Constitution considered themselves part of a covenant with all Americans. "We the People"—not the government, not even the states—established the Constitution. The words "common," "general," and "ourselves" all confirm the understanding this covenant was written on behalf of all Americans.

In his essay, "The Forgotten Key to American Freedom," Os Guinness reminds Americans of the unique nature of our republic's founding and of the importance of keeping our covenant with each other and God.

> If the notions of covenant and constitution are central to the founding of the American republic, then the health or malignancy of their condition must be central to any assessment of the State of the Union, for quite literally they constitute America. A founding creates a nation's DNA, and establishes the lines along which it will develop until and unless the nation is defeated or its founding arrangements replaced. No one can hope to make America great again in any direction without understanding what made America great in the first place. America can neither be understood correctly, nor led well, unless the covenantal and constitutional character of American freedom is taken into account. Covenantalism [sic] and the essential responsibility it requires of citizens provide the missing key to restoring American freedom.[6]

Fundamentally, a covenant is a promise. In declaring fealty to the equality and mutual striving of all men, the Constitution promises the

American government will do its best to create a society in which everyone may equally aspire to happiness—"the lasting and justified satisfaction with one's life as a whole."[7]

The Aristotelian tradition of happiness generally defines lasting satisfaction as grounded in reality, in accord with virtue, and springing from four sources: family, vocation, community and faith. If this seems too simplistic, try thinking of a source of lasting and justified satisfaction that doesn't fit into one of those four. It's hard.

But the other half of that promise is we, as individuals and as communities, will seek to ensure our own happiness—and, more broadly, that of others. Effort, self-donation, individual care, and commitment are required.

This need for individual participation, for people "to take trouble over important things," is what makes the American covenant unique. Alexis de Tocqueville, the great observer of the American character, highlighted it back in 1835 as one of the critical nuances keeping America free and flourishing:

> There are some nations in Europe whose inhabitants think of themselves in a sense as colonists, indifferent to the fate of the place they live in. The greatest changes occur in their country without their cooperation. They are not even aware of precisely what has taken place. They suspect it; they have heard of the event by chance. More than that, they are unconcerned with the fortunes of their village, the safety of their streets, the fate of their church and its vestry. They think that such things have nothing to do with them, that they belong to a powerful stranger called "the government." They enjoy these goods as tenants, without a sense of ownership, and never give a thought to how they might be improved. They are so divorced from their own interests that even when their own security and that of their children is finally compromised, they do not seek to avert the danger themselves but cross their arms and wait for the nation as a whole to come to their aid. Yet as utterly as they sacrifice their own free will, they are no fonder of obedience than anyone else. They submit, it is true, to the whims of a clerk, but no sooner is force removed than they are glad to defy the law as a defeated enemy. Thus one finds them ever wavering between servitude and license.[8]

Lately, this "ownership" of and responsibility for our mutual liberties have been misconstrued as an entitlement. The covenant language of our

Constitution has been replaced with contractual attitudes—"I'm here, I'm an American, my government owes me!" The sacrifices and vision of those who strained to build this nation are now treated as a trust fund to be accessed, rather than a tradition to be sustained.

Essayist Marilynne Robinson characterizes this distinction deftly in describing the growth of the phrase "taxpayers" to define Americans, rather than the term "citizen."

> There has been a fundamental shift in the American consciousness. The Citizen has become the Taxpayer. In consequence of the shift, public assets have become public burdens. [...]. While the Citizen can entertain aspirations for the society as a whole and take pride in its achievements, the Taxpayer, as presently imagined, simply does not want to pay taxes.
>
> [...] Citizenship, which once implied obligation, is now deflated. It is treated as a limited good that ought to be limited further. Of course, the degree to which the Citizen and the Taxpayer ever existed, exist now, or can be set apart as distinct types is a question complicated by the fact that they are imposed on public consciousness by interest groups, by politicians playing to constituencies, and by journalism that repeats and reinforces unreflectingly whatever gimmicky notion is in the air. It can be said, however, that whenever the Taxpayer is invoked as the protagonist in the public drama, a stalwart defender of his own, and a past and potential martyr to a culture of dependency and governmental overreach, we need not look for generosity, imagination, wit, poetry, or eloquence. We certainly need not look for the humanism Tocqueville saw as the moving force behind democracy.[9]

This is not at all what America, a country founded on a "covenant of covenants," promises us. Before we can know what else to keep, we must re-learn how to keep our covenants.

America's Covenant: Two Parties Equally Yoked

"All men have equal rights," wrote Edmund Burke, "but not to equal things." In other words, your citizenship grants you nothing but a level playing field, what Abraham Lincoln called, "an unfettered start and a fair chance in the race of life." We—as individuals and as part of our communities—must do the rest.

This is where the idea of a covenant descends from the realm of the philosophical onto terra firma. Our Constitution establishes that all men, being equal, shall have an equal right to the pursuit of happiness. But what does that look like, in practice?

When it comes to the pursuit of happiness, philosophers from Aristotle to Charles Murray to the rapper Tupac Shakur have observed that happiness can't be found in a vacuum. It occurs in the context of communities, where people's core needs are met and their individuality developed. Indeed, before there is individual flourishing, there must be community flourishing. As Robert Nisbet wrote in *The Quest for Community*, it is the family, religious associations, and local community that "are essentially prior to the individual and are the indispensable supports of belief and conduct."[10]

A good community is simply our larger constitutional covenant writ small. It is neighbors attending to neighbors, creating rules about how they will live together, caring for their shared goals and contributing individually to a shared ideal, a corporate whole. Burke called this mutual striving of neighbors the "little platoons."

> To be attached to the subdivision, to love the little platoon we belong to in society, is the first principle (the germ as it were) of public affections. It is the first link in the series by which we proceed towards a love of our country, and to mankind.

Social organization in communities is vital to individual flourishing and to the pursuit of happiness. It makes sense. Where else can you experience the greatest joys, sorrows, satisfactions, and general preoccupations of daily life but in your community?

The pursuit of happiness, then, comes when an individual is allowed to form a community: a little platoon of people voluntarily doing important things together. As Murray put it in his larger meditation on happiness and good government,

> No one has to teach people how to pursue happiness. Unless impeded, people form communities that allow them to get the most satisfaction from the material resources they have. Unless impeded, they enforce norms of safety that they find adequate. Unless impeded, they develop

norms of self-respect that are satisfying and realistic for members of that community[...].[11]

The government's side of the equation—its role in this covenant among citizens—is thus made clear: to create the "enabling conditions" for individuals to freely form communities and pursue meaning by freely choosing, risking, and cultivating rewards. In other words, to leave "the important things in life for people to do for themselves," and protecting people from the roadblocks that would hinder them in those pursuits.

This covenant relationship becomes distorted when either side of it becomes coercive; when the government centralizes a solution to community problems, or when a majority faction of individuals uses the state to impose their vision of the good on the rest of society. Fundamentally, this distorts the balance of power in the covenant relationship and thus, the free pursuit of happiness.

As the Hungarian psychologist Mihaly Csikszentmihalyi has formulated, people are happiest when they are able to balance challenge and skills. The possibility of failure is something centralized governments often seek to prohibit—but it is in the possibility of failure that the concept of "measuring up" resides. Take away the ability to fail and you take away the capacity to triumph, removing the ability to develop the self-respect that makes life meaningful.

Though it seems counterintuitive, a government that allows individuals to face and overcome challenge to some extent is one that facilitates the development of a mature citizenry able to pursue meaningful lives. Tocqueville put it another way: "Happiness is impossible unless people are left alone to take trouble over important things."

A government keeping its covenant under the American Constitution is one with a stopping point; that limits what it does for people—not just because of budgets, but because humanity depends on the exercise of human potential.

People who keep their covenants nourish and sustain them. They give of themselves to their communities, each derived of small or large covenants, to care for one another's well-being across income, social, and racial divides toward the larger purpose of protecting and promoting a collective commitment to individual liberty.

25

How Covenants Can Lift Us—and Replace the Forces Tearing Us Down

The distinction between a social contract—the idea that we are entitled to services as a condition of citizenship—and a social covenant—the belief that our citizenship is made up of thousands of individuals freely giving of themselves in community—has never been more central to our national dialogue.

The deep divisions in America today are caused, in large part, by people who don't consider themselves in covenant with their fellow citizens or their government. Many see themselves in blind competition with others to get better placement for themselves in society and more resources from the government. Others have fallen prey to the false notion that to pursue social change, one most uproot and remake the system entirely.

All these distort the fundamental nature of the American covenant, which is cooperative rather than competitive, and, when implemented correctly, prioritizes the liberty of the individual to pursue his own happiness rather than regressing his potential to that of the mean.

But covenants also contain the seeds of social reform, a critical point missed by those who would upend America's covenant rather than work within it. A covenant relationship seeks to better each person in it, to strive to be the best version of oneself—whether in individual relationships, community relationships, or, particularly, in the constitutional covenant Americans make with one another.

Indeed, the American founding was an affirmation of human beings' potential to build the best of all possible earthly worlds. Bernard Bailyn surmised the founders' optimism in *The Ideological Origins of the American Revolution*:

> The details of this new world were not as yet clearly depicted; but faith ran high that a better world than any that had ever been known could be built where authority was distrusted and held in constant scrutiny; where the status of men flowed from their achievements and from their personal qualities, not from distinctions ascribed to them at birth; and where the use of power over the lives of men was jealously guarded and severely restricted. It was only where there was this defiance, this refusal to truckle, this distrust of all authority, political or social, that institutions could express human aspirations.

But the founders were also distrustful of the innate human impulse toward self-interest. James Madison, specifically, warned against men collectively destroying their freedoms via factions—that is, "a number of citizens, whether amounting to a majority or a minority of the whole, who are united and actuated by some common impulse of passion, or of interest, adverse to the rights of other citizens, or to the permanent and aggregate interests of the community."[12]

Suppressing factions is not an option—because banning them or demanding everyone share the same views and opinions requires a totalitarian state. (Indeed, diversity of thought and preservation of free discourse in the public square is something we will touch on later as a critical value America must, without question, keep.)

The founders sought instead to create a Constitution that was the ultimate covenant—a dispersal of power among various branches, each with a contributing responsibility to the betterment of the other. No branch can exist independently, but each is interdependent and reliant on the others to, at times, sharpen, mollify, or encourage its exercise of its powers.

This is what the founders intended for individuals too. A representative government deriving its character from the people at once provides a forum for individuals to exercise their freedoms, as well as a requirement they seek to hold the government accountable to protecting the founders' image of man: autonomous actors sharing equal dignity and rights, full of potential, and able to pursue happiness that accompanies the free working-out of his or her life.

In other words, the Constitution-as-covenant pushes us always to strive toward the "better angels of our nature," to use Abraham Lincoln's phrase. It pushes us to become the best version of ourselves and our government a continual reflection of that aspiration.

This is at odds with how many currently view the American covenant—be it the order of our communities, government, values, or traditions. Groups like Antifa heckle the police, belittle America's history as racist, and deem our cherished symbols as patriarchal. Factions on the Left reject long-held American value systems as systemic obstacles to progress. Groups like Black Lives Matter and white supremacy groups on the alt-Right further seek to divide Americans into racial groups, suggesting some groups deserve different treatment than others.

All of this runs directly counter to how the American system was designed to work. Justice, equality, opportunity—all these ends are noble; in fact, we could call them covenantal pursuits. But to pursue these ends by blowing up the system that made their attainment possible is short-sighted.

A Continual Betterment

The American constitutional covenant demands our continual betterment as individuals and a society. The key to reform is the reapplication of our unchanging ideals to our ever-changing times. The equal rights to life, liberty, and the pursuit of happiness are unifying—indeed, universal—principles. The fact that injustice persists does not mean justice is a lie; it means we need to constantly recommit ourselves to it. Reform is only sustainable when it is an inclusive reassertion of our covenant.

The civil rights movement accomplished some of the greatest social triumphs of the 20th century. Martin Luther King Jr., who inspired many of the movement's victories, did so by appealing to the very virtues on which the country's covenant is based. King considered our founding documents to be "promissory notes" in need of redemption.

"All we say to America," he said in 1968, "is 'Be true to what you said on paper.'" He went on:

> If I lived in China or even Russia, or any totalitarian country, maybe I could understand the denial of certain basic First Amendment privileges, because they hadn't committed themselves to that over there. But somewhere I read of the freedom of assembly. Somewhere I read of the freedom of speech. Somewhere I read of the freedom of press. Somewhere I read that the greatness of America is the right to protest for right.[13]

By appealing to our constitutional virtues, King made the case that the injustices being done to black Americans were the result of America's failure to keep its covenant—not the result of the covenant itself.

To be clear, King used more than just words to achieve much-needed social reform. He preached a strategy of non-violence, but one using his constitutional rights to their fullest; he spoke, wrote, assembled, marched, boycotted, peacefully protested, and rallied countrywide. He did so while facing terror, violence, unjust imprisonment, mobs, dogs, and tear gas.

Yet King and his movement never once declared America—the country that had perpetuated generations of injustice against blacks—as a failure, as an effigy to be burned, or as a failed system to be dismantled.

"I criticize America because I love her," King said in a speech about the Vietnam War, "and because I want to see her stand as the moral example of the world."

King continued to lift the American covenant as something not yet fully achieved. His speeches reminded Americans our shared constitutional covenant declares all men equal, and until that was true in practice and in law, our shared commitment to America meant we all had a responsibility to make it right.

For King, his movement was as much about all Americans as it was about black Americans. "Let us be dissatisfied until that day when nobody will shout, 'White Power!' when nobody will shout 'Black Power!' but everybody will talk about God's power and human power," he said in a speech in 1967.[14]

Indeed, King's late wife, Coretta Scott King, characterized her husband's legacy as a mutual commitment of all people—not just black Americans—to America's betterment. "It is a day of interracial and intercultural cooperation," she said of the federal holiday which honors her husband.

> Whether you are African-American, Hispanic or Native American, whether you are a Caucasian or Asian-American, you are part of the great dream Martin Luther King, Jr. had for America. This is not a black holiday; it is a peoples' holiday. And it is the young people of all races and religions who hold the keys to the fulfillment of his dream [...]. The holiday celebrates his vision of ecumenical solidarity, his insistence that all faiths had something meaningful to contribute to building the beloved community.[15]

King's words and actions were at times harshly critical of the country, the government, and its social policies. But at no point did he lose hope the nation could be made better. For King, it was not about upending the system, despite how terribly it treated him. It was about fulfilling the vision of America as a nation of equals—for black Americans and for everyone.

His oft-repeated quote, "injustice anywhere is a threat to justice everywhere" has been used by the Left as a cudgel against their perceived opponents, as a means to justify violent protests and rhetoric that seeks to de-legitimize America as a country rather than to improve it. Those who do so miss the key context of King's quote which is found in his "Letter from a Birmingham Jail."[16]

> Injustice anywhere is a threat to justice everywhere. We are caught in an inescapable network of mutuality, tied in a single garment of destiny. Whatever affects one directly, affects all indirectly. Never again can we afford to live with the narrow, provincial "outside agitator" idea. Anyone who lives inside the United States can never be considered an outsider anywhere within its bounds.

In other words, despite our differences, we are all in this together. Keeping our covenants requires us to do so across neighborhoods, political affiliations, religious differences, racial differences, and social class. Dragging down one class or one group and dismissing them as unworthy of the American ideal or the reverse, elevating one group for special treatment over another—whatever the reason—leads to the same outcome. We all suffer.

Where Modern Movements Fail

Compare King's soaring appeals to unimpeachable sources—the Constitution and the Declaration of Independence—to contemporary protest movements, which seem to value the act of protest and destruction over the articulation of an actual unifying and sustainable vision.

Justifying violence, physical harm, foul language, and destruction of property in the name of "social justice" or "equality" completely misses the point. Members of Antifa and other violent groups justify violent behavior by seeking to reject the system they feel has betrayed them. There is no appeal to a higher ideal, nor is there a unifying message that seeks to restore America to a shared vision.

Voicing grievances against the government is a long American tradition, but, as King demonstrated, sustainable change comes from working within our shared ideals—not demanding they be destroyed and rebuilt in an externally-imposed image.

And it's not just King's example we can point to. Movements that are critical of America, but ones whose criticism resides within a deep sense of patriotism and adherence to America's shared values, have given root to many important and lasting social changes. Historian Michael Kazin summarizes a few:

> Thomas Paine, born in England, praised his adopted homeland as an "asylum for mankind"—which gave him a forum to denounce regressive taxes and propose free public education. Elizabeth Cady Stanton co-authored a "Declaration of Rights of Women" on the centennial of the Declaration of Independence and argued that denying the vote to women was a violation of the 14th Amendment. The Populists vowed to "restore the Government of the Republic to the hands of the 'plain people' with which class it originated" through such methods as an eight-hour day and nationalization of the railroads. In the 1930s, sit-down strikers proudly carried American flags into the auto plants they occupied and announced that they were battling for "industrial democracy." Twenty years later, Martin Luther King Jr. told his fellow bus boycotters, "If we are wrong—the Supreme Court of this nation is wrong" and proclaimed that "the great glory of American democracy is the right to protest for right."
>
> One could list analogous statements from pioneering reformers such as Jane Addams and Betty Friedan, industrial unionists John L. Lewis and Cesar Chavez, and the gay liberationist Harvey Milk. Without patriotic appeals, the great social movements that weakened inequalities of class, gender and race in the United States—and spread their message around the world—never would have gotten off the ground.[17]

Moreover, as Kazin points out, "it is difficult to think of any American radical or reformer who repudiated the national belief system and still had a major impact on U.S. politics and policy."

Even the movement against the Vietnam War remained on the fringes when it was led by Abbie Hoffman and marked by flag burning, waving Viet-Cong symbols, and violence by the Weather Underground. It wasn't until the movement drew in the leadership of such Liberal patriots as Walter Reuther and Eugene McCarthy—men who truly believed in the values of America as much as they believed in their cause—that the country began to take it seriously.

Successful and lasting social change comes from working within our covenantal system rather than attempting to upend it. Our nation has a long tradition of being bettered by people who understood this. After all, how can one seriously engage in a conversation about improving America, or protecting her, if the nation does not hold a privileged place in one's heart? As Russell Kirk pointed out, "Men cannot improve a society by setting fire to it: they must seek out its old virtues, and bring them back into the light."[18]

Keeping Our Covenants

Those who love America have always fought to change it when it fails to live up to its founding vision. This is America's covenant. But we are in danger of losing it—not just to those who reject its covenant traditions, but to a government that seeks to displace the core functions of communities, remove the risk inherent in individual striving, and take unto itself the tending of important things.

America, as a covenant, requires us to set aside what divides us— creed, class, race, religion—and instead focus on what it is that unites us: our shared citizenship and shared striving to make our communities, our country, and our world a better place.

During the Civil War, the greatest period of national fragmentation we have yet faced, Abraham Lincoln again and again appealed to the shared love of country, and to America's long tradition of striving to meet its aspirational vision.

> They [the founders] meant to set up a standard maxim for free society, which should be familiar to all, and revered by all; constantly looked to, constantly labored for, and even though never perfectly attained, constantly approximated, and thereby constantly spreading and deepening its influence, and augmenting the happiness and value of life to all people of all colors everywhere.[19]

Our social fabric can only be repaired by millions of Americans deciding to reach across boundaries and make the local covenants that are the tradition of our shared, collective life. In an interview in 2016, Sen. Cory Booker (D-N.J.) articulated this by distinguishing between mere tolerance and the patriotism that defines our American covenant. Tolerance, he said, means, "I'm going to stomach your right to be different, but if you disappear off the face of the earth I'm no worse off."

Patriotism, on the other hand, means "love of country, which necessitates love of each other, that we have to be a nation that aspires for love, which recognizes that you have worth and dignity and I need you. You are part of my whole, part of the promise of this country."[20]

Fundamentally, America's covenant is a promise of continual striving, of a constant aspiration to improve ourselves as communities and a nation—improvements which will then be reflected in our government. But our larger covenants must be sealed every day by the thousands of tiny covenants we make in our local sphere, within our communities. To return to Burke, we must learn to love our little platoons. That is, before we can grow our wider public affection (love of country), we must first cultivate our smaller loyalties to family and community.

The benefits of citizenship require us as individuals to keep our covenants. This means we must deliberately choose to engage one another as fellow travelers, to weigh in with thoughtfulness and passion rather than to opt out with a social media riposte or a tawdry meme, and to build up those individuals and institutions around us rather than to dismiss their legitimacy and tear them down for some historical betrayal.

In a letter to his friend David Hartley in 1787, Thomas Jefferson called this notion of America "our experiment." It remains so. America was never an immutable concept written in stone as a guide for the ruling to govern the ruled. Rather, as a covenant among equal citizens, America as a concept has the room to grow, change, evolve, and be made better, to pursue what James Madison called "a new and more noble course."

Ultimately, the American covenant asks that before we claim anything for ourselves, we give of ourselves first. The first thing to keep is our covenant.

CHAPTER 2

Keeping Our Faith

It was religion that gave birth to the English colonies in America. One must never forget that [...] I can see the whole destiny of America contained in the first Puritan who landed on those shores [...] Despotism may be able to do without faith, but freedom cannot [...] When a people's religion is destroyed [...] then not only will they let their freedom be taken from them, but often they actually hand it over themselves.[1]

—ALEXIS DE TOCQUEVILLE

When we think about what to keep it helps to put first things first. And the first thing—the one thing more important than everything else—is religion. Put simply, our relationship with God—including exercising one's choice not to have one—defines all our other relationships: with our families; our friends and neighbors; and even our country and governments. Freedom of religion secures our covenant as "We the People" with our fellow citizens and with God.

Your authors are Christians—DeMint is evangelical, and Bovard is Roman Catholic—so maybe you're thinking that while religion is important to us, it's not necessarily to everyone or to the country as a whole. Religion, however, is essential to keeping everything we all care about, and you don't have to take our word for it.

There is a reason the first freedom singled out for special protection in the First Amendment to the U.S. Constitution was religious freedom:

"Congress shall make no law respecting an establishment of religion, or prohibiting the free exercise thereof [...]"

Why would religion come first, even before freedom of speech, freedom of the press, or the freedom of peaceful assembly, which on the surface might seem to be more important to a healthy constitutional republic?

The father of the Constitution, James Madison, provided a hint of an answer in an essay he wrote in 1785, opposing a bill in the Virginia Legislature that would have provided government subsidies for Christian teachers:

> "It is the duty of every man to render to the Creator such homage and such only as he believes to be acceptable to Him. This duty is precedent, both in order of time and in degree of obligation, to the claims of Civil Society."[2]

"Precedent," Madison wrote, as in preceding—coming first. As Yuval Levin of the Ethics and Public Policy Foundation puts it: "Religious liberty, in this view [...] is not a freedom to do what you want, but a freedom to do what you must."

This is the key difference separating religion and religious freedom from other political concerns, both in the building of our own lives and in the making of public policy. As John F. Kennedy famously put it in 1962, "To govern is to choose." But, when it comes to faithfully practicing one's religion, there is no choice. Evangelical Christians must accept Jesus Christ as their personal savior. Roman Catholics must attend mass on holy days of obligation. Practicing Muslims must fast during Ramadan and pray five times a day. Orthodox Jews must keep to a kosher diet. Pick any religion or denomination and you'll find spiritual or practical red lines its adherents may not cross—no matter what.

Most Americans not only understand this but embrace it. Partially, this is just good manners. After all, the United States has been an ethnically, culturally, and religiously diverse society since before we were one country. As we all know from our own life experiences—often even within our own families—the best way to navigate diversity is with mutual respect and tolerance. As George Mason and his coauthors, including James Madison, affirmed in the Virginia Declaration of Rights in 1776:

> Religion, or the duty which we owe to our Creator, and the manner of discharging it, can be directed only by reason and conviction, not by

force or violence; and therefore all men are equally entitled to the free exercise of religion, according to the dictates of conscience; and that it is the mutual duty of all to practise Christian forbearance, love, and charity toward each other.

In this sense, America's long tradition of religious freedom amounts to a society-wide agreement to protect everyone's freedom of conscience by agreeing to infringe on no one's.

But, as our founders knew, and our history affirms, there's more to it than that.

Civic Order and Transcendent Order

Russell Kirk, our guide in knowing what to keep, insisted that a belief in a "transcendent order" must be the first tenet of a free society and the most essential pillar of Conservatism.

> Among the props of order in democratic societies, the chief is religion; and Tocqueville found in his American observation some reassurance on this score. Democratic peoples simplify religion, certainly; but it may remain with them as an abiding force, helping to counteract that materialism which leads to democratic despotism.[3]

Religion, in this sense, is not simply something to keep because it satisfies individuals' consciences, but because, collectively, the byproducts of religion protect our society and sustain our republic. Religious freedom by itself doesn't necessarily make Christianity, Judaism, Islam, or any other religion better off, but it has been proved to make America better off.

George Washington thought so:

> Of all the dispositions and habits which lead to political prosperity, religion and morality are indispensable supports. In vain would that man claim the tribute of patriotism, who should labor to subvert these great pillars of human happiness, these firmest props of the duties of men and citizens. The mere politician, equally with the pious man, ought to respect and to cherish them. A volume could not trace all their connections with private and public felicity. Let it simply be asked where is the security for property, for reputation, for life, if the sense of religious obligation deserts the oaths, which are the instruments of investigation in Courts of Justice? And let us with caution indulge

the supposition that morality can be maintained without religion. Whatever may be conceded to the influence of refined education on minds of peculiar structure, reason and experience both forbid us to expect that National morality can prevail in exclusion of religious principle.[4]

John Adams, too:

We have no government armed with powers capable of contending with human passions unbridled by morality and religion. Avarice, ambition, revenge, or gallantry would break the strongest cords of our Constitution as a whale goes through a net. Our Constitution was made only for a moral and religious people. It is wholly inadequate to the government of any other.[5]

Thomas Jefferson wrote the "Statute of Virginia for Religious Liberty" and considered it one of the crowning achievements of his life.

Alexis de Tocqueville, the French historian considered the most insightful observer of the young American republic, saw it too:

It was religion that gave birth to the English colonies in America. One must never forget that [...] Despotism may be able to do without faith, but freedom cannot [...] When a people's religion is destroyed [...] then not only will they let their freedom be taken from them, but often they actually hand it over themselves.[6]

More recently, President Dwight Eisenhower, who signed the law adding "under God" to our Pledge of Allegiance, said:

"Without God, there could be no American form of Government, nor an American way of life. Recognition of the Supreme Being is the first, the most basic, expression of Americanism."

Fast forward to the 1980s, and President Ronald Reagan—just a few months before winning a forty-nine-state landslide re-election—said this to an ecumenical prayer breakfast in Texas:

"Without God, there is a coarsening of the society. And without God, democracy will not and cannot long endure. If we ever forget that we're one nation under God, then we will be a nation gone under."[7]

Importantly, these men came not only from diverse cultures—spanning across a continent and centuries of time—but held divergent religious beliefs. Washington was an Anglican from the Southern aristocracy.

Adams was a Unitarian from Puritan-inflected Massachusetts. Jefferson was a kind of Deist who famously edited his Bible, cutting out parts he disliked. Tocqueville was a French Catholic. Eisenhower was a Midwestern Presbyterian. Reagan considered himself a "born-again" Christian.

Despite their differences—or maybe, in part, because of them—they all embraced the principle of religious freedom, both out of the due respect deserving individuals' consciences and for the benefits a religious citizenry bequeathed to the republic. Those benefits are not merely spiritual; they are practical.

Our founders—and generations of American leaders from every political party—understood that the success of the American experiment depended utterly on religion and the freedom to practice it. They understood the foundation of democratic self-government is moral self-government—smaller government depends on bigger citizens.

Religion and Individual Freedom

America—even before the founding of the republic—drew on a cultural heritage rooted in ancient Greece and Rome and on vibrant religious traditions.

Biblical tenets were not practiced by everyone who lived in the early American colonies, but biblical values, principles, and practices created "morally meaningful communities" throughout the New World. The connection between God, the Bible, Christianity, virtue, law, individual responsibility, citizenship, and freedom were unquestioned by those who shaped America's founding.

Both Catholicism and Protestantism, in particular, ran in the veins of America's founding. The Protestants, urged on by the independent spirit of Martin Luther, embodied modern notions of freedom by emphasizing individuality and freedom of conscience in life and worship. These early adherents flocked to the American colonies, bringing with them a strong faith in God, a deep sense of individual responsibility, and an unwavering demand for freedom to worship according to the dictates of their conscience.

The Catholics, though raised in a religious and intellectual tradition that formed many of the bulwarks of western civilization—individualism, virtue and morality, science, capitalism, and fixed laws—initially were discriminated against under British imperialism. Under British rule, "Catholics could not practice their faith openly, raise their children in faith or send them to Catholic schools, they could not vote, service in the legislature or in professions like law, and their lands were double taxed."[8, 9]

But all denominations in the early colonies understood the shared ideals of freedom, individual rights, and the ability of all to worship in the way they saw fit. Men of all religious denominations signed the Declaration of Independence: Episcopalians, Presbyterians, Deists, Quakers, Unitarians, Catholics, and Congregationalists.

They were not blind to the role religion played in enshrining individual rights. In fact, service to God was what defined the early concepts of American freedom. As Conservative columnist George Will wrote:

> Because freedom is God-given, it requires responsibility as well as gratitude. Freedom does not mean the right to do whatever a person pleases. That would not be freedom but would be chaos and anarchy— the worst kind of bondage. The Biblical concept of freedom involves the ability to make choices and to assume responsibility for those choices.[10]

Charles Carroll, the classically trained patriot who was the sole Roman Catholic signer of the Declaration, put a finer point on it:

> "What are deserving of immortality? They who serve God in truth, and they who have rendered great, essential and disinterested services and benefits to their country."

Progressivism Is the Left's Religion

In time, this spiritual decentralization took hold in politics as well—most especially in the new American republic. The founders' vision of popular sovereignty and equal justice under the law mirrored Luther's theory of a "universal priesthood." Both placed the individual—governed first and foremost by his or her own conscience—at the center of the story. As the Declaration of Independence shouted to all history:

> We hold these truths to be self-evident, that all men are created equal, that they are endowed, by their Creator, with certain unalienable Rights, that among these are Life, Liberty, and the pursuit of Happiness.

Given the primacy of conscience to the founders, the government they forged was specifically prohibited from either imposing religious ideas on the citizenry or hindering an individual citizen's endeavors to live out their faith in society. The only centralized authority government was given regarding religion was the power to protect citizens' space to practice theirs. In this way, the United States would not serve any one creed, and by doing so, would serve all of them equally.

The Progressive Left today rejects this with extreme prejudice. It's not because they hate religion. They just hate everyone else's. For Progressives today, politics is the one true faith.

Their causes—from environmentalism to gun control to abortion to health care or welfare policy to their identity politics extremism—are not policy positions but transcendent moral principles. Listen to the way they advocate their preferred reforms.

They don't engage Conservatives as opponents but accuse them as heretics full of hateful ideas warranting no place in public debate. People who disagree with their energy regulation ideas are "climate deniers," borrowing a term originally coined for neo-Nazis. Pro-Life activists, including Catholic nuns or moms with young children, are portrayed as "haters of women." Congressman Paul Ryan (R-WI), who proposed a plan to save Social Security and Medicare from the fiscal death-spiral they are about to enter, was portrayed in a political attack ad as killing an old woman. And any politician who publicly supports the plain language of the Second Amendment is held responsible for—and indeed, bloodthirsty for—mass murders.

If you follow the Left's rhetoric and tactics closely, a frightening realization settles in. They're not trying to erect a wall between church and state, but rather build walls around their own church and imprison every heart, mind, and conscience in America within them. They're not trying to sweep the public sphere of religion altogether. They're trying to establish a new, official, state religion—like medieval kings or sultans—in which "error has no rights."[11]

The Left's Crusade

Consider the Progressive Left's most recent skirmishes against religious Conservatives, and a clear pattern emerges.

Exhibit A: "Not Someone Who This Country Is Supposed to Be About"

In 2018, Russell Vought testified before the Senate Budget Committee. He was nominated by President Trump to serve as Deputy Director of the Office of Management and Budget. Ranking Committee Democrat Bernie Sanders of Vermont accused Vought of being "hateful" and "Islamophobic." Sanders took issue with a piece Vought wrote in January 2016 about a controversy at the nominee's alma mater, Wheaton College. The Christian school fired a political science professor for expressing solidarity with Islam. Vought defended the school saying a religious school had the right to employ only those who supported its views. Senator Sanders took particular umbrage with Mr. Vought's statement that Muslims "do not know God because they have rejected Jesus Christ his Son, and they stand condemned."[12]

Sanders repeatedly demanded Vought explain his theological beliefs about salvation and judgment, and repeatedly cut Vought off as he tried to educate Sanders about Christianity 101. Senator Sanders insisted the traditional view of all Christians—that a personal faith in Jesus Christ is the only way to Heaven—was grounds for disqualification from public office.

"In my view," Sanders said, "the statement made by Mr. Vought is indefensible, it is hateful, it is Islamophobic, and it is an insult to over a billion Muslims throughout the world [...]. This country, since its inception, has struggled, sometimes with great pain, to overcome discrimination of all forms [...] we must not go backwards."[13]

He concluded his questioning by saying, "I would simply say, Mr. Chairman, that this nominee is really not someone who this country is supposed to be about." Mr. Vought was confirmed for the position in the Budget office, but not one Democrat senator voted to confirm him.[14]

Exhibit B: "The Dogma Lives Loudly with You."

In 2017, a law professor from the University of Notre Dame named Amy Coney Barrett was nominated by President Trump to serve on the federal Court of Appeals in Chicago. Barrett was viewed as "controversial" by Progressive Democrats because she (a) was Catholic, (b) was involved in a popular ecumenical Christian fellowship group, and, most importantly, (c) had seven kids and so seemed likely to be pro-life.

At Barrett's confirmation hearing, Senate Assistant Democratic Leader Dick Durbin of Illinois asked Barrett if she considered herself "an orthodox Catholic."

Later, Democratic Senator Dianne Feinstein of California opened her questioning of Barrett like this:

> [...] dogma and law are two different things. [...] And I think whatever a religion is, it has its own dogma. The law is totally different. And I think in your case, professor, when you read your speeches, the conclusion one draws is that the dogma lives loudly within you, and that's of concern [...].[15]

In both these cases, Democratic Senators who took oaths to uphold the Constitution brazenly violated its sixth Article:

> "[...]no religious Test shall ever be required as a Qualification to any Office or public Trust under the United States."

Sanders, Durbin, and Feinstein were not acting like custodians of the Senate's advice and consent role; rather, they were acting like Grand Inquisitors, testing the theological purity of Christians trying to live out their faith. They do not believe in religious equality or tolerance. They think people who hold differing theological beliefs should be barred, for that reason, from public service.

Exhibit C: The Boy Scout Oath

This oath pledged by members of the Boy Scouts resulted in decades of harassment and more than thirty lawsuits:

> On my honor I will do my best to do my duty to God and my country, and to obey the Scout Law, to help other people at all times, to keep myself physically strong, mentally awake, and morally straight.

Because of this oath and the moral standards the Boy Scouts required for their members and leaders, they were forced to spend millions of dollars fighting ACLU lawsuits, they were thrown out of public meeting places, denied access to military bases for their traditional jamborees, and suffered the loss of millions of dollars from corporate sponsors. After decades of resistance, the Boy Scouts finally did what many organizations have done;

they abandoned their religious and moral foundations. They gave in to the Inquisition.

Exhibit D: Masterpiece Cake Shop

In the wake of the Supreme Court overturning dozens of state laws prohibiting gay marriage, many Progressive activists immediately turned their attention to the wedding industry. Lawyers, political groups, and government bureaucrats sought out florists and bakers who, because of their religious convictions, might refuse to cater gay weddings.

These bakers and florists were happy to sell their products to gay customers and couples. They simply weren't comfortable endorsing same-sex marriage by either attending the ceremony or, for instance, having to decorate a wedding cake with sentiments that violated their religious beliefs. In every case, there were plenty of other bakeries and flower shops in town whose owners had no problem catering gay weddings. No couple was being denied service; no wedding was being denied flowers or cakes.

Business owners were simply being sued for disagreeing with the bureaucrats' religious beliefs—what George Orwell's terrorizing dictators in *1984* called "wrongthink."

In 2018, one such case triggered by government bureaucrats in Colorado (*Masterpiece Cakeshop v. Colorado Civil Rights Commission*) made it all the way to the Supreme Court. The Court ruled narrowly in favor of the baker but refused to set a larger precedent protecting Americans' religious freedom in cases like this.

In every instance above, the goal is the same. It is not merely to tell religious believers how and where they may practice their faith. It is to use the power of the state to make all Americans avow the Left's preferred religious beliefs—like Henry VIII or Spanish conquistadors or Iran's Ayatollahs. They want to replace the primacy of the individual and his conscience with the centralized power of a dogmatic elite. In the Left's secular sect, politics is God, government is the church, and politicians, academics, and media and corporate elites are the college of cardinals who will tell us what to believe and what not to believe.

This worldview is not just ahistorical and inhuman; it's fundamentally un-American. Religious freedom made America.

It was freedom from religious persecution in the Old World that led so many early Americans to come here in the first place. The Great Awakening of the 18th century stoked the fires of liberty and revolution in the colonies. As John Adams put it:

> What do we mean by the American Revolution? Do we mean the American war? The Revolution was effected before the war commenced. The Revolution was in the minds and hearts of the people; a change in their religious sentiments of their duties and obligations.[16]

Faith sustained General Washington and the Continental Army through the Revolution. One of the first things President Washington and the new American Congress did was declare a national day of Thanksgiving. (Who do they think Americans still thank over turkey and pie on the fourth Thursday of every November?)

It was religion that turned the American people against slavery. It was the religious moral principles of human equality that won equal rights for women. It was religion that drove Martin Luther King Jr. (talk about "dogma living loudly" in someone!) and the civil rights movement to victory over segregation. It was our religious convictions about human dignity that sustained the West during the long, dark struggle against Soviet Communism during the Cold War.

We are not suggesting in any way that our lawmakers create laws following Old Testament Jewish laws and customs or any Christian denomination's theology. Nor are we saying atheists and people of other religions cannot participate freely and constructively in an America with a Judeo-Christian foundation. We simply agree with Martin Luther King, who wrote in his famous "Letter from a Birmingham Jail":

> A just law is a man-made code that squares with the moral law or the law of God. An unjust law is a code that is out of harmony with the moral law. To put it in the terms of St. Thomas Aquinas: An unjust law is a human law that is not rooted in eternal law and natural law. Any law that uplifts human personality is just. Any law that degrades human personality is unjust.[17]

Everyone, regardless their religious beliefs, will benefit from the freedom, prosperity, and security created when cultural and political institutions are founded on biblical precepts of love, charity, and the primacy of conscience and human dignity.

There is no question about the essential role of religion in America's success, but there is an important distinction between the voluntary practice of religion and how government interfaces with religious principles. A free society is not the direct result of the belief in God or the practice of religion. Instead, history teaches the foundations of freedom are derived indirectly from people who hold themselves accountable to God and adhere to moral boundaries. The benefits derived from these beliefs include the essential elements of freedom: individual internal disciplines (virtue and self-governance), societal behavioral expectations (cultural mores), and voluntary adherence to the laws created by democratically elected representatives (respect for the law).

Freedom relies on millions of people making their own political, economic, social, and religious decisions from a wide array of choices provided by many competing interests.

Government must not force religious doctrine or morality onto the people—whether that doctrine is sectarian or secular. Our Constitution, especially given the innate diversity of a continental nation of 300 million souls, must allow the free operation of religion, freedom of association, and the practice of religious-based values throughout society. Freedom of religion guarantees freedom of the people.

Religion is a threat to dictators, Communists, Socialists, the alt-Right and the Progressive Left because it supersedes government authority. Socialism and Progressivism, the primary political and economic threat to freedom in America, requires an all-powerful central government to force societal compliance and uniformity.

Secular-Socialist uniformity is based on the lowest common denominators of values and behaviors because it is based on the minimum standards of external law. A pervasive religious culture creates an internal moral code based on society's highest values and aspirations.

Progressives feign a commitment to religion but insist it must be private and stricken from public discourse. Progressives demand a secular culture but, as Richard John Neuhaus writes:

The notion of the secular state can become the prelude to totalitarianism. That is, once religion is reduced to nothing more than privatized conscience, the public square has only two actors in it—the state and the individual. Religion as a mediating structure—a community that generates and transmits moral values—is no longer available as a countervailing force to the ambitions of the state [...]. No, the chief attack is upon the institutions that bear and promulgate belief in a transcendent reality by which the state can be called to judgment. Such institutions threaten the totalitarian proposition that everything is to be within the state, nothing is to be outside the state.[18]

Neuhaus observed the cascading effects of the Left's desire to create a "naked public square," free of any religious actors or institutions and rejected them as doomed to tragic failure. The "naked public square," as Neuhaus pointed out, is never really naked. As the 20th century proved, the secular state will inevitably create strange, new gods of its own. As Neuhaus noted, "The public square will not and cannot remain naked. If it is not clothed with the 'meanings' borne by religion, new 'meanings' will be imposed by the virtue of the ambitions of the modern state."[19]

For proof of this, look no further than Soviet Russia, Nazi Germany, or Communist China, where religion was purged, replaced, instead, by the godhead of the state and a political order that rejects the inherent and inalienable dignity of the human person. Secularism is itself its own religion, and a self-undermining one at that. It doesn't result in a freer country or a "safer" space. It results in persecution of those who disagree with elite consensus.

This is not to say that secularist thought should be purged from public life. Rather, contrary to the Left, who would sanitize the public square from any discussion with which they disagree, both Kirk and Neuhaus freely embraced the dissent and the contention that defines democracy.

They recognized, as we do, America is and has been frequently transformed by dissent as much as she has been improved by those who speak up in defense of her founding principles. What shape our country takes depends largely on the outcome of this public debate. That being the case, why wouldn't we want the public square to be as vibrant and robust as possible?

As Neuhaus wrote,

There is an inherent and necessary relationship between democracy and pluralism. Pluralism . . . does not mean simply that there are many different kinds of people and institutions in societal play. More radically than that, it means that there are contenders striving with one another to define what the play is about—what are the rules and what goal [...]. He strives to sustain that contention within the bond of civility, also, because he recognizes that totalitarianism is the presently available alternative to such democratic contention.[20]

It is this contentious striving that keeps America free, thriving, and ever evolving around our foundational principles. It is our ability to have, express, and practice our beliefs about how we ought to live together at the root of our political tradition.

That's why the founders enshrined freedom of conscience first of all rights protected by the Bill of Rights. And that's why religion is first among the things Americans should know we must keep.

CHAPTER 3

Keeping Our Differences

Conservatives have an "Affection for the proliferating variety and mystery of human existence, as opposed to the narrowing uniformity, egalitarianism, and utilitarian aims of most radical systems."

—RUSSELL KIRK

Few principles are as publicly celebrated in America today as diversity and tolerance. Yes, these words are a part of the vocabulary of political correctness. But the ideas behind them are a part of American history. Long before the United States declared its independence or ratified the Constitution, we were the most diverse collection of people ever bound together as one nation. We were many before we were one.

Modern Conservatives may resist embracing these buzzwords of the PC Left. But American Conservatism—up to and including Russell Kirk's "affection for the proliferating variety and mystery of human existence"— has always embraced diversity. It's the Left, as we will see, that has a problem with tolerating different people and ideas.

Conservatism is often described as a "worldview." In truth, Conservatism isn't based on a view of the world, but a clear-eyed view of the human person—the good and the bad of human nature. This Conservative perspective is derived from the Judeo-Christian belief that man is God's most awesome creation, made in His image and likeness. At the same time, Conservatives accept the fact we have fallen into sin and selfishness and are therefore ever capable of evils great and small. From this perspective—which the founders called, "self-evident truth"—Conservative ideas click into place like the well-worn pieces of a child's puzzle.

There is a reason why classic stories—from the Bible and Aesop to *The Iliad* and the tale of Robin Hood—still resonate with modern readers. It's because, in the words of Boston University Professor Glenn Loury, "human nature has no history." People today are basically the same as people one hundred or one thousand years ago, no matter their race, religion, or region. Cultures and individuals may have very different means of pursuing what they want, but deep down, we all want the same things—knowledge, power, love, wealth, freedom, security, truth, and so forth. This is the core insight of Conservatism—human nature doesn't change this side of the grave.

According to this view, history shows that attempts to remold human nature from on high always fail and usually end in catastrophe.

Progressives, on the other hand, seem to overlook the carnage left in the wakes of bloody cataclysms like the French Revolution and the Russian Revolution and think to themselves, "Shame about all the bodies, but 'A' for effort!" They believe the right combination of laws and pressures can change human nature to finally make people behave the way Progressives want. That's why they pursue their ideas of reform with such tireless zeal. That's why they always seem to be in such a hurry to change this, that, or the other thing. Progressivism is not a campaign; it's a crusade.

Progressives agree with Conservatives that people, as we are, may not be perfect. But Progressives believe their theories and policies can improve on God's creation. They theorize if only they could tweak this tax rate or that welfare program or that healthcare regulation, they could create a new version of mankind in their dreamed image—Adam and Eve 2.0—and finally make a new kingdom of heaven here on earth.

To Progressives, this is just idealism. They don't understand that for everyone else, it's intolerance—often backed up by intimidation and violence.

Our younger readers may be shocked at our assertion that Progressives—the most vocal proponents of "diversity"—don't practice what they preach. But it's true. Progressives are the strongest opponents of individual differences. They only embrace superficial differences such as race and ethnicity. (They even create make-believe differences, such as claiming minority status for someone with 5 percent Native American DNA.) Progressives oppose and are offended by differences in opinions, beliefs, religions, behaviors, and lifestyles—and label dissenters from their views as "deplorable," "bitter clingers" or much worse.

It is the Left's contempt for true diversity, and the quasi-religious crusade they wage against the rest of us, that is tearing America apart.

Out of Many, One

Conservatives believe in an America where individuals with a wide variety of intrinsic, philosophical, and lifestyle differences are united into one common community. This is the whole idea behind our national motto, "E Pluribus Unum": out of many, one.

Diversity has always been with us. Since before America's founding, men, women, and children have come here from every corner of the world as soon as they could get here. That's still true. Today, the United States is so large we have a literal melting pot within our own borders. In America, the "pluribus" is easy. It's the "unum" that has been harder to manage.

How did America come together in the first place, given its unprecedented differences in culture, language, religion, and lifestyle? By cutting through all these differences in one swing, by treating everyone here as an individual. In the American community, everyone is free to be different, to be themselves. But everyone is equal under the law and under God—treated with respect, and free to think and live as they will.

Here, we put the individual at the center of our society, our culture, our politics, and our economy. As a result, our diverse citizenry did not pull apart; they pulled together. Free citizens formed strong marriages and communities, families and businesses, churches and clubs—the great American constellation of associations our late President George H.W. Bush called our "thousand points of light."

America has experimented with exceptions to this rule in the past and we still regret it. Slavery, Jim Crow, unequal rights for women, the internment of Japanese Americans during World War II, the eugenic forced sterilization of "undesirables," the legalized killing of the unborn. The United States' record on individual human rights and dignity is the best in the world, but even we have fallen short of our ideals and continue to suffer for it. Individualism isn't perfect—far from it—but it does more to protect human rights and dignity than any other political system.

Conservative Individualism

Progressives often accuse Conservatives of pretending people are islands, isolated from one another. But, in truth, the Left seeks to isolate and atomize citizens from one another, using the power of government to divide and conquer us. Happy lives are created by the relationships between individuals in families and communities, and the unity of our country is based on the freedom of individuals to build those relationships and to associate with those they choose. That's what Conservative individualism is all about.

In economics, the free enterprise system does not isolate individuals. It connects us in a huge, diverse web of buyers, sellers, bosses, employees, coworkers, partners, and investors. The market economy is the most diverse institution on earth—comprising everything from rockets to sprockets, from spring water to springboards.

Likewise, in politics, for all its emphasis on individual liberties, the Constitution does not isolate us at all. It invites us into the concentric governing circles of the neighborhood, town, the county, the state, and the nation. The differences of each individual, family, community, and region thus strengthens the nation as a whole, by giving each layer of authority the right to set its own course. By giving Catholics and Protestants, Jews and gentiles, big cities and small towns, rich people and poor people, the young, the old, and the middle aged an equal right to self-determination, our Constitution harnesses our variety to the good of the whole.

In our culture, too, it is Americans' emphasis on the freedom of the individual—the individual student, the individual artist or writer, the individual scholar, the individual church or churchgoer—that creates the space for creative flourishing. New ideas spring from the respectful interaction of old ideas. Consider all the cultural innovations America has produced in a relatively brief two and half centuries. Jazz and rock and roll. Movies. The best universities in the world. Giants of literature from Emily Dickinson to William Faulkner. Our proliferation of charitable organizations, religious institutions, and popular sports. In our culture, we can all move forward together even if we're not always marching to the same beat.

It may seem ironic that individual freedom is what brings Americans together, but by putting every citizen—every person—at the center of our society, we really can transcend the suspicious tribalism that defined so much of human history before 1776.

By taking each other as individuals, what really matters in life—what we are on the inside—transcends the superficial facts of our skin color or ethnicity, or religious heritage, our class, where we grew up, or who our parents were. Here, we conduct politics, commerce, and culture not only eye to eye, but I to I—as equals and fellow citizens, no matter our differences. As unique individuals, our freedom to be ourselves is what we have in common, what binds us.

Through Conservatism, individual freedom draws out the best in us, making us simultaneously distinct and yet more attentive to others. It makes us more respectful and respectable, more tolerant and more tolerable. Through Conservative individualism, our diversity becomes our greatest strength and our differences miraculously unite us.

Progressive Conformism

The Left can't stand all this. At every turn, they see diversity as an inefficiency or a threat. They believe the only reasons people disagree—disagree with them—is ignorance or hate. They don't believe there are different paths to happiness; there is just one: theirs.

President Barack Obama summed up this mindset in a common refrain from his speeches. "We know what works," he would say. "We know what we have to do. We've just got to put aside the stale and outmoded debates." He took it as a given and communicated to the American people, that anyone who disagreed with him was indulging in "stale and outmoded" politics. President Obama was a talented politician, but he never got more than 53 percent of the popular vote. Is it remotely fair to win an election with 53 percent of the vote, and then declare the 47 percent who disagree with you as no longer engaging in good faith debates? This isn't an argument: it's a cudgel. It's bullying contempt: do what we say, you deplorable bitter clingers, or we will make you.

This attitude runs through the Left's agenda, which ultimately comes down to the denial of and even the criminalization of diversity in economics, politics, and culture.

Socialism Attacks Economic Individualism

The free enterprise system is based on individuals' right to spend their money how they want—thus driving resources and innovative creativity toward the most customer-pleasing goods and services. Socialism is the opposite. Socialism is the use of government power to ban economic choice among individuals, giving government officials the power to choose for the rest of us. It's not generosity; it's greed and contempt for the choices all those stupid people—that is, you and me—keep making.

Self-styled Socialist New York Mayor Bill de Blasio recently complained "the hardest thing" he's had to deal with in office has been the American legal system's respect for private property rights. "I think people all over this city," he said, "of every background, would like to have the city government be able to determine which building goes where, how high it will be, who gets to live in it, what the rent will be."[1] Of course, like Bernie Sanders, de Blasio is a millionaire. He owns two rental homes in New York City, worth in excess of a million dollars, and he hasn't handed them over to "the city government." He is perfectly happy with his private property rights; it's everyone else's property rights that bothers him. Nor would de Blasio be okay with a different mayor, a Conservative mayor like Rudy Giuliani or New York City native Donald Trump, having that same power. Socialism is never about empowering people or even empowering government. Socialism is just about empowering the Socialists.

During his presidential campaign in 2015, Sanders went off on a rant—as Bernie tends to do—about capitalism:

> You can't just continue growth for the sake of growth in a world in which we are struggling with climate change and all kinds of environmental problems. All right? You don't necessarily need a choice of twenty-three underarm spray deodorants or of eighteen different pairs of sneakers when children are hungry in this country.

Here's another take on Bernie's argument. If you think about it, humans only need one kind of drink: water. Why should our grocery stories be so cluttered with all those sodas, juices, milks, let alone beer and wine? Well, because people buy them. Why should there be so many fast food restaurants selling slight variations of the exact same thing? Because the people getting Happy Meals at McDonalds and Whoppers at Burger King and chicken sandwiches at Chick-fil-A have as much right to their choice of food as Bernie Sanders or Donald Trump or anyone else.

That's the moral genius of the free market; it rewards people for delivering increasingly more appealing goods and services at ever lower prices to the people who want them. The fact that this system also happens to make people richer and makes countries stronger and more peaceful than any other economic system is just an ancillary benefit—one of several trillion all Americans enjoy in the United States today, Bernie Sanders and Bill de Blasio included.

Free-market economics doesn't judge people's diversity. It allows people to choose how they want to spend their money, or not spend it—as the free market provides people the largest range of savings and investment options, too. It allows people to choose their own economic path in life—prioritizing work or home time, maximizing income or flexibility, consuming or saving. People are different, and the free market lets everyone make their own way.

Again, the Left hates diversity and individualism in economics, so leftists embrace socialism as a means of making everyone spend money the way Bernie Sanders or Bill de Blasio want them to. And don't kid yourself: the end result of socialism is never equality. The vast majority of people do end up equally miserable, yes. But the misery never reaches the Progressive politicians.

The best illustration of this truth is the famous nighttime satellite images of the Korean peninsula. You've probably seen a version of it: it depicts South Korea aglow in lights all over the country. By contrast, North Korea looks like a black hole. The contrast is often noted to show the difference of economic prosperity between a Communist and a market-based economy. But, to me, the more salient point is North Korea isn't entirely in the dark. If you look closely, you'll see there's one medium-sized bright dot. It's Pyongyang, the capital, where the tyrant Kim Jong-un and his henchmen live in comfort while their starving subjects mire in the dark.

Socialism isn't just economically stagnating; it's morally unjust. It's always nice for the Socialists; it's everyone else who suffers.

In the Conservative worldview, all people are equal; in the leftist worldview, some people are more equal than others. We'll come back to this in more detail in Part II.

Constitutionalism vs. Identity Politics

The Left doesn't like diversity in politics any more than it likes it in economics. But the Left's insistence on uniformity defies the infinite and wonderful differences in human beings. People see the world, the individual, the role of government, and the nature of community differently. It's only natural for people to lean politically left on some issues and right on other issues.

America's founders believed in the innate diversity of human communities. That's why they created a constitutional system designed to channel those differences toward compromise and consensus at different levels of government. This frustrates the Left because Progressives know they cannot impose their will on a nation of diverse, unique, individual citizens who think for themselves. So Progressives want to destroy diversity.

The cutting edge of intolerant and conformist leftism in America today is so-called "identity politics." This is the idea that an individual's social, political, and economic ideas should be based not on one's own personal experience and judgment, but derived from one's membership in certain, preferred demographic groups.

Under identity politics, 160 million American women from all walks of life, all regions of the country, of every age and religious and ethnic group, are supposed to share a political ideology. Same for young people. Same for black people and Latinos. Same for immigrants, though American immigrants are one of the most culturally diverse collections of people in the world. Same for poor people. According to identity politics, these people are not flesh-and-blood individuals with hopes, dreams, and agency to achieve them, but pawns in a political game played by their supposed ideological betters.

Identity politics is not just an attack against diversity itself; it's an attack launched from the highest echelons of American society. For identity politics' purpose is not to cultivate or promote the diverse identities of historically marginalized communities, but to permanently yoke them all to the political preferences of the richest, most powerful, and privileged men in the world.

Look around. This is the dirty little secret of "identity politics." We're told it's the way to empower the downtrodden or ignored, the "little guy." But the most prominent promoters of identity politics are political elites, media elites, academic elites, cultural elites, entertainment elites, corporate elites, and technology elites.[2] Turn on the news or go to the movies. Spend some time at an Ivy League university or a Silicon Valley campus. Listen to the Masters of the Universe who run the 21st century boomtowns of New York, San Francisco, or Washington, D.C., and you'll hear all about how important it is to open our eyes and ears to the voices of the marginalized communities. After a while, you'll realize it's all nonsense. They don't mean a word of it.

These elites are not interested in women's voices, as such. They can't stand outspoken Conservative women like Laura Ingraham, Candace Owens, or Ivanka Trump. By women, they really mean Progressives. They have no time for Supreme Court Justice Clarence Thomas or U.S. Department of Housing and Urban Development Secretary Ben Carson, one of the great surgeons of his generation. They're not interested in hearing from African Americans—just Progressives.

Leftist leaders who demand greater inclusion for Latin Americans don't mean Conservatives like former congressman and native Puerto Rican Raul Labrador, or Cuban-American Senators Ted Cruz and Marco Rubio. They mean Progressives, period.

The Left loves superficial diversity because it allows them to portray themselves on television as an open, inclusive coalition—which is how they like to see themselves. But, under identity politics, real diversity—of thought and values and priorities—is rejected out of hand. There are right answers and there are wrong answers. The right answers have been worked out by the most powerful and privileged people in society. All that is left is for everyone to either acquiesce or be condemned. Progressive elites are like caricatures of medieval Catholic missionaries who try to convert heathens to the one true faith—at the tip of a sword.

What the Left refuses to acknowledge is that while their values and beliefs and worldview might work for them, they don't necessarily work for everyone. And, because everyone is endowed with equal dignity, everyone should therefore have the same right to pursue happiness in his own way. That's the basic idea behind the United States of America, our Constitution, our economy, and our exceptional way of life.

The ugly, cruel consequence of identity politics—the politics of class, race, ethnicity, or religion—is why most Americans became Americans in the first place. "I have a dream," Martin Luther King said, "that my four little children will one day live in a nation where they will not be judged by the color of their skin, but by the content of their character."[3] When Dr. King gave his speech in 1963, being judged only by the content of our character was supposed to be the goal of every American. The character, skills and contributions of the individual, not the group from which he or she came, should determine our societal esteem. Identity politics turns that foundational American principle on its head. Identity politics says you're not really you, you're just a proxy for whatever racial, ethnic, religious, or cultural or demographic group Progressives say you belong to.

But think about what that means. The logical endpoint of identity politics would lead us to adjusting the respect we owe to individual rights depending on whether someone is black, white, Asian, or of mixed race. It means we should protect the property rights of, say, Christians but not Jews, or, say, men but not women. It means granting free speech rights to native-born Americans but not to immigrants, or not allowing people of certain ethnicities or sexual orientations to serve on juries.

This is insane. These are literally the disgusting, cruel ideas America was founded to resist. Identity politics is just fancy words for prejudice and bigotry. And, in the end, it will end up targeting and hurting the very people it pretends to empower.

Diversity in Culture

Progressives' crusade against diversity doesn't stop at economics and politics. It doesn't stop anywhere. Progressive conformism is a totalitarian impulse and it extends beyond public policy into citizens' private lives. Once again, don't let the talking points fool you. So-called "multiculturalist" Progressives are really cultural chauvinists and supremacists; they are as intolerant toward alternative cultural attitudes as theocratic monarchs.

Look at colleges and universities, which leftists control the same way they hope to control the whole of society. Conservative speakers are routinely shouted down, disinvited, and even injured for daring to show up. Many universities have stopped inviting speakers who might offend Progressive students and professors.

The Boston Globe published an account of one of the many disturbances launched against Conservative speakers:

> The normally peaceful campus of Middlebury College, with its mountain backdrop and elite reputation, was shaken last week after violent student protesters shut down a talk by controversial Conservative social scientist Charles Murray and injured a Middlebury professor who was with him.
>
> Many on campus, including the college president and leaders of the student organization who invited him, disagree vehemently with Murray's views on social welfare programs and race, but on Saturday they said the campus failed in its duty to exemplify how to debate unpopular ideas with civility.[4]

These Progressives don't just want to avoid opposing opinions themselves; they want to make sure no one hears them. It's not enough for them to avoid an event with a Conservative speaker. They want to ban Conservative speakers altogether.

Some go farther. Consider the rise of the Antifa movement. This is a loose organization of self-styled Progressives—mostly young, affluent, and white—who don black clothes and masks and sometimes carry weapons while staging law-breaking, often violent marches and demonstrations. They declare themselves the enemies of fascism ("anti-fascism.") The problem is: they define fascist as anyone who disagrees with them—which is more or less the definition of fascism itself. Their purpose seems to be to make Republicans afraid to ever go outside.

So rabid has the cultural left's crusade against wrongthink become that many innocent people are finding themselves in the crosshairs too.

Late in 2018, comedian and actor Kevin Hart was forced to withdraw from his contract to host the 2019 Academy Awards show. Hart is a wildly popular comic and star of the hit movie *Jumanji: Welcome to the Jungle* with Dwayne Johnson. He's not known for his politics one way or another and is the kind of talent who might be able to reverse the Oscars' recent tilt toward politics, and toward lower viewership. Unfortunately, several years ago, Hart made some insensitive comments about homosexuality—comments he's long since apologized for. But an apology wasn't good enough for the Progressive Internet mob: Hart had to go.[5]

The thing is, though, nobody believes Hart is homophobic. Nobody believes he hates LBGT people. Nobody believes it would be homophobic or insensitive for Hollywood stars and directors to continue working with him—according to IMDb, Hart has no fewer than five future movies already in the works. Nobody believes his hosting of the Oscars would, in fact, signal that Hollywood—Hollywood!—is homophobic or hateful toward the LBGT community. This ritual public shaming serves no purpose of forgiveness and reconciliation—it's simply a show of raw strength, a threat to anyone else who might dare to disagree with Progressive elite orthodoxy.

The same goes for the Left's newest weapon of mass distraction: "cultural appropriation." According to Oxford Dictionaries, cultural appropriation is, "the unacknowledged or inappropriate adoption of the customs, practices, ideas, etc. of one people or society by members of another and typically more dominant people or society." Cultural appropriation is what Progressives call cultural diversity they don't like.

The problem is, there is no such thing as cultural appropriation—there's just culture. When people from different backgrounds or traditions interact, new ideas emerge. For instance, did you know the national dish of Great Britain, and incidentally, it's most popular dish, is chicken tikka masala—chicken in curry sauce? It's an Indian dish, which made its way to England during British colonialism. Have you ever had spaghetti and meatballs? Ever practice yoga, meditation, or martial arts? Or drink tea? Or listen to rock music? Ever vote in an election? Ever wear a suit or play football? Do you really believe Protestant, Catholic, and Islamic cultures are all totally distinct from one another, or all three don't possess at least some shared origins?

In an essay titled "Every Culture Appropriates," *The Atlantic*'s David Frum recounts a recent mini-controversy about a high school girl in Utah who was attacked by the Progressive internet mob for wearing a Chinese-style cheongsam dress to a school dance. Upon seeing her post, one Asian-American responded on social media, "My culture is not your prom dress." Thousands of Progressive hate mongers on Twitter and Instagram followed suit, trashing this young woman for being white and wearing an Asian-inspired dress.

Happily, as Frum writes:

"Good sense and kindness prevailed, and instead of her prom being ruined, the young woman exited the dance buoyed by worldwide support and affirmation, most of all from within China."[6]

As with Kevin Hart, nobody thought the young woman in Salt Lake City was doing anything wrong. The Left's cultural chauvinism is not about preserving one or another cultural heritage; it's about asserting their own cultural power. It's about telling other people what they can and cannot do. It's about attacking the natural human process of sharing, threatening people who might express their individuality and imposing on them the rigid monoculture of Progressive elites.

The freedom to be yourself is supposed to be universal. That's why American culture is so dynamic—and so beloved around the world. Walk through a grocery store or a mall. Drive down a country highway and see the wild diversity of churches and homes you'll see; turn on the radio and find any variety of talk or music you could wish.

What the Left doesn't understand—or, rather, hates—is that all this diversity is unifying. The reason Americans are so divided today is due to the intolerant Left trying to smother our natural diversity. Progressive elites are trying to impose conformism about religion, economics, politics, and culture from their every perch—from Washington to Wall Street to Hollywood to Silicon Valley, to Brussels.

Not only is this strategy—trampling the innate individuality of all people—morally wrong, it's also foolish and counterproductive. President Obama was wrong when he said, "We know what works." As Conservatives, we do believe history and tradition can show us many things that have worked for society as a whole. But none of us knows what works, or what is preferred, by every individual. Different things work for different people at different times. Ask any parent, any teacher or coach, any priest or pastor or rabbi. People want and need different things.

Progress is a process of trial and error—we succeed only by experimenting, failing, learning from our mistakes, and doing it all over again. We build on each other's success and knowledge and work together— even if we don't know it—toward goals we set for ourselves and each other. Not goals set for us by far-off elites who look down on our values and ways of life.

Progressives, in their arrogant belief they already have all the right answers, trample this process. Instead of trial and error, they leave us with just error. They snuff out the "thousand points of light" Americans need to guide our way, leaving us all in darkness.

In America, it is our freedom that makes us great. But it is very much our differences that make us free. Our nation is great because our people are different. Freedom makes our diversity a unifying strength; Progressivism makes us less free, less diverse, less united.

CHAPTER 4

Keeping Our Republic

Let the objects of government be few and clearly defined; let all important powers, in America, be reserved to the states (as the framers of the Constitution intended), outside the scope of federal authority. Astute lovers of freedom will assert state powers constantly, so that personal and local liberties may endure; the smaller the unit of government, the less possibility of usurpation, and the more immediate and powerful the operation of prescriptive influences.[1]

—RUSSELL KIRK

If you are convinced the intrinsic differences and the variety of preferences in America are worth celebrating and protecting, then you will find our arguments for the decentralization of political power to be good common sense. As we have already mentioned, common sense is not common in government. The American people, however, intuitively understand the value of differences.

There are countless examples of Americans—the most diverse group of people in the world—enjoying and often having fun with our differences. One of these examples is in Texas. If you think Texas is one ubiquitous group of people, think again. In a sea of rootin'-tootin', gun-toting, God-loving cowboys and cowgirls, there's the capital city of Austin: an island of Left-leaning, artsy, crunchy, hippie-dippy types. Years ago, the city fathers in Austin developed the marketing slogan, "Keep Austin Weird" to promote the city's distinct identity.

It was all in good fun, but it made an important point. Austin is different from the rest of the state and they are proud of it. It sounds defiant—like the Right-leaning groups that wave flags with the slogan "don't tread on me"—and it is defiant. It is a declaration of independence. Unfortunately, most of the Progressives in Austin don't understand the bigger, more important point; Austin's relationship to Texas is similar to Texas's relationship to the rest of the country. Texas is weird compared to California and New York. And that's okay!

Too much of our politics today is about whether blue-state city people will tell red-state rural people how to live or vice versa—when the whole point of the Constitution is to do neither. America is actually stronger and happier when we respect each other's weirdness.

Most Americans understand the positive aspects of diversity. We live peacefully and constructively with diverse people and ideas in all areas of our lives. But too many politicians—especially federal-level politicians—build their political power base by grouping people according to their differences, fomenting distrust and pitting factions against one another.

Frustrated voters often ask, "What happens to people after they go to Washington?" Reasonable candidates seem to quickly become unreasoning politicians. They divide the country into warring groups, but then insist one-size-fits-all programs will work for everyone. We call this "Potomac Fever." After seeing people work in Washington as a congressman, senator, or senior staffer, we can report first-hand why good people catch Potomac Fever and become part of the "swamp."

The most prevalent cause of Potomac Fever is the goal of re-election, so voter expectations drive the behavior of elected officials. Voters tend to think of government as a continuous hierarchy from local, to state, to federal. They don't make clear distinctions between separation of powers or functions for the different levels of government. And they can no longer conceive of a federal government with limited jurisdiction or authority. Quite the contrary.

Voters think of the federal government as the "boss" over state and local governments. If voters have a problem—whether with potholes or trash pickup—they often look to the top of the pecking order for assistance. And the expectation for assistance from the federal "boss" now goes well beyond public services to personal needs such as jobs, income, food, housing, healthcare, and retirement security.

Voter expectations drive the development of public policy. Russell Kirk wrote about the changing expectations of the American voter in the early 1950s, and we can now see how those expectations resulted in the creation of major federal programs such as Social Security, Medicare, Medicaid, Welfare, the Department of Education, and Obamacare.

> Among the strange notions which have been broached since I have been in the political theatre, there is one which has lately seized the minds of men, that all things must be done for them by the Government, and that they are to do nothing for themselves: the Government is not only to attend to the great concerns which are its province, but it must step in and ease individuals of their natural and moral obligations. A more pernicious notion cannot prevail.[2]

Congressmen and Senators who take an oath to protect the Constitution, which limits federal jurisdiction, quickly turn their focus back to the local and personal interests of the people who elected them and to the special interest demands of those who funded their campaigns. There is always the urge to "do something"—or even just to *appear* to be doing something for constituents, reporters, and campaign supporters. The good of the country as a whole and the constitutional limits on federal power have been the casualties of this focus by federal officials on "particular matters" as Kirk describes them.

Kirk, when writing of the early 19th century statesman John Randolph—a Conservative whom Kirk called "the most singular great man in American history"—wrote:

> He (Randolph) was the Conservative of particularism, of localism. Without the spirit of particularism, the idea of local associations and local rights, perhaps no sort of Conservatism is practicable.[3]

Randolph was not suggesting congressmen and senators focus on "particular" matters. He was insisting on the opposite. Freedom and Conservatism can only exist when decision-making is decentralized— when individuals and local officials have the rights to make their own choices about how they live and to take responsibility for their themselves and their neighbors.

Kirk writes that politics ("democratic methods") should not be used to address every issue.

"The application of 'democratic methods' arbitrarily to every controversy, heedless of particular circumstances and intricacies, is consummate stupidity."[4]

We would argue it is not stupidity that drives Progressives to centralize power and dissolve our federation of states into one national government. It is by design. Progressives can only accomplish their goals through centralized political control. Federalism, republican government, and individual freedom are their enemies.

Failures of Centralized Governance

The parochial focus of federal officials has created a cascading set of problems for America. First, before a Congressman or Senator from one state can get federal money for the local needs of constituents, he or she must get the votes of a majority of other Congressman and Senators. This is most easily accomplished by funding similar needs for every state and congressional district. The result has been the creation of massive federal programs to address almost every issue and need—poverty, retirement security, transportation infrastructure, education, environment, healthcare, employee benefits, hiring practices, workplace safety, product safety, marriage, and many more.

Massive federal programs have created a staggering national debt along with widespread waste and corruption. And, importantly, few federal programs have accomplished their stated goals. Despite trillions of dollars spent for the war on poverty, there has been little reduction in poverty. The quality of education has actually declined relative to other countries. Health care has become more expensive and harder to access. Poor Americans who use Medicaid for their insurance have the same health status as people who have no insurance at all. And even popular programs that seem to be working, like Social Security and Medicare for seniors, are fiscally unsustainable and careening toward bankruptcy.

Compounding these problems are the hundreds of thousands of pages of regulations created to control these massive federal programs. These regulations are intended to manage the one-size-fits-all implementation of federal programs for hundreds of millions of Americans. Everyone in every state must be treated the same, regardless of the different needs or preferences of individuals. To the Progressive mindset, manifested in all these rules and regulations, people must not merely be equal, but totally interchangeable. The result has been the elimination of competition, the subversion of the authority of local and state officials, and the loss of freedom and personal responsibility by individual Americans.

Despite the failures and unsustainability of these federal programs, public demand makes it politically difficult, if not impossible, to eliminate or even change them. Few politicians have the courage to tell their constituents the truth: These programs don't work and they are bankrupting the country.

Worse than the waste, incompetence, and debt of federal programs is the divisiveness and incivility caused by forced compliance of one-size-fits-all solutions from Washington. Federal regulations popular with the people in California, might be anathema to the majority of people in thirty other states. But, instead of fighting for the freedom of states and individuals to make their own decisions, politicians try to pass legislation that will force their beliefs and preferences on all the other states. This is not how a republic should work—in large part because it doesn't work.

The centralization of lawmaking has resulted not only in the concentration of political power at the federal level. It has also led to the concentration of economic, media, academic, and overall cultural power. The big players get what they want, and the little guys are forced to take what comes down from the top. This creates frustration, disillusionment, incivility and—as we are seeing in America and all around the world—violence.

Many of the biggest problems we face in America today were created by Washington, D.C. And yet too many Americans continue to look to Washington to Make America Great Again. We're writing this book to tell you Washington cannot do it. Washington will not do it.

Our national government was never meant to be what it is today. It's treated almost as if it were our god—and it behaves almost as if it were our god.

But Washington isn't the master of the people—the people are supposed to be its master. The federal government didn't create the states—the states created the federal government. Congress isn't our provider—it is we, the people, and the work of our hands, the sweat of our brows, the industries we create, and the businesses we run that provide both the money and the authority Congress wields.

America Is a Constitutional Republic, Not Just a Nation

The antidote for America's dysfunction and debt is a return to constitutional governance. America was founded as a federation of states—a republic made up of smaller republics. The main purpose of the Constitution was to guarantee state authority over most issues and to codify the limits of federal power. This is something we should keep!

The differences between the states—and the freedom of each state to leverage its unique qualities—make the union itself stronger. Progressives and those on the Left presume strength only comes through the rational efficiencies of consolidation and scale. They think the nation works like a machine. It does not. It's a community, and communities are weakened by externally imposed conformity. In America, strength comes from letting each state—each community—be itself. A strong country is like a strong marriage, where the strength of the union is reinforced—not undermined—by the individuality of each spouse.

Unfortunately, the precedents established by decades of executive, legislative, and judicial overreach have effectively destroyed the original constitutional limits on federal power. Any Congressman or Senator who appeals to the Constitution when opposing a piece of legislation is considered naïve or radical. And, because there are no requirements to limit federal spending or to ever balance the budget, Congress will continue to create new programs and increase the debt until America experiences a potentially devastating financial collapse.

The only way Americans can avoid division, incivility, and an inevitable fiscal disaster is for voters to decide they want to restore our republican form of government—to fight against the Progressive goal of an all-powerful, centralized national government. We must keep our federation of states. Conservatives call this approach "federalism."

Federalism—a misnomer that means the opposite of federal control—is best defined using the 10th Amendment to the Constitution, an overriding principle that protects and enables the other nine amendments of the Bill of Rights.

> "The powers not delegated to the United States by the Constitution, nor prohibited by it to the states, are reserved to the states respectively, or to the people."

The Constitution limits federal functions primarily to defense, international trade, immigration, regulating commerce between states, and minting currency. The states, along with the people in each state, were supposed to have the responsibility and control over other public and private issues.

The traditional argument for federalism is the "laboratories of democracy" argument, which holds the states are essentially fifty farm-team governments developing policy and private practices, the most successful of which are inevitably scaled up to D.C. for national application. An even better argument for federalism is we should never scale them up without national consensus. If Kansas and Florida and Vermont want different answers to certain public questions, the people there have every right to apply their preferences to the policies in their states.

The independent actions of the states will accomplish two things: first, it will lower the temperature of our overheated national political debate, both by lowering the stakes and localizing the battlefield (people don't talk to their neighbors the way we torch people on Twitter); and, second, it will allow the more homogeneous populations of the different states to set policies more in line with their values.

Much of the incivility in America today is caused by interest groups who are aggressively working to convince 51 percent of our federal representatives to pass legislation that will cram their interests, values, and beliefs down the throats of all Americans—even when a large majority of Americans in most states disagree with the policies. This is the opposite of how the Constitution and federalism are supposed to work.

Senator Mike Lee from Utah, one of the most thoughtful and civil Conservatives in America, wrote, "In the absence of national consensus, there shouldn't be federal policy." Sounds simple and reasonable, but too many politicians in D.C. view the lack of a centralized national policy on any issue as a failure to "do something." In reality, divergent approaches in fifty states means free Americans are agreeing to allow others to live the way they want.

What Progressives so often ignore or forget is that many of the differences they want to erase are not simply personal or cultural preferences—which should usually be good enough reasons to tolerate that diversity. Rather, sometimes different approaches are driven by concrete differences that can't be changed. For instance, because New York and Los Angeles are America's two biggest cities, it's easy to think of them as very similar. But New York has more than twice as many people—more than eight million residents to L.A.'s four million—living in a much smaller area—three hundred square miles to five hundred square miles in Los Angeles. Those may seem irrelevant differences to someone living in small home towns in South Carolina. But, to the mayors and city councils of those cities, the differences are huge. It would be crazy for a congressman from Ohio or Oklahoma (simply because he's sat on a certain committee for the longest time) to have the power to declare New York's and Los Angeles's housing or public transportation, taxi services, trash collection, or utilities provision must be the same.

Ask a country doctor and a city doctor if their practices are the same. Ask teachers from poor and rich school districts if their workdays are the same. We all know these kinds of differences exist because we all live with them every day. It's only in Washington that we pretend the human beings in our diverse national community are as interchangeable as numbers on a bureaucrat's spreadsheet.

Obamacare and federal health care policies in general are perfect examples of why the federal government shouldn't try to prescribe solutions for the entire nation. Under nationalized Obamacare policies, a small number of Americans found more affordable health insurance, while the large majority pay much more for inferior policies with less coverage than the policies they lost when the federal government took control.

It's no mystery why Americans are angry. The mystery is why Americans continue to vote for the people who have created one failed federal program after another. Perhaps it's because they don't understand the benefits of federalism. Or, perhaps, too many American voters just don't understand our Constitution or the uniqueness of our republic.

CHAPTER 5

Keeping Our Institutions and Traditions

Custom, convention, and old prescription are checks both upon man's anarchic impulse and upon the innovator's lust for power[...]. Society must alter, for prudent change is the means of social preservation; but a statesman must take Providence into his calculations, and a statesman's chief virtue, according to Plato and Burke, is prudence.

—Russell Kirk

Everything we want to keep as Conservatives is dependent on our ability as citizens to restrain the power and growth of government. Limited government is essential for a free society, but how can government be limited? By offsetting the power of government with an even more powerful force: the collective institutional power of "We the People."

A limited, decentralized, republican form of government is not possible without prevalent and thriving voluntary institutions and unifying cultural traditions. The public and private spheres are two parts of a power equation that always add up to the same total. As mentioned earlier, smaller government depends on bigger citizens. If the public sphere grows in power, the private sphere will shrink and vice versa. Whatever powers are added to the public sphere are subtracted from the private sphere. As Thomas Jefferson said, "The natural progress of things is for liberty to yield and government to gain ground."[1] Only private-sphere institutions and associations can keep liberty from yielding.

Institutions and Associations

The terms "institution" and "association" apply to both informal and formal convening entities that support voluntary activities, traditions and standards (societal norms, customs, and expected patterns of behavior). While America's republican form of government is certainly one of our institutions, it is not voluntary, and its laws are not optional. Government coercion is a necessity for a free society, but it is also the primary threat to freedom.

Voluntary, private sphere institutions and associations are often referred to as "mediating institutions" because they serve to transform and redirect the natural self-interests of individuals into behaviors that support the common good. They also serve as "mediators" between individuals and government by using the collective power of their membership to advocate on behalf of their priorities. Voluntary institutions and associations are essential to freedom because they are, as Tocqueville pointed out, "a bulwark of freedom against the encroaching power of the state."[2]

Voluntary institutions and associations can be any group organized around common interests: churches, parent-teachers' associations, bowling leagues, Rotary clubs, the United Way and other charities, cycling clubs, garden clubs, dinner clubs, chambers of commerce, business and industry associations, professional associations, boys' and girls' clubs, and bridge clubs. They also include larger, overarching institutional concepts such as our free enterprise economic system, Judeo-Christian values, and financial and educational institutions.

Self-improvement requires a lot of work; individuals cannot do it on their own. We need our families, churches, communities, and a network of other societal institutions to help us. When these break down, it becomes harder for each of us to check our inner nature. As Burke warned his fellow Englishmen when the horrors of the French Revolution unfolded across the channel, "Society requires not only that the passions of individuals should be subjected, but that even in the mass and body, as well as in the individuals, the inclinations of men should frequently be thwarted, their will controlled, and their passions brought into subjection."[3]

Government cannot control human passions; it can only punish them after they are manifested in destructive behavior. Private sphere institutions and associations can more effectively shape constructive human behavior through friendships, shared goals and activities, positive peer pressure, societal esteem, and stigma.

Burke rightly understood anything is possible—and much is to be feared—once we discard the inner check in each of us. The inner check Burke spoke of is shaped and guarded by institutions, particularly the church. When inner checks are discarded, "public benefit would soon become the pretext and perfidy and murder the end—until rapacity, malice, revenge, and fear more dreadful than revenge, could satiate their insatiable appetites."[4]

Standards

Some of the most essential products of voluntary institutions and associations are standards—fixed expectations about behavior, morality, performance, and quality. Standards are a free society's alternatives to government laws because when people voluntarily adhere to societal expectations, fewer laws are needed. Institutions and associations are the guardians of voluntary standards.

Many of the original societal standards in America and Europe were derived directly or indirectly from the Bible, which is why Kirk considered a respect for a transcendent order to be the first and most important "thought" of the Conservative mind. And much of what we want and need to keep for our security and freedom—our covenants, our faith, our differences, our republic, our opportunities, and our traditions—is only possible with individual and collective submission to God.

Religious institutions establish varying standards for religious practice, individual morality, and duties. While different for each religion, these standards' commonality collectively shape and elevate societal norms. Families adopt many of these expectations and add their own standards for spouses, children, and extended family members.

Business and industry also establish voluntary standards. These are standards for best practices including quality, benefits for employees, management integrity, fair competition, fair profit, and customer service.

We are not suggesting all businesses currently keep these standards, but collectively the presence of standards establishes implicit measurements allowing customers and the public to judge how businesses perform.

Individuals, businesses, and organizations establish their credibility and reputations based on how they match up to societal standards. Those who perform well against standards are rewarded with gifts like public esteem and financial gain. Those who perform poorly against societal norms suffer stigma and are incentivized to improve.

Traditions

Traditions are what individuals, families, communities, and nations keep.

Traditions are the gift-wrapped packages containing the directions for a better life passed from one generation to the next. Kirk refers to traditions as "custom, convention and old prescription,"[5] but traditions are anything but old. They are each new generation's guide to the future and the closest any society can come to eternal life.

But, when it comes to Conservatism, there is probably nothing more fraught with meaning—or misunderstanding—than the role of tradition. The Left has given it many synonyms: patriarchy; white supremacy; oppression; "the closet," i.e., bigotry; or an unrepentant nostalgia for the so-called halcyon days of the 1950s and '60s. None of this could be further from the truth. So, before we get into why our traditions are so vital to keep, we have to define the role tradition plays in Conservatism.

Conservatism and the Great Tradition

The word "tradition" comes from the Latin verb "tradere" which means "to hand down" or "hand over." The experiences and wisdom of one generation identifies principles, practices, and solutions that make life better, which are then handed down to the next generation.

In this sense, tradition is hardly the set of rigid, inflexible, outdated rules Liberals make it out to be. Rather, the notion of tradition refers to the customs, beliefs, and habits developed over time; it contains the accumulated wisdom of those who have lived, labored, failed, dreamed, and triumphed before us. The concept of tradition, fundamentally, is that over time, human nature hasn't changed, so maybe we could learn a thing or two about what's worked and what's failed. Kirk put it more eloquently when he said Conservatives work for the "preservation of the ancient moral traditions of humanity."[6]

The word "moral" doesn't necessarily mean Christian or religious, though faith certainly plays a role. Rather, it refers to what has, over time, worked to make people virtuous—that is, happy, fulfilled, and able to serve as productive members of families, neighborhoods, and communities.

Ultimately, while our customs and habits may change and evolve over time, human nature does not. And, over time, our collective wisdom (or, in other words, our tradition) has sorted through what works—and what doesn't—for governing ourselves. Deference to this accumulated wisdom is what separates Conservatives and Liberals. This divide is centuries old, tracing its roots all the way back to the French Revolution, where an Irish Whig named Edmund Burke reacted to the excesses of Maximilien Robespierre's Jacobins by articulating the Conservative argument for the importance of the past and a belief in private property, religion, and the complexity of life.

Burke rejected the position of the Jacobins that French society could only be reformed through radical revolution and abject destruction, upending every aspect of a centuries-old system and starting anew. Rather, Burke believed—as Conservatives do now—in the accumulated wisdom of constitutions and in gradual, tempered change that draws lessons from the past about what works and what doesn't. Russell Kirk, writing centuries later, framed this as "the politics of prudence."

The use of the word prudence does not suggest timidity or fearfulness about reform and change, but, instead, a thoughtfulness that takes into account the fullness of society, the need for an ordered liberty, and the unchanging truths about human nature. The Conservative tradition, in this sense, sharply differs from Progressivism. Whereas the Left embraces the state as the shaper of public life, Conservatives see politics as merely a part of society. For Conservatives, the proper goal of political institutions is to protect and nurture our local institutions and associations: churches, schools, homes, and families.

Conversely, the Left places the state at the center of their ideology and gives it the role of disruptive, destructive innovator. Progressives believe government, to achieve the highest good, should direct the constant remaking of society based upon new and constantly shifting norms. But, if the Conservative tradition has taught us anything, it is that placing a centralized and intrusive state at the center of our society has poor outcomes. As James Madison observed, men are not angels. A long and violent human history has taught us this truth.

This is why Conservatives seek so vigorously to defend the cause of individual liberty: for a free society which allows us to embody and pass on the time-tested habits that make us fulfilled individuals, good citizens, strong families, and free people. This is the great tradition of Conservatism: a handing down of wisdom from one generation to the next; a collection of timeless truths won by those who have struggled before us. As Kirk put it, "modern people are dwarfs on the shoulders of giants" and we are "able to see farther than their ancestors only because of the great stature of those who have preceded us in time."[7]

The Conservative tradition prizes continuity between the ages. To quote Burke, "Society is a contract between the generations: a partnership between those who are living, those who have lived before us, and those who have yet to be born."[8]

Progressives have distorted the concept of institutions and traditions in an attempt to escape the "chains of the past." They use the successes of people like Steve Jobs, founder of Apple, to make their case that ideas from the past are oppressive. The following quote from Jobs suggests he is recommending a complete break from the past.

> Your time is limited, so don't waste it living someone else's life. Don't be trapped by dogma—which is living with the results of other people's thinking. Don't let the noise of others' opinions drown out your own inner voice. And most important, have the courage to follow your heart and intuition.[9]

This may sound inspiring to Progressives, but it is precisely America's traditions of independence, adventure, entrepreneurship, innovation, competition, and profit that create opportunities for people like Jobs and the millions of people who have benefited from his products. Apple's success would not have been possible in a country without these respected traditions. It was America's tradition of innovation and market capitalism that allowed Apple to build on previous generations' work on the transistor, punch-card computers, the silicon chip, and on and on. Ironically, Progressives advocate Socialistic economic policies that would destroy the opportunities they claim to support.

Progressives have a different view of institutions and traditions. As former Vice President Joe Biden once said, "Government is what we do together." But this is not true—quite the opposite. Government is not America's overarching and all-powerful institution. It is only a part of what we do together, and we should never forget: for people outside the political class, government is what we are *forced* to do together. Government is only supposed to establish and enforce the rules to assure the freedom of individuals and voluntary societal institutions. The government is the institution established by the people to guard their freedom, not direct their lives.

When former first lady and Progressive leader Hillary Clinton said, "It takes a village to raise a child," she wasn't referring to the families and all the voluntary institutions working together to guiding children into adulthood. Progressives like Clinton often change the meaning of words. She was referring to the myriad government programs she believed were necessary to raise children. Progressives believe only government can correct and even perfect the human condition.

Kirk explains that Conservatives like Edmund Burke are "contemptuous of the notion of human perfectibility."[10] The notion that laws and government-forced conformity can fix inequality and vice has led to all sorts of Progressive experimentations and tyranny. Burke writes, "Poverty, brutality, and misfortune are indeed portions of the eternal order of things; sin is a terribly real and demonstrable fact, the consequence of our depravity, not of erring institutions; religion is the consolation for these ills, which never can be removed by legislation or revolution. Religious faith makes existence tolerable; ambition without pious restraint must end in failure."[11]

> Rejecting the notion of a world subject only to sudden impulse and physical appetite, he (Burke) expounded the idea of a world governed by strong and subtle purpose [...]. Revelation, reason, and an assurance beyond the senses tell us that the Author of our being exists, and that He is omniscient; and man and the state are creations of God's beneficence. This Christian orthodoxy is the kernel of Burke's philosophy. God's purpose among men is revealed through the unrolling of history. How

are we to know God's mind and will? Through the prejudices and traditions which millennia of human experience with divine means and judgements have implanted in the mind of the species. And what is our purpose in this world? Not to indulge our appetites, but to render obedience to divine ordinance.[12]

Institutions are how traditions are kept and maintained. The institution of the church keeps traditions that include regular worship, morality, marriage, child christening, communion, bar mitzvah, marriage, Easter, Christmas, Hanukkah, and funerals. The institution of family keeps many of the same traditions and adds the traditions of education for children, celebrating birthdays, holidays, vacations, and continues many other practices passed down from parents and grandparents. Families and churches guide the moral and character development of individuals, establish standards of behavior, and provide voluntarily societal accountability for results.

The institution of the market keeps the traditions of entrepreneurship, innovation, work, employee pay and benefits, production, service, pricing, trade, competition, and profit. The institution of academia and education encompasses a broad range of traditions from early childhood development to graduate level universities to continuing education. The institution of the media keeps the public informed and entertained. Voluntary institutions, such as charities and civic societies, keep the traditions of compassion, humanitarianism, and community service.

The absence of well-developed voluntary institutions in many countries around the world has created obstacles to freedom. American politicians and military leaders have painfully discovered that establishing democratic governments in undeveloped countries usually creates more problems than it solves. When President George W. Bush took America to war in Iraq, we were promised the liberation of Iraq would quickly lead to a free and prosperous country. But, once Iraq was liberated and the people voted with great celebration, the country devolved into chaos.

The reason freedom hasn't worked in Iraq and many other countries is that there were no free and voluntary institutions to make freedom work. There was no network of financial institutions, so everyone—including soldiers—had to be paid with cash from a central location. Widespread corruption ensued. The media was undeveloped, and state controlled, so the population was poorly informed and government propaganda was prevalent. Religious practice was controlled by Islamic leaders enmeshed with government leaders. Other religions were not tolerated. Schools became laboratories of Islamic indoctrination. And there were essentially no market institutions to build a free and prosperous economy.

The politically incorrect truth is: Iraq wasn't ready for 21st-century American-style freedom and neither are most peoples or countries around the world. And, sadly, even in America—in the land of the free—our people are increasingly unprepared to live in freedom. This, in large part, is because of the deterioration of traditions and "mediating" institutions. Much of this deterioration has been caused by government intrusion.

Tradition and Change

Keeping our traditions as Conservatives does not mean we do not think, or question, or change. Rather, we say "remember." Think, but remember. Question, but recall. Change, but do so with the wisdom and experiences transmitted to us from generations prior on how to live a full and meaningful life.

In this way, tradition ensures the best possible change. Traditions keep successive generations of imperfect people progressing in a positive direction by leaving the bad behind and sifting the good into the future. Traditions aren't hostile to change; they are essential to positive change.

Consider the benefits of weekly attendance to religious services. It is something families do together. It is something we do as submission to a transcendent authority. We are socialized with others who are on their best behavior, which raises expectations and creates accountability. Children are exposed to examples of good adult behavior. They see the process of child-rearing, marriage, new family formation, and respect for life and death.

Within this "little platoon" of community, relationships with other like-minded individuals and families create the first affections and appreciation for the larger community and nation. The love of family and community developed on a small scale at home and in a church or synagogue can be transferred to a larger and larger sphere.

There is much room for positive change with traditions, even traditions as old as religious practice. Today, many families worship in a more casual environment with contemporary music. There are thousands of home churches where small groups of neighbors meet. There are millions of prayer groups meeting every day of the week. The formats may change, but the positive benefits of maintaining the tradition of religious gatherings are the same.

Now consider the implications of the loss of this one tradition. Many Americans have forgotten the reasons and benefits associated with attending religious services, which has resulted in the decline of religious gatherings for several decades. It's no coincidence that destructive and costly social pathologies have replaced this sacred but increasingly optional tradition.

Family formation has declined, and unwed births have skyrocketed. A near majority of Americans are now born out of wedlock, with three-fourths of black children born to unmarried mothers. Nearly as many black children are aborted as are born every year. The government has redefined marriage and moral standards and has generally lowered expectations for responsibility and work.

This is far from just a religious or moral issue. The societal costs associated with the loss of traditional worship are astronomical. Research shows conclusively that unwed births and fatherless homes lead to high school dropouts, unemployment, drug use, crime, incarceration and another generation of unwed births. Nearly half of Americans will have a sexually transmitted disease during their lifetime.[13] States and the federal government spend trillions of dollars every year on the direct and indirect costs of the decline in traditional worship, including welfare, Medicaid, unemployment benefits, law enforcement, and prisons.

Change is necessary and can be positive. Edmund Burke acknowledged, "a state without the means of some change is without the means of its conservation."[14] But Kirk adds, "True progress, improvement, is unthinkable without tradition [...] because progress rests upon addition, not subtraction."[15]

Similarly, George Santayana observed, "Progress, far from consisting in change, depends on retentiveness. When change is absolute there remains no being to improve and no direction is set for possible improvement; when experience is not retained[...]infancy is perpetual. *Those who cannot remember the past are condemned to repeat it*."[16] Tradition is how we remember the lessons of the past and use these lessons to build a better future.

Change is inevitable. Consequently, Kirk believed the role of Conservatives is "to patch and polish the old order of things, trying to discern the difference between a profound, slow, natural alteration and some infatuation of the hour."[17]

This role for Conservatives is especially necessary now, where public infatuations are enhanced by a twenty-four-hour news cycle and amplified by social media. Distinguishing between today's fleeting obsession and what T.S. Eliot called "the permanent things" is more difficult than ever. This is why the constant reflection toward what has been, what has worked, and what has failed is so vital.

This does not, however, mean Conservatives should blindly follow tradition or cling to the status quo. Kirk acknowledged tradition is only a guide; there are both good and bad traditions—often bad specifically because they undermine creativity and put an end to "variety and change."[18] Traditions should be evergreen and ever-changing; maintaining them requires constant reflection.

"In a healthy nation," Kirk writes, "tradition must be balanced by some strong element of curiosity and individual dissent."[19] Distinguishing between good and bad tradition is "a question of degree and balance."[20]

Progressives use examples of bad tradition to discredit the good ones. But despite their claims, the greatest danger today is not being "crushed beneath the dead weight of tradition" but arises from "the flux of ceaseless change, the repudiation of all enduring values."[21]

If the freedom and success of America depends on the collective strength of millions of different individuals, then America is dependent on institutions, association, traditions, and standards to build the strength of every individual.

Individuals must have the character and skills to succeed in a free economy and society. They must have the confidence in themselves and the external institutional support "system" to take risks and reach beyond their own expectations. This can only be achieved through the practice of traditions and presence of enduring public and private institutions that pass on traditions from one generation to another.

How Progressives Have Undermined Tradition and Institutions

Voluntary institutional standards are anathema to Progressives who eschew any notion of moral absolutes or permanent truth—except from government edicts. Early Progressives, such as Rousseau, created evolving humanistic standards or what Kirk called, "a false morality." Kirk wrote:

> A new-fangled morality was a monstrous imposture; Burke turned in this matter, as in most, to prescription and precedent, old materials ready to the true reformer's hand, to supply this opposing morality which might heal the wounds inflicted by revolutionary moral doctrines.[22]

Much of the decline of America—the debt, the public rancor, the divisiveness, the violence, the absence of moral standards, and the decline of marriage—can be attributed to government intrusions into the roles of voluntary institutions. During the 20th century, the federal government replaced many of the functions of societal institutions. This has been the goal and work of the Progressive movement.

The major shift from voluntary to government institutional control occurred in the 1960s. Federal courts disallowed prayer (of any kind) in public schools. New welfare programs created disincentives for marriage and work. Universities receiving any public funding were immediately pressured to drop any religious teachings. Organizations, such as the Boy Scouts, also founded on traditional moral principles, found themselves under attack. Progressives have seized upon these government edicts as weapons against any public religious display or private insistence on religious morality.

Burke warned against a society set adrift:

> When ancient opinions and rules of life are taken away, the loss cannot possibly be estimated. From that moment we have no compass to govern us, nor can we know distinctly to what port we steer.[23]

The federal government has also intruded heavily into America's institution of the free market. Government laws and regulations now prescribe wages and benefits, create pressure for unionization, define workplace safety rules from hundreds of miles away, control America's banking and lending institutions, direct investment practices, impose restrictive and costly environmental regulations, and much more. Conservatives agree some regulations are needed, but the heavy hand of government has done more to create powerful monopolies and oligopolies than protect consumers or the environment.

When voluntary institutions shape the future with traditions and standards, you can be assured Americans will be free and prosperous. But wherever the government replaces volunteerism with laws, regulations, and judicial edicts, Conservatives should be concerned standards will be lowered and freedom lost. Without some moral consensus and voluntary high standards among the public, progress is impossible.

Americans need to know what institutions, associations, traditions, and standards we should keep. As Kirk wrote, "The Conservative is a champion of[…]the standards and institutions which humanity has discovered or created by a long and painful process."[24] Our most important tradition is tradition itself. What are traditions? They are the accumulated results of generations worth of trial and error. The things we call "traditions" today were once new and called "solutions." Traditions are simply how we know what to keep.

CHAPTER 6

Keeping Our Land of Opportunity

The uniform, constant, and uninterrupted effort of every man to better his condition, the principle from which public and national, as well as private opulence is originally derived, is frequently powerful enough to maintain the natural progress of things toward improvement, in spite both of the extravagance of government and of the greatest errors of administration.[1]

—ADAM SMITH

Freedom is just an abstraction unless it is paired with opportunity. Primitive men living in a jungle were free, but they had little opportunity to change their condition. America has long been known as the land of opportunity because, more than any other country, it offers an abundance of choices, means, and methods for people to build a better life.

For centuries, opportunity has inspired people to trek to America—traveling thousands of miles, crossing oceans, risking their lives, waiting for years in visa lines, taking any job they can find and working long hours with diligence just for the chance to succeed—to create a better life for themselves and their families. The whole world knows America offers something unique: the ability for everyone to change their destinies, stations, and outcomes with dedicated labor, grit, and maybe a little bit of good fortune, regardless of where they start.

You may have the best ideas or a massive IQ but, without opportunity, your plans and brains go nowhere. Opportunity is the bridge that connects a person's hopes and dreams with their achievements, fulfilment, and ultimate success. Throughout history, there has never been a bridge like the United States of America.

America's recipe for opportunity is multifaceted. Our institutions, traditions, and adherence to the rule of law prepare individuals on one side of the bridge with the skills and capabilities necessary to cross over, and on the other side, these same institutions and traditions create many paths for achievement and success.

America's commitment to the traditions of education, character, hard work, risk-taking, persistence, and vision prepare and empower individuals to seek and seize opportunities as they arise. Voluntary institutions of family, church, and myriad community organizations inculcate individuals with the attitudes and skills they need to make the most of these opportunities along the way.

Ultimately, opportunity is the means for a journey to a secure and prosperous end: strong social and family connection, a thriving community, economic security, a sense of personal safety and interpersonal belonging.

This "end" is the magnet calling Americans and all who are inspired to cross the bridge of opportunity, persisting in the face of circumstance, disabilities, disasters, and limitations compounded by the barriers and obstacles placed along the way by people and bureaucracies.

Americans are known for their striving, for their grit and determination to succeed. But, as we strive to improve our own lives, we aspire to make sure everyone—regardless their background, skin color, or financial circumstance—has equal access to the same opportunities.

This is what sets American apart. And it is rooted most fundamentally in America's economic system—the institution of capitalism.

The Power of Capitalism

Capitalism provides both the means and ends for opportunity and success. It builds the bridge of opportunity and creates the prosperity to fuel the city on the hill.

Capitalism is the voluntary trading of dollars (capital) for goods and services—from a cup of coffee or a haircut to a home or lawn service. Every transaction by an individual or business creates more opportunities and wealth for hundreds and perhaps thousands of others. This wealth-creating phenomenon is akin to the idea of the small wind from butterfly wings in one part of the world eventually growing into a hurricane on the other side of the world. Capitalism has the power to expand wealth exponentially.

But, today in America, capitalism is increasingly maligned by the Left: Progressives, Liberals and the Democratic political party. This economic institution that has created more prosperity for America and the world—lifting more people out of poverty than all government programs throughout history—is in danger of being replaced by the failed economic and political system of socialism.

The battle between capitalism and socialism is one of the major sources of division in America today. The Left has pushed for government control of the economy since America's founding, but only recently has the word "socialism" been openly used by its proponents. Socialism, exalted by the union movements in 19th century Europe, captivated most of the world's economies during the 19th and 20th centuries. And, not surprisingly, Socialist economies were usually controlled by political dictators or sham democracies.

But America, from its inception—with its democratic and decentralized political system, faith-based institutions, and spirit of individual freedom—chose the opposite of socialism by adopting the principles of capitalism advocated by a controversial British economist.

Adam Smith published *The Wealth of Nations* in Britain in 1776, the same year of America's Declaration of Independence. Smith documented the societal benefits derived from individuals pursuing personal gain through business activity. Smith even took the idea of capitalism to the highest level by describing it as "unfolding at least part of a Devine [sic] Plan; a Plan which is given substantial expression by virtue of the activities of individuals who are unconscious of the end which these activities help to promote."[2]

Smith's *Wealth of Nations* popularized the notion that, under a free-market system, an "invisible hand" guided the actions of those in pursuit of selfish gain to serve the good of others. The book enraged anti-capitalists who blamed greedy businessmen for all societal ills. But Americans, because of their diversity, independent natures, decentralized political control—and simply out of necessity—became the first country to fully deploy Adam Smith's ideas of capitalism. The results were described more than a hundred years later by Andrew Bacevich.

> By the end of World War II, the country possessed nearly two-thirds of the world's gold reserves and more than half its entire manufacturing capacity. In 1947, the United States by itself accounted for one-third of world exports. Its foreign trade balance was comfortably in the black. As measured by value, its exports more than doubled its imports. The dollar had displaced the British pound sterling as the global reserve currency [...] Among the world's producers of oil, steel, airplanes, automobiles, and electronics, it ranked first in each category. In 1948, American per capita income exceeded by a factor of four the combined per capita income of Great Britain, France, West Germany, and Italy. [3]

This is the economic miracle of capitalism few Americans are taught today. Rather, Americans in large numbers have accepted the Left's lie that capitalism is an economic system that benefits the rich at the expense of the poor. Rather than looking at the fertile, multi-level fabric of opportunities created by capitalism—opportunities that have turned millions of poor dreamers into rich success stories—it's become fashionable to dismiss the whole system as unredeemable, inherently bad, and fatally corrupted by greed.

Many college-aged students, in fact, believe socialism is better than capitalism—ironic, because their colleges are only made possible by the wealth created by our capitalist economy. The only reason all those students, deans, and professors are not subsistence farmers slopping around in the muck is the prosperity created here in America and around the world by the competitive innovation and cooperative progress of free markets and private property.

Merriam-Webster's dictionary defines capitalism as: *an economic system characterized by private or corporate ownership of capital goods, by investments that are determined by private decision, and by prices, production, and the distribution of goods that are determined mainly by competition in a free market.* [4]

Translated, this means capitalism is an economic system that allows the prices of goods and services to be set by buyers and sellers, all of whose property and rights are equally protected by the law and government. In such a system, sellers compete for dollars from buyers by offering customers the most value for their money. Every transaction—from the purchase of a giant corporation to the purchase of a candy bar—is voluntary and, therefore, beneficial in the eyes of both the buyer and the seller. (Otherwise, it wouldn't happen.)

Consider eBay, maybe the *least* Socialistic mini-economy in America today. Have you ever been wronged on eBay? Ever been forced to buy a product at gouging prices? Ever been bullied into buying something you didn't want? No. The worst that could happen is some seller misrepresents his product or fails to ship it to you on time. And, when that happens, it's inconvenient, but you get your money back and the seller gets a black mark on his ratings, warning other customers away. That last bit—real-time reputation self-defense—is a much greater incentive for good and honest behavior than government regulations, which always come with fine print and can be amended by well-paid lobbyists.

Voluntary transactions in the free market are more than just the exchange of products and services for money. Each transaction creates tiny elevators raising the standard of living for many people. Take a close look at something as mundane as the purchase of a Happy Meal™ lunch at McDonald's and you'll see. From the outside, it looks like someone forked over five bucks to the corporate fat cats at McDonald's in exchange for a little burger, fries, a drink, some apple slices, and a cheap little toy. And maybe to the customer, that's all it is—a tasty meal at a low price.

But look and see who else benefits. The cashier behind the counter, making minimum wage. The teenager dropping baskets of fries into the hot oil. The shift manager supervising the restaurant. The ranchers who raise the cattle the hamburger is made from, the workers at the packing plant who processed it, and the truck drivers who transported the meat and potatoes all the way to the store. The guy at the plastic cup factory. The family who owns the orchard where the apple was grown. The gal who works at the plant where they make the cardboard Happy Meal™ and French fry boxes and paper hamburger wrappers. And the napkins. The companies that make the paper and the ink used to print the receipt. And all *their* suppliers and distributors and salesmen and marketers. And on and on and on.

And the whole thing happens spontaneously and voluntarily, without any necessary involvement from a politician or bureaucrat or cost to taxpayers. Under the free enterprise system, money is not redistributed by a central government bureau. It goes wherever people see value. Those who create value are rewarded, which then signals to the rest of the economy to up their game. It's a continuous democracy.

Capitalism gets a bad rap for its supposed dog-eat-dog competition. But why are all those businesses working together and competing so fiercely to give people more for less? Because they want to make a profit. They want to improve their own lives. And, when they do, they improve the lives of many others.

How can this be? After all, isn't everyone in the free market out for themselves?

For the most part, yes. But, remember the Conservative view of human nature. There's no way around it. Whether an economy is free or Socialistic, whether a political system is democratic or monarchic, or whether the legal system is just or corrupt, people will always look out for themselves, their families, and their friends more than they will look out for everyone else.

The free market doesn't make people self-interested; human nature does.

But here's the "magic." Instead of finger wagging at people to be better, capitalism and free enterprise harness people's inherent self-interest and direct it to the good of the wider society. In a free market system, the only way to get ahead—to succeed, to profit, and maybe even get rich—is to *help other people get ahead too.* Consider some well-known American billionaires. How did they earn their money?

Bill Gates' Microsoft Corporation made the DOS and Windows operating systems, made personal computers user-friendly for everyone, increased productivity, and improved the lives of millions of people around the world.

The late Steve Jobs did the same with Apple Computers, then went even further developing portable digital devices like the iPod, iPad, and iPhone. Jobs made billions of dollars for himself while improving the lives of millions of others.

Jeff Bezos of Amazon figured out how to sell books, and then almost everything else, for lower prices than traditional retailers. He has saved his customers trillions of dollars over the last two decades.

Los Angeles Lakers legend Earvin "Magic" Johnson became a millionaire by creating value as one of the greatest basketball players who ever lived. With the money he earned on the court, he created even more value by building movie theaters and coffee shops in urban neighborhoods around the country.

What's true of billionaires is true of most millionaires and thousandaires and even hundredaires just starting out. If you create value for other people in a free enterprise economy, you'll be rewarded for it. Adam Smith called this process the "invisible hand" because it constantly shifts resources from less valuable to more valuable endeavors—and, critically, does so without any visible central management.

But there is more to the "invisible hand" than just money and economic benefits. Capitalism also moves the hearts and minds of people. To create value in other people's lives, you first must empathize with them. You have to put yourself in their shoes, think about what they want, what product or service or idea would help them improve their lives or achieve their dreams. Capitalism aligns each individual's self-interest with everyone else's—it unites us.

Consider the following chart from the World Bank. It shows global gross domestic product—that is, the aggregate wealth of planet Earth—from the turn of the last millennium to today. From the dawn of time until around 1800, human beings all lived in their natural state of poverty. There were a handful of kings and nobles who lived in comparative splendor (though "affluence" five hundred years ago would make the poorest Americans today look like kings), but life until the 19th century was, in Thomas Hobbes' famous words, "solitary, poor, nasty, brutish, and short."

Then, a little less than a generation after the United States declared its independence from Great Britain and Adam Smith published his defense of free markets, it all changed. First in Great Britain and America, where Smith's ideas were put into practice, and slowly expanding around the world, human beings started getting richer. We haven't really stopped since. Almost all the wealth creation in the history of the world, and almost all poverty that has *ever* been eliminated, have happened since the founding of the United States of America.

Not just here, not just in Europe, but everywhere. The material prosperity enjoyed today on every continent, in every culture and every country, is owed to the free exchange of goods, services, and ideas made possible by capitalism—*American* capitalism.

Now, capitalism gets a bad rap in large part due to the dark shadows cast by crony capitalism—the alliance of big business with big government. The big Wall Street bankers, the big multinational corporations, the big pharmaceutical companies, the big corporate farmers, and the big media moguls are all protected and enriched by entrenched federal politicians and lobbyists. Unfortunately, Americans in the 21st century are more familiar with crony capitalism than real capitalism.

The political campaigns of Bernie Sanders and other Socialists have flourished because of the angst many Americans feel about capitalist greed, corporate welfare, and their belief our government cares more for Wall Street than it does for ordinary families. It's an understandable feeling. During the 2008 financial crisis, Congress bailed out bad decisions by politicians and Wall Street to the tune of billions of dollars. This was crony

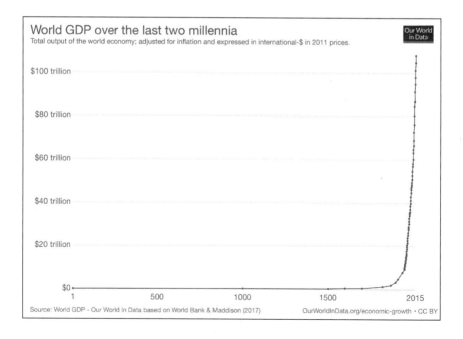

World GDP over the last two millennia
Total output of the world economy; adjusted for inflation and expressed in international-$ in 2011 prices.

Source: World GDP - Our World In Data based on World Bank & Maddison (2017)   OurWorldInData.org/economic-growth · CC BY

capitalism at its worst. Meanwhile, on Main Street, thousands of families lost their homes, their retirement savings, and received not a pittance.

Very few on Wall Street were punished. After sending what amounted to a wrecking ball through the world economy, hardly anyone went to jail. And, after all the dust settled, Congress passed the Dodd-Frank financial reform legislation that rewarded the big guys who caused the problems and punished their little competitors.

Crony capitalism is a big problem in America, but socialism is not the solution.

Anti-capitalists and Progressive politicians today continue to be offended by Adam Smith's conclusions, but the results in America and around the world are measurable and conclusive: capitalism and free markets—when allowed to work—lift more people out of poverty and improve the quality of life for more people than any government program.

Capitalism Extends the Realm of Individual Freedom

Capitalism is nothing more or less than the extension of individual freedom from the political and cultural realms to the economy. Just as government isn't supposed to tell you how to pray, or what to think, or what sports teams to follow or books to read, it's not supposed to tell you what to do with your own money and property. Rather, government's primary economic duty is to protect citizens' property from any who would try to seize, destroy, or defraud them out of it.

Free enterprise (another term for capitalism) has been so successful in the United States and around the world—successful at creating wealth and opportunity, pulling people out of poverty, improving the health and wealth of previously broken societies—that, in 21st century America, it's easy to take it for granted.

We expect businesses to compete for our dollars by constantly offering lower prices, innovative products, and better customer service. *We expect* the stock market, over time, to always go up, up, up and even non-wealthy savers and investors to amass small fortunes for their retirement. *We expect* there to always be jobs aplenty, with rising wages and easy access to credit. *We expect* supermarket shelves to be stocked with tens of thousands of products to meet the demands of everyone from all income levels. And *we expect* the government to respect all citizens' property rights, enforce contracts, punish thieves and frauds, and mete out equal justice to all. The benefits of capitalism are so pervasive that it's hard for Americans to appreciate how radical, new, and still rare this idea is.

The idea that societies and governments should organize their economies around legally protected individual property rights is only about 250 years old and it has been controversial the whole time.

Property and the Rule of Law

According to Friedrich Hayek:

> Nothing distinguishes more clearly the condition in a free country from those in a country under arbitrary government than the observance in the former of the great principles known as the Rule of Law. Stripped of all technicalities, this means that government in all its actions is bound by rules fixed and announced beforehand—rules which make it possible to address with fair certainty how the authority will use its coercive affairs on the basis of this knowledge.[5]

Under capitalism, private property is the "capital" that makes America's economic system work. Private property means individual ownership and ownership must be protected by the rule of law. Without private property, there is no prosperity and, without the rule of law, there is no private property.

Every parent should understand how property and ownership can change a person for the better, especially if the person works and buys something with his or her own money. When a teenager gets a job, saves, and buys his own car—even if the car is an old model in disrepair—that car will be taken care of and prized much more than a new luxury model borrowed from his parents.

"My own" is the concept that creates responsible citizens. From my own toy, to my own car, to my own house, to my own children, to my own country—ownership drives the "service above self" behaviors that create opportunities for individuals and their communities. Far from causing selfishness—Progressives' constant critique of capitalism—property ownership drives people to assume more responsibility for themselves and the good of others.

Ownership of private property is the basis of capitalism. When property rights are protected by the rule of law, people will work hard to acquire property—including cash, land, homes, commercial buildings, and production equipment. Ownership creates incentives to work harder, add value to property, use property for wealth creation, and to invest in more property. All of this builds an economic cycle requiring professional services, construction, production equipment, the hiring of workers, and the purchasing of products created by other workers. This is how jobs and opportunities are created.

Two of the ten amendments in America's Bill of Rights focus specifically on the protection of private property. The third amendment protects private homes from being used by the military without the consent of the owner, and the fourth amendment protects people, houses, papers and personal "effects" from unreasonable searches and seizures (that is, without warrants and probable cause). Other amendments, such as the first and second amendments, also address the freedom to "own" our own opinions, religions, and guns. The rights of persons and property are inseparable.

The Constitution is the basis for the rule of law and it is the first covenant between the American people and their government. This covenant establishes the foundation of limited governance and free people. America's founders intended for the republic to be ruled by fixed and knowable laws written by elected representatives of the people instead of the arbitrary decisions of unelected rulers ("the rule of men"), which had been their experience under the English king. But much of the intent of our founders has been lost since the ratification of our Constitution. As Frederic Bastiat said, "The law has been perverted by the influence of two entirely different causes: stupid greed and false philanthropy."[6]

In Part II of *CONSERVATIVE,* we will detail how the Left has perverted the rule of law to advance their Progressive agenda. And we will discuss how this has resulted in the loss or diminishment of opportunities for many Americans. It is essential for thinking Americans to be aware of how secular Socialists on the Left are using the government and the law to promote their hypocritical compassion and false philanthropy.

This threat is fast becoming a reality. Several freshman members of the newly elected Democrat majority of the House of Representatives in 2019 began to openly advocate for radical Socialistic policies such as extreme taxes on the rich, curtailing of free speech, economically paralyzing environmental regulations, and Medicare for All.

One of these new congresswomen, Alexandria Ocasio-Cortez, a self-described Socialist from New York, openly declared it is immoral for any society to allow the existence of billionaires. She stated, "a system that allows billionaires to exist when there are parts of Alabama where people are still getting ringworms because they don't have access to public health is wrong."[7]

Ocasio-Cortez, who proposed a 70 percent tax on the income of over $10 million continued, "Do we want to live in a city where billionaires have their own personal Uber helipads in the same city and same society as people who are working eighty-hour weeks and can't feed their kids?" According to Ocasio-Cortez, it should be a crime for billionaires to exist. [8]

There is an obvious truth missed by Ocasio-Cortez and other Socialist politicians: a billion dollars left in the hands of a billionaire who earned it will create exponentially more jobs and prosperity for more people than a billion dollars put in the hands of Washington politicians and bureaucrats.

Socialism sounds good and fair until you understand Socialists are merely levelers. They'd rather have everyone live "equally" at a lower standard of living than have anyone succeed, no matter how hard they work, no matter what they've overcome, no matter the value of their ideas. But the scourge of economic leveling is why over two million Venezuelans have fled their Socialist "paradise"—many of them immigrating to the United States—because they'd rather have the opportunity to succeed than be equally oppressed and poor.

Frederic Bastiat said:

> Socialism, like the ancient ideas from which it springs, confuses the distinction between government and society. As a result of this, every time we object to a thing being done by government, the socialists conclude that we object to its being done at all [...] We disapprove of state education. Then the socialists say that we are opposed to any education. We object to a state religion. Then the socialists say that we want no religion at all. We object to a state-enforced equality. Then they say that we are against equality. And so on, and so on. It is as if the socialists were to accuse u of not wanting persons to eat because we do not want the state to raise grain.[9]

Keeping our land of opportunity for all Americans requires an under-standing of how opportunities are created. Our previous chapters—and all of Russell Kirk's Conservative principles—lay the foundations for the creation of opportunity, prosperity, and wealth. The covenant between "We the People" builds the trust, confidence, and community spirit necessary for free markets to flourish. Religious faith imbues people with the integrity to transact freely with each other without the heavy hand of government regulation. Respecting and encouraging our differences multiplies market and employment opportunities by diversifying demand and the corre-sponding incentives to produce a wide variety of goods and services. And keeping our republican form of government creates competition between the states for the best social, cultural, and economic outcomes.

When it comes to creating opportunities, our capitalistic free market economy is the "goose that lays the golden eggs." You are probably familiar with the children's story by that name. The special goose in the story lays a golden egg every day until its owner decides he wants more than one egg at a time. So he kills the goose in hopes of getting all the golden eggs at once. But there weren't any eggs. They had to be made one at a time.

The man who killed the goose is like the Socialists who want a 70 percent tax on the earnings of the rich, or to raise property taxes, or take property from land owners, or heavily regulate businesses, or have govern-ment takeover businesses. Socialists don't understand wealth has to be created incrementally by individuals who are free to make their own deci-sions. Wealth cannot be created by government or taken from one person and given to another. That's like killing the goose to take the gold.

Wealth is the result of free people working, investing, and taking risks in a free market economy. If good people are given the opportunities and protected by the rule of law, they will produce enough gold for everyone to share. This is what creates the land of opportunity Conservatives want to keep.

PART II

KNOWING
WHAT TO FIX

Overview of Chapters 7–12

It has been said by Liberal intellectuals that the Conservative believes all social questions, at heart, to be questions of private morality. Properly understood, this statement is quite true. A society in which men and women are governed by belief in an enduring moral order, by a strong sense of right and wrong, by personal convictions about justice and honor, will be a good society—whatever political machinery it may utilize; while a society in which men and women are morally adrift, ignorant of norms, and intent chiefly upon gratification of appetites, will be a bad society—no matter how many people vote and no matter how Liberal its formal constitution may be.[1]

—Russell Kirk

Liberals and Progressives

Liberals are good people. Conservatives are good people. Most people are "good" in a general sense (certainly in our own minds), but the natural bent of all humans requires internal and external restraints to bring out the best in each of us. We all need guardrails to keep us on the straight and narrow. Guardrails are simply the things Conservatives want to keep. Part II of *CONSERVATIVE* reveals the motives, goals, and strategies of those who believe these guardrails are obstacles to progress and should be removed.

The opponents of Conservative guardrails come in two ideological flavors: Liberals and Progressives. Both flavors are generally served by the Democratic Party, but they are sometimes swirled with Moderates in the

Republican Party. Liberals are on the Left of an ideological continuum that merges in the middle with Conservatives on the Right. Liberals often share goals with Conservatives (i.e., economic opportunity), but they advocate for a larger and more active federal government to achieve these goals. Historically, there has been some common ground and room for compromises in the middle between Liberals and Conservatives. Progressives, however, have moved so far to the Left on this continuum the gap with Conservatives is almost impossible to bridge.

Most Liberals have good intentions. This is a notion Conservatives should keep in mind as we criticize their policy positions. In truth, outside of political grandstanding, Liberals are almost indistinguishable from Conservatives in their day-to-day lives. They work hard and play by the rules. They take care of their families and look out for their neighbors. Some of them, like Progressive candidate for president, Sen. Kamala Harris (D-Calif.) are even gun owners (though her policy prescriptions would, ironically, curtail that right).[2] They make up about a third of the country, so they can be credited with many of the things that make our world and our communities better through their courage, work, and love.

In a healthier political era, differences between Conservatives and Liberals could be viewed as a healthy tension—a necessary conflict between traditional values and the need for reform. Unfortunately, the growing dominance of Progressives on the Left and in the Democratic Party has produced such viciousness and division, civil discourse and compromise has all but disappeared.

Progressives are impulsive and angry. Their solutions often teeter on absurdity (we offer a detailed review of the Left's policies in later chapters), but they will not accept any criticism. In fact, Progressives attack their critics as traitors and heretics. The media amplifies their attacks and drowns out constructive dialogue. Like it or not, a new generation of Progressive corporate elites, not working-class Liberals, are now the dominant force on the Left, and they control the institutional structures of the Democratic Party.

Progressive philosophy is difficult for the rational Conservative mind to process. Progressive solutions offer no connection between cause and effect—between actions and outcomes. Russell Kirk described the Progressive ("radical") rush to action:

Any public measure ought to be judged by its probable long-run consequences, not merely by temporary advantage or popularity. Liberals and radicals, the Conservative says, are imprudent: for they dash at their objectives without giving much heed to the risk of new abuses worse than the evils they hope to sweep away. As John Randolph of Roanoke put it, Providence moves slowly, but the devil always hurries. Human society being complex, remedies cannot be simple if they are to be efficacious. The Conservative acts only after sufficient reflection, having weighed the consequences. Sudden and slashing reforms are as perilous as sudden and slashing surgery.[3]

Progressive actions are often at odds with their rhetoric. For example, Progressives accuse others of hate and social injustice, but, when you listen to them, you discover they mostly hate Conservatives and the things we want to keep. We cannot hate them back. The Conservative battle is not against the people who call themselves Progressives. We want to solve the same problems Progressives claim they want to solve. Our fight is against Progressive policy recklessness that actually makes our problems worse.

Conservatives want to address the high costs of health care and the poor quality of public education. We want to protect the environment and conserve our natural resources. We want to make home ownership more affordable and child care more available. We want to stop the cronyism and corruption between big government and big business. We want more economic opportunities and higher wages for low-skilled and highly educated workers. And we want to stop the violence and chaos on America's southern border.

These are not Conservative, Liberal, or Progressive issues. These are American issues. These are problems we must solve together. But solving problems requires open and civil debates.

Conservatives believe, if our principles and policy ideas are intelligently applied at the appropriate levels of government, that Americans can solve or, at least, greatly diminish our most serious problems. We are convinced, if given an open and honest forum with the American people, we can prove our ideas—the things we want to keep—will secure freedom, prosperity, opportunity, meaning, and create many paths for people from all walks of life to pursue and find happiness. These ideas and policy solutions will be presented later in Part II.

No "fix" is permanent. Constant change requires constant vigilance. As soon as one problem is solved, new problems will be staring us in the face. Problems and challenges are part of life. Progressives will always have one easy-to-understand answer to every challenge: let the government ban it or throw money at it. It's not enough for Conservatives to assert that such simplistic and ham-handed policies never work. We must go further by proposing positive ideas to address the continuous challenges always accompanying changing times.

Political success in a democracy is not about crushing your enemies. Victory means turning opponents into friends. Winning elections is about winning *converts*. Progressives may be unwinnable at this point, but Conservatives can find common ground with Liberals if we work outside the leadership of the two political parties. To attract Liberals, we must first understand them. Ironically, the relentless leftward slant in the movies, on TV, and in the media has given Conservatives an opportunity to understand the Left *much better* than the Left understands Conservatives.[4]

What Liberals Want

If Conservatives are motivated by gratitude for all the good our society enjoys, Liberals are motivated by indignation toward stubborn injustices our society still endures or indulges. Both impulses are equally human and virtuous—even divine. After all, the same carpenter-turned-rabbi who taught us to love our neighbors also horse-whipped blaspheming money changers out of the temple in Jerusalem.

Both gratitude and indignation are essential to any human association, from individual families to businesses and churches—all the way up to nations. Recall, as Edmund Burke put it:

> A state without the means of some change is without the means of its conservation. Without such means it might even risk the loss of that part of the constitution [sic] which it wished the most religiously to preserve.[5]

Put another way: Conservatives help their society succeed by constantly reminding it what to keep. Liberals help those same societies succeed by constantly suggesting what might be fixed. Conservatives serve as a check on imprudence, Liberals as a check on complacency. Both impulses are essential to justice and, therefore, to happiness.

But these impulses of gratitude and indignation are not neatly split between Conservatives and Liberals. Conservatives are also indignant about the indefensible parts of America's status quo. Think of an issue like abortion, where the Supreme Court usurped the laws of all fifty states and dictated, literally, the most expansive abortion regime in the world on a country that didn't, and still doesn't, want it.[6] You can say the same about the national debt or Washington's blasé attitude toward illegal immigration for the last thirty years. Conservatives around the country are fed up and want to fix these problems.

In these cases, Conservatives are the ones who are outraged—and they're right to be. We can be grateful for our constitutional republic and still fume over the refusal of our representatives in government to do their jobs. On those issues—and so many others today—it's the Left leaning on their gratitude and trying to preserve what *they* "want to keep." Healthy political debate—especially in a country whose diversity is one of our defining strengths—is in the give-and-take between the desire to preserve what's working and to change what's not.

This respect for opposing views doesn't fit the typical partisan style today, where Democrats and Republicans blame each other for every problem under the sun, and even for *intentionally* hurting the country with their ideas. The current approach by both political parties has created chaos and dysfunction in Washington and has spread division and discord across America. More importantly, the current approach in Washington is not solving America's problems. It is making our problems worse.

Where Government Comes In

To Conservatives, the fact problems persist even in our strong, prosperous, free nation is not a surprise or a scandal. It doesn't mean we shouldn't try to fix these problems. It only means we are still human, still fallible. *Of course*, there are pockets of injustice, of poverty or homelessness, of substandard schools or rundown neighborhoods. Of course, there are healthcare problems like addiction and as-yet-uncured diseases. These have been a part of *every* human society since the dawn of man. To Conservatives, the fact that, in America, there are *only* pockets of these miseries is something close to a miracle. Most everywhere else in the world, and at almost any moment in history before today, things have been and remain much worse.

To Liberals, however, the persistence of these kinds of problems proves our society is not good, strong, prosperous, or free at all. They see these maladies as an indictment of our political and economic systems—even our country as a whole. To the Left, the combination of capitalism and constitutionalism are not the near-miraculous engines of opportunity, prosperity, and happiness Conservatives think they are. Rather, the Left views these institutions as culprits, as flawed experiments at best, and, at worst, as weapons wielded by the powerful to hurt everyone else.

This is why the split between Right and Left is often framed in the shorthand of Big Government vs. Small Government.

The Right sees an undeniable track record of success from the organic, interpersonal, bottom-up institutions of the market economy and civil society voluntarism. Free enterprise and community spirit have created unmatched social opportunities and economic prosperity for the vast majority of Americans. Conservatives want to keep these things that have worked and continuously try to make them work better for all the people who have yet to get a firm grip on the ladder of opportunity.

The Left, on the other hand, sees all the people who are being "left behind" by capitalism and voluntarism—people still struggling and suffering—and concludes voluntary institutions must be replaced with government programs. Absent from the Left's consideration is whether less government might actually help more people by allowing the private sector to work better.

Most major policy debates in Washington follows this pattern. A problem is identified—usually, but not always—by those on the Left. The Left declares the existence of the problem as evidence of the inadequacy of America's free market and civil society—and proposes a government program to ban things they don't like or subsidize things they do. Conservatives counter that either (a) the source of the problem is not the free market, but the unintended consequences of *previous* government meddling in it, or (b) this new plan for government intervention would create more negative unintended consequences. The Left hears the Right's prudence as hard-heartedness, while the Right hears the Left's idealistic confidence as utopian hubris—and round and round they go.

Conservative Reformers

Ideally, this natural tension yields reform—continuous improvement. And Conservatives, at their heart, must always be reformers. The argument of the Left is, no matter how good things may seem, nothing is perfect. This is actually a *Conservative* insight. No Conservative believes free enterprise or voluntary associations are perfect. They are human institutions and, therefore, inherently flawed. Conservatives must always pay close attention to the problems Liberals highlight. These are opportunities to propose Conservative solutions.

Conservatives are right to trust existing institutions, up to a point, simply because their continuing existence suggests they have proved useful in the past. But times change, and, to be effective, Conservatives must always change with them. The most effective solutions are usually found in tweaking the law so existing voluntary institutions and the private sector as a whole can work better for more people. Replacing proven institutions with more layers of dysfunctional government programs is, unfortunately, the natural default solution of the Left.

Conservatives should not change our principles—our time-tested and proven covenants of faith, diversity, and the like—nor can we insist on protecting the status quo when real problems emerge. We must constantly reapply our principles to discover creative answers to new challenges.

In this life, as the economist Thomas Sowell says, "there are no solutions; only trade-offs."[7] Even good ideas eventually become obsolete if they are not adapted to our constantly changing world.

In the 1980s, Ronald Reagan heated up the Cold War with massive defense spending and escalated rhetoric against the Soviet Union. He thought it was essential to challenge the long stalemate between what he considered the free people of the world and "the evil empire." History now proves Reagan was right. His strategy forced the Soviet Union to destroy itself without firing a shot. But no sooner had his strategy worked than the United States found itself in a new era of global challenges—in China, Europe, Iran, North Korea, and in a reemerging Russia.

After 9/11, George W. Bush knew the United States needed to answer the threat posed by Al Qaeda. We did. But, as soon as Al Qaeda was defeated, ISIS exploded into the region.

In the 1930s, senior citizens were the poorest age cohort of Americans. The federal government created the Social Security program as a national social insurance system for the elderly. This program made a huge dent in senior poverty—so much so that, today, senior citizens are America's *wealthiest* age cohort. Mission accomplished? No question. But now Social Security is fiscally unsustainable, less than a decade away from insolvency. New ideas are always needed.

This is not to criticize the Cold War, the War on Terror, or Social Security. It's simply to illustrate the point even successful strategies eventually require updating.

In the free market, where competition drives creative destruction of the status quo, this process of continuous improvement happens all the time without any help from government. New products, services, and business models replace old ones. Companies who cannot adapt—even huge, profitable, international corporations—go under. Economists often talk about capitalism's "invisible hand"—which directs resources to their most efficient uses. But equally important to a functioning market is the "invisible foot," which spurs every business to constantly improve itself or face failure.

McDonald's has Burger King to keep it honest. The Yankees have the Red Sox. FedEx has UPS. Amazon has Google. When the big guys make mistakes, competitors immediately capitalize on them. The invisible foot of market competition forces businesses to stay sharp, or else. No business wants to end up like VHS tapes or rotary phones. Government alone is immune to market forces.

When a government program fails or falls behind, there is no competitor or customer who has the power to impose real-time discipline on the politicians and bureaucrats who created it. There's only We the People attempting to referee from a distance the great debate between the Right and Left about whether to improve the free institutions of the market economy and civil society, or to replace them with the coercive programs and edicts of the government.

Understanding this debate—the arguments and issues—is the responsibility of citizenship. Every American who abdicates this responsibility because they think politics is too boring, too mean, too confusing, or too frustrating becomes a willing partner with the authors and beneficiaries of the status quo.

The Left would have all Americans believe policy is just too complicated for ordinary people to understand—we're all better off leaving it up to the expert politicians and bureaucrats. But, even if we know nothing about politics, we still know one thing about experts: They're human. And, if experts are human, they are just like the rest of us: filled with pride, selfishness, greed, and vulnerable to the same temptations we all face. The theory of Liberalism says government politicians and bureaucrats can be trusted not to fall prey to these temptations, but the long record of human history screams otherwise.

It was this realistic view of human nature that compelled the Framers of the U.S. Constitution to create our government system with "checks and balances." They gave us two houses of Congress, one to represent our diverse people and the other to represent our diverse states and geography. They gave us a president who can propose and sign laws, implement and enforce laws, but not allowed to create laws. They gave us judges with the power to strike down unconstitutional laws, but subject to presidential appointment and congressional confirmation and impeachment. They gave the federal government specific and limited powers but reserved vast powers for the states and the people.

But, as Part I has shown, sufficiently clever and motivated politicians have figured out how to get around a lot of these institutional checks on their power and mischief. At the end of the day, neither the House nor the Senate nor the presidency nor the courts are the real checks and balances of American political power; only the people can safeguard freedom.

Unless We the People keep close watch on the politicians and bureaucrats, the politicians and bureaucrats will look out for themselves instead of the rest of us. The United States of America belongs to the people, not Washington. The politicians work for us, not the other way around. If we want to reclaim our birthright of freedom, Conservatives are going to have to fight for it.

Inside the Fight

Part II of *CONSERVATIVE* will take you inside the ongoing and escalating fight between the Left and Right and between the government and the governed. Now that you know what Conservatives want to keep, you also need to know *what* we've lost and *how* we plan to get it back. In other words, Part II is about knowing what to fix and how to fix it.

Chapter 7 will reveal the motives and goals of the Left and describe how the Left has changed in recent years, from the optimistic Liberal champions of the working class to the servants of Progressive global elites who look down on the rest of the country. Where Liberals used to be impatient with problems, Progressives today are just intolerant of Conservatives and traditional American values. What does this new, angry Progressive Left really want and what are they willing to do to get it? And, just as important, what threats and opportunities does the Democratic Party's embrace of this new (actually, old) ideology offer to Conservatives and Republicans?

Chapter 8 will detail the global and domestic networks of Progressive money, institutions, and influence. You've heard of George Soros and you know about Progressive dominance of popular culture and the academy. But the Left's tentacles reach far beyond the people and institutions we know and into almost invisible local, national, and international organizations, all working hand-in-hand to persuade, misguide, or just overthrow We the People in America and around the world.

Chapter 9 will expose the Left's dangerous pursuit of Socialist economic policies and Chapter 10 will survey the damage the Left has already done (what we've lost), both here in the United States and everywhere their policies have been imposed on free societies. From the wartime power-grabs of Woodrow Wilson to the psychotic lunacy of Communism, from the destruction of vibrant nations like Cuba and Venezuela to the slow-motion breakdown of blue states like California and New York, everywhere the Left succeeds in replacing covenants, faith, diversity, traditions, institutions, and opportunity with centralized government planning and control, families, communities, and economies fall into dysfunction.

Finally, Chapters 11 and 12 will lay out specific policy reforms, political and cultural strategies that can take the fight to the Left—and win!

If Conservatives are to prevail in keeping the things that made America great, we need to know who is trying to replace them, why they want to replace them, and how they intend to do it. We also need to know what things need fixing in America and how to apply our principles to fix them.

CHAPTER 7

The Motivation
and Goals of the Left

*None but the people can forge their own chains; and to flatter the
people and delude them by promises never meant to be performed is
the stale but successful practice of the demagogue, as of the seducer
in private life.*[1]

—JOHN RANDOLPH

Why? Why do Progressives, Liberals, and Democrats work so hard and
spend so much money to tear down the things Conservatives want to
keep—things we can prove make life better for everyone? It's a fair question: what motivates the Left?

Discovering motives is essential to knowing the truth. Unless you
understand the motivation of the Left, you will not know why they are so
intolerant of Conservative thought. You will not know why Conservatives
and Progressives can't compromise and "just get along." And you will not
see the grave danger in the policies pursued by the Left with such anger and
self-righteous zeal.

If you want to understand the motivation of the Left at its most
simplistic level, a good place to start is John Lennon's 1971 mega-hit song
"Imagine." The song imagines no religion, no heaven, no hell, no countries, and no possessions—nothing worth dying or taking life for. Lennon

imagines if these traditional ideas were eliminated, all people would live in peace, sharing all the world as a brotherhood of man. It is the Left's utopian dream.

Lennon was matter-of-fact about the song's extremism—and how easy it was to convince people his imaginings were reasonable. "'Imagine' is anti-religious, anti-nationalistic, anti-conventional, anti-capitalistic," Geoffrey Giuliano, one of Lennon's biographers, wrote, "but because it is sugar-coated, it is accepted."[2] The Left, by necessity, has become adept at "sugar-coating" their positions because if Americans understood their ultimate goals, their ideas would be rejected.

John Lennon was not a political activist with plans to establish a one-world government. But his perspective represents the one-dimensional default logic of the natural man. In other words, this is how most people will assess issues without an understanding of the causes and effects of public policy. Think about it; most wars are between countries and many conflicts have been about religion. So, logically, if there are no countries and no religion, there will be no wars. Right?

Without religion, heaven or hell, there would be no moral judgement or guilt—only peace. And if people didn't have possessions, there would be no greed or crime. If everything was shared, there would be no poverty or hunger. It all makes perfect sense, unless you know history and understand human nature.

As a practical matter, religion and a fixed transcendent order is the basis of all human morality. Attempts to divorce societies from their natural preferences for their faith, families, neighborhoods, and nations have resulted in blood-drenched failures. And the call for an end to earthly possessions—odd coming from Lennon, one of the wealthiest entertainers of all time—is just absurd.

Over the last thirty years, mankind has successfully reduced poverty and hunger more than at any time in the history of the world—specifically because market capitalism has spread to Asia and Africa, while the only places in the world sinking deeper into poverty are "possession-free" paradises like North Korea and Venezuela. You don't need to imagine it; you just have to turn on the news.

Few on the Left will admit they are anti-country, anti-capitalism, anti-military, anti-tradition, and anti-religion. Most would likely say they support all of these, but their political views and policies work to diminish the relevance of these ideas in America. Consider a few examples.

The Left may say they love America, but their policy positions of open borders, non-citizen voting rights, and citizenship for illegal aliens reveal a devalued notion of nationhood. Prominent Democrats have called for the abolishment of the U.S. Immigration and Customs Enforcement, the agency which enforces immigration laws throughout the country.[3] They call border walls "immoral," and have stated in plain terms that even existing border walls should be removed.[4] In early 2019, all House Democrats voted to defend localities that allow illegal immigrants to vote in their elections.[5]

And the Left consistently works to transfer American authority to global organizations such as the United Nations, the World Trade Organization, the World Court, and the International Monetary Fund. Just take two examples. In 1995, President Clinton signed the UN Convention on the Rights of the Child, which gives children a full right to abortion and contraceptives (regardless of their parents' ethics, desires, or consent), a right to privacy (even in the home) and the legal mechanisms to challenge in court their parents' authority. The Senate failed to ratify the treaty, but not for lack of trying by the Left.[6]

The Left also seeks to impose their agenda on the rest of the world using taxpayer dollars. "The U.S. has deployed its diplomats and spent tens of millions of dollars to try to block anti-gay laws, punish countries that enacted them, and tie financial assistance to respect for LGBTQ rights," read the lead in one NBC news story written during the Obama years. As a result of a 2011 memorandum signed by President Obama to "promote and protect the human rights of LGBT persons" in other countries, U.S. embassies began taking part in gay pride celebrations and raising rainbow flags alongside American ones.[7]

The same article quotes Susan Rice, President Obama's national security advisor, as saying she "walked into a very backward environment in 2009," presumably referring to the Bush administration's position of allowing other countries to make their own policies with respect to social issues.

The Left claims to support capitalism and oppose socialism (although many Democrats are now openly advocating for socialism), but their policies say otherwise. Remember, socialism means the government—rather than individuals—own the means of production, distribution, and exchange.

Leading Democrats now support policies promoting government control of large swaths of the American economy, including healthcare, education, energy production, and taxation. We will discuss these areas more in depth later in Part II.

If you want to understand the policy goals of the Left, consider what would be required for John Lennon's imaginings to become reality. Without countries, we would need a global central government (think United Nations or European Union as a pretext to global governance). This is why leftist leaders and globalist corporations around the world opposed Brexit—the effort of the British people to extract themselves from the bureaucratic morass and corruption of the European Union. And this is why the Left in both political parties promote trade agreements and international treaties that supersede the authority of American laws.

In this context, it's easy to understand why the Left was apoplectic about President Donald Trump's slogans of "Make America Great Again" and "America First." Trump's call for definitive and secure borders and his prioritization of American jobs and American greatness were anathema to the Left's core beliefs. Contrast this to the time, early in his presidency, when Barack Obama watered down the idea of "American exceptionalism" altogether. "I believe in American exceptionalism," he said, "just as I suspect that the Brits believe in British exceptionalism and the Greeks believe in Greek exceptionalism."[8]

The Left's anger with Trump was further stoked by their political predicament; they couldn't let the public know they disagreed with Trump's nationalistic themes. So they agreed rhetorically with "border security" while opposing everything that would bring it about. The Left supports sanctuary cities and states for illegal immigrants and continuously pushes for citizenship and voting rights for those who come to America illegally. The Left knows if American citizenship is available to everyone in the world, citizenship means nothing—no loyalty, and no shared values. Just everyone living as many, and none as one—none, that is, as Americans.

Let's imagine a religion-free America. The Left will never admit to being anti-religious. But, as we've already pointed out, Democrats have become increasing bold in their public denigration of Christian beliefs during the nomination and confirmation process for judges and executive branch officials. They are applying an unconstitutional religious test to candidates for public office, accusing one nominee of Islamophobia for holding traditional evangelical Christian beliefs about salvation and telling another her Catholicism would make her a biased judge.[9] In early 2019, the Democratic majority in the House of Representatives couldn't even agree to condemn anti-Semitic comments by one of their freshman members.[10] The Left's strategy is to discredit and denigrate religious values by stigmatizing religious beliefs and moral standards for public officials.

When religious people, including Christians, are persecuted, harassed, sued, and fined for attempting to keep traditional values in their own lives and small businesses, the foundational source of righteousness and virtue in America is pushed into the shadows of public life. If not for the private efforts of churches and people of faith in America, our federal government would have already completely vanquished Kirk's "transcendent order."

Imagine no property or possessions in America. Most on the Left will feign outrage if you accuse them of opposing private property, but their policies expose their true beliefs. For years, the Left has supported heavy taxes and regulation on private property, which gives them the means to control what individual Americans can do on their own land.

The Environmental Protection Agency, in particular, has waged a long war with property owners over things like "ephemeral streams"—streams that form only when it rains. Just ask eighty-year old Charlie Johnson, a Massachusetts cranberry farmer and Korean war veteran who spent twenty-two years fighting the EPA for the right to expand his cranberry farm by fifty acres. He eventually gave up after running out of money. He had already spent $2.5 million. The EPA, on the other hand, spent $10 million in taxpayer money going after Charlie and his fifty acres.

Charlie's attorney, a former EPA official, framed the attitude of these government officials in stark terms: "They had it out for Charlie from the beginning [...] they don't accept anyone who stands up to them, so they will punish you."[11]

This kind of control and abuse of private property—one of America's most fundamental rights—is supported by Left. Every time Conservatives have tried to amend the Clean Water Act to prevent these kinds of abuses, the Left blocks it.

It's easy to dismiss Lennon's "Imagine" as an anthem to leftist utopian silliness. Yet the ideas in the song continue to motivate the Left despite reality's refutation of it in the decades since its release. Billions of people around the world have been pulled out of poverty not by ending property rights, but by finally extending them to places and people where those rights were previously precluded. Wars are rarer and less bloody than they were decades ago, in large part because the United States has asserted its role as the strongest military force in the world, and the Communist regimes that took Lennon's economic advice are no longer around to terrorize the globe.

The motivation and goals of the Left are easy to figure out if one is willing to take a few minutes to study the facts, but average Americans getting their news from the mainstream media may never know the truth. There is usually a great chasm between what the Left says and what they actually believe.

The great irony of the Left is the conflict between their motivation and goals, and their means to achieve them. Their goal is to unify everyone under a central political and economic structure and to move toward global governance, but, to achieve this goal, the Left must divide and create discord between an increasing number of disadvantaged and "victimized" groups of people. The Left divides to unite. They work to convince people only government can protect them from the sources of their victimization. This was the poisonous logic behind President Obama's 2010 exhortation to Democratic voters to "punish our enemies," meaning Republicans.[12]

Without the resources and protection of government, in this mindset, people are supposedly powerless against "white nationalists," "greedy capitalists," "religious bigots," "homophobes," "traditionalists" who enslave with old morals, and Conservatives who "cling to their guns and religion" (according to Obama).

The Left must create fear and discontent to gain public support for centralizing power. The spirit of gratitude to God and country—the prevailing attitude of Conservatives—is viewed as a type of blindness and an unwillingness to recognize and address systemic problems.

The Road to Hell Is Paved with Good Intentions

We are not suggesting all Progressives, Liberals, and Democrats have evil motives or bad intentions. Certainly, John Lennon wanted love and peace for everyone. The problem is the Left considers their goals so noble they are willing to abandon their integrity to achieve them. While their intentions may be lofty, their strategies and actions can become tyrannical and have often proved destructive to individuals and nations.

Good intentions have always been a characteristic of the Left—at least, for the rank and file, if not for their leaders. In the early 20th century, there were many calls in America to imitate the German models of universal welfare and pension systems. "[B]y 1910 […] actual pensions or prospective eligibility for them [Germans] reached 52 percent of the economically active German population."[13] If only Americans could have seen then the tyranny that would result from a population anesthetized by government largess. German tyrants caused two world wars and tens of millions of deaths before the middle of the century.

The good intentions of European socialism and government dependency were brought to America by advocates such as Dr. I. M. Rubinow, a Socialist Party member and author of *Social Insurance* (1913) and *The Quest for Security* (1934). Rubinow wrote government-sponsored social insurance:

> may and has been decried as rank paternalism, and this indictment must be readily admitted. For social insurance, when properly developed, is nothing if not a well-defined effort of the organized state to come to the assistance of the wage-earner and furnish him something he individually is quite unable to attain for himself.[14]

Professor Henry Rogers Seager, another influential proponent of government paternalism in the early 20th century, wanted America to move toward a view of government as a moral agency with a humanitarian mission.

> To become a "truly civilized society," the United States must develop a "deepening sense of social solidarity and quickening of appreciation of our common interest." And that Americas must "begin to think of government as […] organized machinery for advancing our common interests."[15]

Americans resisted European-style paternalism until the Great Depression and two World Wars caused the seeds of socialism to take root. President Franklin D. Roosevelt used America's insecurities and vulnerabilities to implement his New Deal, which included: massive expansions of the welfare state like the nearly-insolvent Social Security program;

preferential treatment of unions; the National Recovery Act, which set prices and wages in specific industries; and a farmer assistance program that manipulates the choices of individual growers and protects big, conglomerate farms from market risks.

Roosevelt's intentions were good, but socialism and dependency grow like a cancer. Roosevelt's predecessors had presided over a republic with a set of checks and balances designed to limit the concentration of political power. His successors presided over a system defined by the concentration of power, both in Washington and, within Washington, in the executive branch.[16] National politics has since been consumed by candidates and political parties attempting to win elections by promising more and more from government.

Roosevelt represented the political philosophy defined by the "Liberal" application of government resources and power to every situation. This is the philosophy that shaped the Democratic Party from the mid-1930s through the turn of the century. But, beginning with the election of Barack Obama in 2008, the Democratic Party has been dominated by Far-Left Progressives intent on a globalist, Socialist agenda. Their motives and intentions now seem far less noble and the results of their policies are potentially far more dangerous.

Misdirection Obscures the Left's Motives and Goals

From abortion to climate change, the true motives of the Left are often hidden behind phrases like "women's health," "saving the planet," "free healthcare," or "tolerance." While these goals are important, and, undoubtedly, many on the Left feel strongly about them, the outcome of policies hidden behind these phrases is usually less pleasant. Abortion is less about women's health than it is about convenience and, increasingly, eugenics. Policies surrounding climate change and health care resort more and more to one tactic: control. Tolerance, meanwhile, has become a buzzword not for the pluralism and diversity America was built upon, but rather "speech with which I agree."

As the Left moves closer to outright promotion of socialism, their policies begin to divide us into hierarchies of the controllers and the controlled, the victims and the aggressors.

Examples from the last few years abound. Recall the case of Master-piece Cakeshop, which we raised in Part I. Jack Phillips, a cake baker in Colorado who sells cakes to anyone but will not make a custom cake for gay weddings that violate his religious beliefs, has been subjected to years of government harassment, as he seeks to simply live out his faith in his own small business. The Supreme Court of Colorado, in a 7–2 decision siding with Phillips, noted he was subjected to "clear and impermissible hostility toward the sincere religious beliefs that motivated his objection."[17]

The same mentality was on display as part of Obamacare, which mandated all employers must pay for employee health insurance that provides contraception and abortion-inducing drugs—even those employers who have strong religious beliefs against it. This logic is how the Little Sisters of the Poor, an order of Catholic nuns, ended up at the Supreme Court, challenging the government's ability to coerce a religious order into doing something diametrically opposed to their religious beliefs and to America's first freedom. The Little Sisters won, by the way.

It's not that the Left is opposed to religious liberty, as such. They just want to limit religious freedom to those religious beliefs that fit with Progressive politics. Some people should be allowed to have free religious expression. Others not. The same Democratic House majority that happily provided religious exceptions for their Muslim members to wear hijabs on the floor of the House (as they should) absolutely refused to give the same deference to the religious beliefs of President Trump's nominees, who were publicly shunned by Senate Democrats for being evangelically Christian, for being Catholic, and for being affiliated with the Knights of Columbus, a Catholic service organization.

The Left's buzzwords also hide a pervasive desire to control. In proposing a Green New Deal with the goal of "remaking" the country's economy, Representative Alexandria Ocasio-Cortez would mandate Americans' choices regarding the cars they drive, how they travel, where their energy comes from, and how much of it they can use.

The same goes for health care. Government policies have mandated the coverage of so many conditions they have priced families out of the marketplace. Under the Medicare for All plans proposed by leading Democrats, the government would decide your best treatment options, rather than you and your doctor.

Even the Left's abortion policies, when you unpack them, are far less about women's health than they are about refusing to recognize the dignity and humanity of new life, even after birth. A woman's health has nothing to do with a baby who has kicked and screamed its way into the world, but that hasn't stopped Democrats from defending outright infanticide as a critical component of "health care."

The Left's policies are easy to sell. Who doesn't like free stuff? Who doesn't oppose hate speech. Who doesn't want to protect the environment and support women's health? But as we will show later in Part II, the policy outcomes of these unobjectionable phrases are far more pernicious.

CHAPTER 8

How the Left Is Organized

The reason it is so important to control government is because government is the source of enormous power. One president in this country...appoints...5,000 people to run the bureaucracy, nonmilitary nonpostal service of 2 million people, who hire 10 million outside outsource contractors—a workforce of 12 million people—that spends $3 trillion a year. That number is larger than the gross domestic product of all but four countries on the face of the earth.[1]

—Rob Stein, founder of the Democracy Alliance

Rob Stein, a leader of the Left and former political operative for Bill and Hillary Clinton, doesn't hide why he wants the Left to control government. It's all about power. And power is all about money. But his statement far understates the power of government control. The Bureau of Labor Statistics reports approximately twenty-two million people are employed by the federal, state, and local governments in the U.S.[2] That's almost twice as many as are employed in the manufacturing sector.

Postal workers add almost another six hundred thousand.[3] And, while no one knows exactly how many civilian contractors are working for the government at all levels, if we add all government workers and a Conservative estimate of the number of government contractors, we can say with some confidence there are close to thirty million direct and indirect employees of government in America. With average family sizes of over three people, we can conclude approximately 100 million Americans are dependent on government for their paychecks. These voters have a vested interest in growing the government.

Approximately one third of all government workers are members of unions (five times the union membership of the private sector).[4] These unions are the largest funders of leftist politicians and causes. Half of all union members in the U.S. now work for the government.[5] A portion of every paycheck of union members is automatically deducted for union dues (a new executive order has made it possible for some government workers to opt out of automatic deductions for union dues). And, as we will detail in this chapter, a large portion of union dues is sent directly to the Democratic Party and leftist initiatives designed to seize more government power.

If you think the leaders on the Left want universal healthcare (Medicare for All) just to help average Americans get better healthcare, think again. Healthcare represents about 1/6 of the total U.S. economy and there are eighteen million healthcare workers.[6] If these workers become government employees and union members, they will become a major new funding source and powerful voting block for the Left.

Dependency on government for income and other vital services makes voters vulnerable to political manipulation. When we add the over 100 million Americans who are beneficiaries of Social Security, Medicare, and Medicaid to the Americans who receive their paychecks directly or indirectly from government sources, the strategies of the Left become apparent. Well over half of all Americans are dependent on the government for at least part of their income and, therefore, are subject to electioneering fear tactics and promises of more benefits from the Left.

As we explore how the Left is organized in America, it will become clear to our readers why they seek to increase the number of dependent voters and union members. And it will become obvious why socialism is the Left's Holy Grail. Socialism means practically everyone is dependent on the government.

It will also become increasingly apparent why the Left literally hates Conservative goals of less government, freedom in the workplace (freedom not to join a union) and more choices of nongovernment services. Conservatism is a direct threat to the elite who want to control people and society.

Philosophical Foundations of the Left

We have been careful to acknowledge that most voters and politicians on the Left have a genuine interest in helping people. They differ from Conservatives because they believe people are best served by a large, powerful, and centralized government. There is another significant but more subtle difference between Conservatives and the leaders of the Left: The Left doesn't believe most people can live independently from government. They do not trust people to make choices for themselves and therefore don't believe they should be allowed to make choices at all. The Left believes dependency on experts and government benefits is a good thing.

Allow us to make a few subjective, statistically unsubstantiated observations about the philosophical foundations of the Left based on our collective thirty years of experience in the political arena. The leftist views society as a large mass of intellectually inferior people who need to be guided and cared for by the benevolent elite. They will vigorously deny this assertion, but all of their strategies and policies suggest otherwise.

The leaders and funders of the Left tend to be people who have attained great wealth, often quickly, such as Wall Street investors, money managers, and young tech innovators such as the founders of Facebook and Google. The elite also include performers, professors, news media anchors, politicians, and bureaucrats who sit above society and look down on average workers, fans, students, audiences, and voters. The elite believe the masses are incapable of guiding their own lives and certainly unqualified to guide society.

In this context, it is easy to see why the Conservative philosophy of less government and more individual freedom is completely irrational to the Left. When Conservatives demand less regulation of business and private property, more education choices, more healthcare competition and choices, more private options for Social Security and Medicare, more incentives for work and less incentives for welfare, more power for states and more overall freedom—the Left becomes enraged. These ideas are anathema to their societal paradigm.

Why Is the Left So Powerful?

The goals and strategies of the Left sound more attractive (free Medicare for All, free college, basic income for all, and so on), and they translate into a significant political advantage. The Left's quest for cultural and economic control is complimentary to their goal of centralized political control. Their policies promote more government power, which translates into more power for the Democratic Party. Centralized political power translates into centralized control of the economy, media, entertainment, and academia. Big begets big. Every new government program enlarges the Left's political and cultural constituencies with more dependence on government—from children in poverty to multinational corporations.

Conservatives have an inherent political weakness. They believe in less government control and decentralized political power. They promote individual freedom and more localized government. These ideas lead to less political leverage and smaller electoral constituencies. Conservative politicians don't want voters to need them, and Conservative voters want less from government. In other words, Conservative policies put political middlemen out of their jobs.

As Progressives, Liberals, and Democrats gain power, they dismantle the constituencies for Conservative ideas and the foundations of a free and civil society. Their policies result in more dependency, division, envy, jealousy, greed, hate, violence, crime, poverty, homelessness, and misery. We see this in major cities like Detroit and states like California, which have been controlled by Progressive Democrat politicians for years. But, instead of creating political problems for the Left, these failures play right into their hands. The people demand more government to fix the problems.

As society deteriorates, the Left portrays freedom as a dangerous free-for-all—everyone left alone to fight for themselves—where only the strong survive. As Janis Joplin, a contemporary of John Lennon, expressed in her song "Me and Bobby McGee," freedom means you have nothing more to lose. The Left has done a good job promoting their worthless form of freedom. Today, when Conservatives call for more freedom, an increasing number of Americans feel threatened and run into the arms of the Left.

It's easy to see why Conservatives accrue less political power. They seek to give more power to the "masses." A true Conservative statesman is a servant leader. In the words of business leader Robert K. Greenleaf:

> The servant leader is a servant first. It begins with the natural feeling that one wants to serve. Then conscious choice brings one to aspire to

lead. The best test is: do those served grow as persons: do they, while being served, become healthier, wiser, freer, more autonomous, more likely themselves to become servants? And, what is the effect on the least privileged in society; will they benefit, or, at least, not be further deprived?[7]

Compare this to statements from leading Democrats like Alexandria Ocasio-Cortez, who addressed policy criticism of her Green New Deal by shooting back, "I'm the boss."[8] Or Hillary Clinton who, while running for president in 2016, referred to Americans supporting then-candidate Trump as an irredeemable "basket of deplorables."[9] To President Barack Obama, much of "red" America was incapable of intellectual thought because they were too busy "cling[ing] to guns or religion."[10] The contempt many on the Left have for the rest of America is surmised in an article that trended on *Gawker* in 2015 with the headline, "Dumb Hicks Are America's Greatest Threat."[11]

We are not claiming all Conservative leaders—and certainly not all Republican politicians—are servant leaders in the aspirational sense described by Mr. Greenleaf. But we can say with confidence: this is the true Conservative ethos. And we can say with equal confidence the actions and policies of the Democratic Party—and especially the Progressives therein—work to achieve the opposite. They want more people on welfare, food stamps, Medicaid, and other benefits, while opposing work requirements, education choices, private health insurance alternatives, personally owned Social Security accounts, and other options to help people become more independent of government.

Certainly, there are many followers on the Left who see those in need and honestly believe government should help them. But the top leaders and funders of the Left foment a "helpless masses" philosophy to propel themselves into positions of power for much less charitable motives. They seek to weaken the close associations that strengthen individuality, character, and skills, such as marriage, family, churches, and voluntary associations. To the Left, these "little platoons" are rivals of big government. The Left promotes more welfare and dependency, while resisting reforms to make people "*healthier, wiser, freer, more autonomous, more likely themselves to become servants.*"

The more you know, the clearer you will see the differences between the Right and Left. On the Right, fellow servants strive to live freely in covenant with each other. On the Left, fellow dependents will live as servants to government.

How the Left Dismantles What Conservatives Want to Keep

Most of the supporters of leftist ideas are not involved in a global conspiracy to create a one-world government. They are pawns in a global chess game controlled by leftist elites who profit from the money and power derived from centralized government. Their political strategies prepare the soil for voters to give away their freedom.

As leftist policies weaken the bonds of marriage and family, faith, community, and voluntary associations, they weaken the societal infrastructure that enables people to live free and independent lives. When leftist propaganda convinces people that they are victims of discrimination and vulnerable to dangerous societal forces, they look to government for protection. And, when national pride is diminished, and citizenship cheapened, people are susceptible to the promises of socialism and international governance.

Consider what has happened to the proud nations of Europe. Most have been part of the European Union for several decades. Workers and their families from EU countries can now move freely throughout Europe. That's a good thing, except most visitors and guest workers can vote in local and some national elections. Even non-European immigrants who have been granted asylum in large numbers into Europe can move freely and vote in some countries. The result has been the election of local and national political leaders with more loyalty to supranational organizations, such as the European Union and the United Nations. When countries like Britain try to escape the chains of the larger whole (Brexit), they are warned their country can no longer survive as an independent nation. Indeed, the EU is now beginning to tighten its budgetary control over member states, who have up to now enjoyed veto power over tax and other national-level fiscal policies.[12]

Globalists have the same designs on America. Since 2000, our decennial census has not included a question about citizenship. Everyone is counted as a citizen and congressional districts are allocated based on the total population for each state. It has been estimated California has between six to ten unwarranted congressional seats because illegal immigrants and legal non-citizens are counted in the census.[13]

Congressional districts translate into electoral votes in presidential elections. So states offering sanctuary cities and attracting illegal immigrants with Liberal social welfare programs gain considerable political power. Federal money is also granted to states based on population and congressional districts. Education funding, money for roads, bridges, and mass transit, welfare and Medicaid funds, and other federal grants are often linked to population.

This is why Democrats filed suit against the administration when the Justice Department under President Trump asked the Census Bureau to include a citizenship question in the 2020 census.

The March 1, 2018 edition of *The Federalist* described the census controversy:

> Democrats disagree. In the words of 17 state attorneys general, including a citizenship question could risk an *"unconstitutional undercount"* by chilling noncitizen respondents.
>
> That those state attorneys general were recently joined by former Obama administration Attorney General Eric Holder indicates the gravity of this issue for the Left. Why? Illegal aliens tend to live in large blue urban areas. The greater the population figures due to the counting of illegal aliens, the more political power and bacon such states can bring in.

The Left disarms the Right by dismantling the foundations of a free country: national pride and the close associations of family and community that hold us together as a nation and imbue individuals with the capabilities to live in freedom. Without confidence in oneself and a sense of covenant with a larger whole, uncertainty and fear drive people into the arms of benevolent-sounding tyrants.

The Left's Transition from Liberal to Radical

Until their two successive defeats in presidential elections in 2000 (Al Gore vs. George W. Bush) and 2004 (John Kerry vs. George W. Bush), the Left kept their focus and resources inside the Democratic Party. Their candidates were center-Left in their ideology, largely traditional Liberals, and the Democratic Party still had some Conservatives ("Blue Dogs"). But all this changed after the 2004 election.

After their defeat in 2000 and looking toward their almost certain victory over Bush in his re-election bid in 2004, a group of leftist donors began to coalesce into an informal coalition called the Phoenix Group—presumably they were "rising from the ashes" of the "stolen" 2000 election. These folks began giving millions to Liberal candidates and political committees, but 2004 still ended in humiliating failure. So, in December 2004, after another defeat, a small group of wealthy donors met in San Francisco. George Soros, Peter Lewis, savings and loan tycoons Herb and Marion Sandler, and a few others met to commiserate about what one called "our Pearl Harbor" and how best to respond.[14]

2004 was supposed to be the turnaround year for the Left. The polls leading into election day—and even exit polls at the precincts said John Kerry would beat George W. Bush. But, the next morning, Bush was not only still president but had increased his numbers among voters in almost every demographic group—including blacks, gays, women, and Hispanics.[15]

In April 2005, the Left's response began in earnest. A larger group of donors—around seventy millionaires and billionaires—met in a secret, long-term planning session in *Phoenix*, Arizona. Three-quarters of the members voted that their "Democracy Alliance," as it was called, should not "retain close ties to the Democratic Party."[16]

Some former Clinton officials were at this meeting; the most important was the attorney Rob Stein. He was an evangelist of sorts among this group, showing them a famous PowerPoint presentation, "The Conservative Message Machine's Money Matrix," which featured groups like the Bradley Foundation, the American Enterprise Institute, and The Heritage Foundation. Stein credited Conservatives' electoral success to four decades of Conservatives' long-term investing in ideas and institutions—"perhaps," he reportedly said, Conservatives have become "the most potent, independent, institutionalized apparatus ever assembled in a democracy to promote one belief system."[17]

Stein would later recall from the Phoenix meeting "an unbelievable frustration, particularly among the donor class [...] with trying to one-off everything—with every single one of them being a single, 'silo' donor and not having the ability to communicate effectively with a network of donors." Stein helped convince this group of wealthy leftist donors the Democratic Party had become a top-down organization run by professional politicians who cared little about donors' concerns. He was convinced the Democratic Party's hierarchy had to be turned upside-down: Donors should fund an ideological movement that would dictate policies to the politicians.[18]

The Phoenix Group officially organized into the Democracy Alliance, a taxable nonprofit that doesn't have to disclose its donors. Leftist millionaires and billionaires funnel their money through Democracy Alliance into myriad Progressive causes. Also, at the top of the pyramid of leftist funding organizations are government and private sector unions. Government unions such as the Service Employees International Union (SEIA—government workers), National Education Association (NEA—teachers' union), American Federation of Teachers (AFT—teachers' union) join private sector unions such as the American Federation of Labor and Congress of Industrial Organizations (AFL-CIO), the Teamsters, and Communications Workers of America (CWA—includes government workers). This massive infusion of "autopilot" money helped Democrats win majorities in Congress in 2006 and Barack Obama win the White House in 2008.

We should note union workers often don't share the ideology of their bosses. As many as 40 percent of union workers sometimes vote Republican. But they, nevertheless, serve as unwilling funders of radical leftist politicians and causes. For example, unionized coal miners in West Virginia are mostly unaware their dues support the Sierra Club, which is trying to close coal mines and eliminate fossil fuels. Union workers in auto plants in Detroit may not know their dues support the Union of Concerned Scientists, which advocates for the elimination of the combustion engine. Union workers in Pennsylvania who voted for Trump in 2016 would not be happy to find their dues supported Hillary Clinton for President.

The Democracy Alliance quickly took control of the agenda of the Democratic Party. Traditional Democrat candidates could not find funding for their campaigns unless they moved to the Left and became more Progressive. Conservative and pro-life Democrats were pushed out of the party. The Democratic Party became an association of many groups with disparate interests, but united by the common benefits of centralized government and the global elite.

One Conservative watchdog group, the Capital Research Center, reported the following list of strategies for the Democracy Alliance from their website: [19]

- **Building power and capacity in key constituencies**: primarily Latinos and young people, as well as African Americans and unmarried women. [note: the Left preys on the young and unmarried, those who perceive themselves to be victims, those who have little association with local faith communities or traditional family units, and minorities susceptible to the idea that they are not in covenant with the broader American citizenry].

- **New media and technology**: content generators, aggregators and distributors that disseminate and amplify Progressive messages. [note: the Left dominates social media and major online sources such as Facebook, Google and Twitter censor Conservative messages].

- **Law and legal systems:** working to advance Progressive values at all levels of the legal system. [note: this includes the nomination and election of judges at the state and federal level].

- **Early-stage idea generators:** including journals, academic networks, books, and *non-traditional* think tanks. [note: this includes schools and universities].

- **Content generation:** traditional and new media vehicles capable of effectively promoting Progressive ideas.

- **Civic engagement coordination:** achieving greater efficiency and effectiveness through collaboration and creating economies of scale.

- **Civic engagement tools:** increasing capacity and availability of data services, including online organizing services for civic engagement groups. [note: this includes quasi-government, "community organizing" groups such as ACORN].

- **Election "reform":** structural changes of our democratic process that will increase voter participation among Progressive constituencies. [note: this includes the promotion of early voting—weeks and months ahead of elections, same-day registration, online voter registration, no voter ID laws, and so forth].

- **Youth leadership development**: the youth part of the leadership pipeline, especially organizations targeting young people who work at scale. [note: this would include universities and Planned Parenthood and NARAL to target young women].

- **Mid-career nonprofit leadership development:** Again, they want to strengthen the "leadership pipeline" into nonprofits and political organizations, especially "organizations working at scale" [such as a small group of activists organizing an entire university to get out the vote].

Saul Alinsky's Rules for Radicals

Much of the organizing philosophy and tactics of today's Progressive Left appear to come from *Rules for Radicals*, a playbook written by Saul D. Alinsky in 1971. Alinsky is generally considered the father of the community organizing movement; his ideas heavily influenced Progressive politicians such as Hillary Clinton and Barack Obama. Unfortunately, the results of Alinsky's influence can be seen all across America today.

> The main goal of Alinskyites is to cause social instability through subversive and divisive rhetoric. One method is to control the outcome of the education system by lowering the standards of education so that it creates a dependent class. As adherents to the Cloward-Piven strategy, they use their political platforms to overload a society with social spending programs and class warfare to the point that hatred and division cause social panic. Once they've created a problem, they propose themselves as the answer and use wealth transfers and the trumping of rights as the method to bring about "equality."[20]

Barack Obama began his career as an activist with a position as a community organizer for the Developing Communities Project (DCP) and the Calumet Community Religious Conference (CCRC) in Chicago. Both the CCRC and the DCP were built on the Alinsky model of community agitation, wherein paid organizers learned, in Alinsky's own words, how to "rub raw the sores of discontent."[21]

Saul Alinsky's stated goal was to improve the conditions of the poor, but his "ends-justify-almost-any-means" approach has proved detrimental and divisive for America. Alinsky's approach is now the playbook for the new Progressive Democratic Party. Democrats view their opponents, especially Conservatives, as the enemy. Any means to defeat Conservative ideas is considered fair game. So why—you ask—is there no bipartisanship in Washington? Compromise becomes impossible when every disagreement is viewed as a declaration of war.

Alinsky was an atheist who sympathized with Communist ideology. The fact he is an icon of the Left should be cause for concern. Like many on the Left today, he believed it necessary to do the wrong things (disruption, division, fomenting discontent and chaos) in order to make things right (help the poor). But his approach rips at the heart of America's strength.

Russell Kirk often referred to those on the Left as radicals. Perhaps Alinsky adopted Kirk's term as a badge of honor. Alinsky dedicated his book, *Rules for Radicals*, to Satan:

> Lest we forget at least an over-the-shoulder acknowledgment to the very first radical: from all our legends, mythology, and history (and who is to know where mythology leaves off and history begins—or which is which), the first radical known to man who rebelled against the establishment and did it so effectively that he at least won his own kingdom—Lucifer.

The Left still seeks a global kingdom and they know they must destroy the things Conservatives want to keep to achieve their goals.

The Expanding Tentacles of the Left

In 2018, the American Legislative Exchange Council (ALEC) completed a comprehensive analysis of how the Left is funded and organized. Their results were presented with detailed matrices and charts showing the flow of funds to educational, media, political, and nonprofit organizations targeting specific groups and activities. The Democracy Alliance and both government and private sector labor unions were featured in all of these charts as the funders and directors of dozens of organizations.

The Democracy Alliance targeted the media by funneling millions of dollars to Media Matters, a leftist group that drives the messaging of the Liberal mainstream media. Controlling the media has become much easier for the Left because of corporate consolidation. In 1983, fifty corporations controlled the national media and thousands of locally-owned newspapers and radio stations kept media messaging decentralized. But, by 2015, most significant locally-owned media had been bought by national companies and, according the *Mother Jones* magazine, eight giant corporations now control the U.S. media.[22] These companies include:

- Disney (market value: $72.8 billion)
- AOL-Time Warner (market value: $90.7 billion)
- Viacom (market value: $53.9 billion)
- General Electric (owner of NBC, market value: $390.6 billion)
- News Corporation (market value: $56.7 billion)
- Yahoo! (market value: $40.1 billion)
- Microsoft (market value: $306.8 billion)
- Google (market value: $154.6 billion)

These corporations (with the possible exception of News Corporation, which owns FOX News and the *Wall Street Journal*), along with most major U.S. corporations, now support the Left through campaign contributions and, as advertisers, control much of the content in the media. The Democracy Alliance has funneled hundreds of millions of dollars into investment firms such as Walden, Zevin, and Trillium that now, as directors and investors, have significant influence on the political and social policies of major corporations. They are also major donors to colleges and universities. These leftist investors continue to buy and control news media outlets such as *HuffPost, The Guardian*, and *The Nation*.

Did you ever wonder why so many corporations supported gender-neutral bathrooms when several state legislatures were embroiled in that illogical debate? Many corporations threatened to boycott states that didn't let boys shower with girls in public schools. A Republican governor in North Carolina who supported single-sex bathrooms lost his re-election bid because of corporate pressure. Corporations have found it more profitable and less risky to join rather than fight the Left. And many corporations pressure their employees to adopt their leftist ideology. Read any employee manual today and you'll likely find the celebration of the LBGTQ lifestyle, but no recognition of traditional marriage or values. Unfortunately, Democracy Alliance has succeeded in making most of corporate America a tool of Left.

The environmental movement in America has also become a tool and pawn of the Left. The Democracy Alliance directs funds into Citizen Engagement Laboratory (CEL) which, in turn, channels funds into groups such as the Energy Action Coalition, Color of Change, and Forecast the Facts. These groups have given up all pretense of promoting clean water and air. Their singular focus is climate change and the consolidation of government control over the economy, which they claim is necessary to control carbon emissions. They are joined by the trial lawyers of America, also major funders of leftist causes, who make sure no scoop of dirt is turned for a new project without the owner or developer facing a "sue and settle" case in court.

Progressive Realignment and Reinvestment in State and Local Politics

The Left is now targeting states and major cities across the U.S. Since 2008, Progressive advocacy and legislative groups have made significant investments in state programs as part of a new, big-money effort to turn back the free market, limited government tide in the states. The Progressive state infrastructure, led by Democracy Alliance donors, has invested in four key areas (ideas, media, leadership, and civic engagement) to cultivate a new American majority and socialize an "economic equality agenda," unfriendly to entrepreneurs and will reduce American competitiveness in global markets.

While the Democracy Alliance purports to advance "a just democracy, a fair economy and an environmentally sustainable future"—all laudable goals—in reality, their mission is all about control. The newfound Progressive focus on the states is ultimately aimed at the 2020 census, redistricting and reshaping the American electorate for years to come.

To achieve their goal, Democracy Alliance enlisted or created grassroots and activist groups such as MoveOn.org., Common Cause, Progress Now,

Citizens for Responsibility and Ethics in Washington (CREW), Citizen Engagement Laboratory, Color of Change, and more than 150 others to manufacture outrage, marginalize Conservative leaders and thinkers, and chill the speech and association rights of everyday Americans.

Colorado was the Left's first test case. They succeeded in turning a Republican state into a solidly Democrat state. And they have continued to push a Liberal agenda in Colorado that attacks traditional marriage and energy production while promoting the legal, recreational use of marijuana. Their next success was North Carolina, where manufactured outrage over single-sex bathrooms resulted in the ouster of a Republican governor. No state can be considered safe from the Left's agenda. In 2018, the Left poured over $100 million into Texas—one of the nation's most Conservative states—and almost defeated Republican Senator Ted Cruz.

The Left's Top-to-Bottom Funding and Control

Democracy Alliance has organized the wealthiest people in the world to fund their leftist agenda from the top down. They fund hundreds of organizations seeking to control the entertainment industry, the news media, corporations, universities, government agencies (through unions), grass roots political groups and the Democratic Party. They have invested heavily in technology that allows the Left to micro-target their messaging and focus their organizational efforts to specific individuals and groups.

The Democratic Party complements the Democracy Alliance by fundraising and organizing from the bottom up. They created ActBlue, an online fundraising resource that allows millions of Americans to send small donations to candidates and specific organizations—many nonprofit, tax-exempt "charities." ActBlue has raised over $3 billion since its inception in 2004.

After eight years of progress during the Obama administration, the Left was poised to solidify their control of the federal government with the election of Hillary Clinton as president in 2016. They didn't count on a wild card opponent like Donald Trump. The Left significantly outspent Trump. The Liberal news media was all in for Clinton. Trump had little support from the Republican Party. None of the "experts" gave Trump a chance.

But Trump out "outraged" the Left and offered positive and simple solutions (i.e., Make America Great Again). His powerful personality—despite many well-known flaws—seemed capable of actually draining "the swamp." His appeal to patriotism was more appealing than the Democrats' appeals to aggrievement. Americans, even in heavily union-ized states like Pennsylvania and Michigan, accepted Trump's challenge of "What do we have to lose?" Trump upset the most powerful political machine in the world.

The Left's anger at their loss has been abundantly evident since Trump's election. They invested billions of dollars and decades of work trying to centralize power in Washington and specifically in the executive branch only to have it hijacked by someone who wanted to dismantle it. After Trump's election, the Left unleashed all of their weapons on Trump creat-ing a continuous barrage of bureaucratic sabotage, biased investigations, negative media, mocking by entertainers, online censorship, university safe spaces for anti-Trumpers, and intimidation of anyone indicating support of Trump's agenda.

The 2018 midterm election proved the Left was still well-organized and well-funded. They shamelessly focused on the failures of America's healthcare system, even though Obamacare had created them. They denied the economy was good despite the evidence. They claimed Trump's tax cuts only helped the rich. And they proclaimed Trump was dividing the nation by spreading hate and bigotry.

The Republicans showed little passion or organization. Many Republi-can candidates distanced themselves from Trump. There was no coordinated message. The Democrats won the majority in the House and only lost two seats in the Senate, despite having to defend a historic number of seats.

If Conservatives hope to save America for freedom and prosperity, we must deliver the right ideas and build an organizational infrastructure for "We the People"—and hope the Republicans follow. We must also point out the failures of leftist Progressive policies which we will do in the follow-ing chapters.

CHAPTER 9

The Progressive Left and Socialism

No discussion of the Progressive Left would be complete without a discussion of their recent lurch toward socialism. Progressives today increasingly embrace this once-taboo label, as well as many of the government-centric policies that go with it. Sen. Bernie Sanders has long been an avowed Socialist. His formerly fringe ideas are now the Democratic Party's mainstream. In the 2016 presidential primary, he received 43 percent of the Democrat vote and came close to upsetting Hillary Clinton for the nomination. Rep. Alexandria Ocasio-Cortez upset long-time Democrat Rep. Joe Crowley in New York's 14th congressional district, running on a "democratic Socialist" platform, and has advocated everything from 70 percent income tax rates to banning airplanes, even to *not having children* because of humans' impact on climate change.

Polls tell us about half of millennial voters embrace socialism.[1] But research also shows most young Americans don't know what socialism really means. Many on the Left, including in the media, portray socialism as a new and fresh approach to national challenges. The problem is, Socialists have been calling their ideas new and fresh for more than one hundred years: when they took over Russia and ruined it; when they took over China and ruined it; when they took over Vietnam, North Korea, Cuba, Venezuela, and even the United Kingdom, and ruined all of them too. It seems every new generation has to learn through hard, painful experience that the problem with socialism is not that it's never been tried, but that it has never worked.

And since socialism is now in the spotlight here in America, it's worth digging deeper into what it really means and how it affects real people.

Government-Mandated Sameness

Socialism is often justified by its proponents because it promises equality. The most charitable interpretation of Progressives is they believe in equality in the same way Conservatives believe in freedom. It's the center of their worldview. This isn't to say Conservatives don't believe in equality or Progressives don't believe in freedom. They simply give these words different meanings. Conservatives' idea of freedom usually has to do with freedom *from* minimizing, artificial, and unnecessary constraints—in particular, the government telling you what to do or how to live.

The Bill of Rights—freedom from government interference in religion, speech, self-defense, personal privacy, and the like—reflects Conservatives' view of freedom. To the Left, however, freedom is less about what the government can't do to you and more about what government must do *for* you. Without, say, guaranteed health insurance, education, redistribution of wealth, a guaranteed income or "living wage," you're not really free—in the Liberals' sense of the word—so government should provide those things and much more.

In the same way, when Conservatives use the word "equal," as in "equal rights" or "equal under the law," they are usually thinking about equality of opportunity. Abraham Lincoln eloquently defended this approach to politics in his first inaugural address when he declared government's leading object, "to afford all an unfettered start, and a fair chance, in the race of life." Notice Lincoln is silent about the finish line. The purpose of government is to let everyone run his or her race to the best of his or her ability, industry, and designs—it's not to make sure the race ends in a 300-million-person tie.

Progressives, however, are more interested in equality of outcome. The Left sees, as we all do, some people succeed more in life than others and assumes inequality of outcome is due to inequality of opportunity. They therefore see government's role as leveling. If you put together the Left's philosophical concepts of "freedom"—defined as government doing things *for* you—and "equality"—as a question of *outcomes* rather than simply opportunity—you reach the Left's defining mission: they believe government should exert every power necessary to mandate and enforce universal sameness.

Alexis de Tocqueville, the French diplomat who traveled and catalogued the early American experience, observed the difference early on:

> There is, in fact, a manly and lawful passion for equality which excites men to wish all to be powerful and honored. This passion tends to elevate the humble to the rank of the great; but there exists also in the human heart a depraved taste for equality, which impels the weak to attempt to lower the powerful to their own level, and reduces men to prefer equality in slavery to inequality in freedom.[2]

Everywhere in the world—and at all times—individuals are born with different strengths and different weaknesses, into different circumstances, and with distinct life stories. What has always made America special is here we allow all our diverse individuals and communities to create opportunities for themselves based on their differing abilities, passions, and perspectives. That's freedom.

Every society has its obstacles to achievement—be they natural, cultural, or familial—but, in a free society, there is not supposed to be an artificial ceiling on individual initiative or flourishing. You are free to strive, as Tocqueville put it, to put your passions to use to elevate yourself from the "humble to the rank of the great." There are an infinite number of paths to happiness and success—as many paths as there are people! Maybe your path is in business or the church or in art or music, teaching, or mastering a trade. Maybe your path is based around your family or friends. Everyone's path is different; in a free society, government's job is not to push you down one path or another, but instead to make sure they are all open to you.

Mandated equality—that is, socialism—says otherwise. State-sponsored sameness says we must all be treated to the same outcome, regardless of our different gifts, effort, and abilities.

There are two ways to do this: to raise everyone to the highest level or to lower everyone to the bottom level. The former has proved impossible over thousands of years of human civilization. The latter happens all the time.

C.S. Lewis's fictional devil Screwtape illustrated it plainly in his speech to the Tempters' Training College of Young Devils. According to Screwtape, the best way to destroy a soul—and society—is to destroy individuality:

Democracy is the word with which you must lead them by the nose[…] You are to use this word purely as an incantation; if you like, purely for its selling power. It is a name they venerate. And, of course, it is connected with the political ideal that men should be equally treated. You then make a stealthy transition in their minds from this political ideal to a factual belief that all men are equal[…] You remember how one of the Greek dictators (they called them "tyrants" then) sent an envoy to another dictator to ask his advice about the principles of government. The second dictator led the envoy into a field of grain, and there he snicked off with his cane the top of every stalk that rose an inch or so above the general level. The moral was plain. Allow no pre-eminence among your subjects. Let no man live who is wiser or better or more famous or even handsomer than the mass. Cut them all down to a level: all slaves, all ciphers, all nobodies. All equals.[3]

The Socialist dream that we are all born into the world with different gifts and talents, yet end up in the same place, regardless of effort, is compelling. But, in practice, it has proven a short road to tyranny. When the government enforces equality of outcome (again, separate from equal rights or equality of opportunity), it strips individuals of personal initiative, undermines the rule of law, empowers the rulers at the expense of the ruled, and invites coercion, abuse, dishonesty, and violence.

As French philosopher Charles le Comte de Montalembert said, "equality cannot be imagined outside of tyranny." It was, he said, "nothing but the canonization of envy, [and it] was never anything but a mask which could not become reality without the abolition of all merit and virtue."[4]

In fact, forced egalitarianism nearly always ends in destruction. As sociologist Robert Nisbet has pointed out, egalitarianism—the preoccupation that all people are not only equal but interchangeable—is the fundamental doctrine of movements that end up toppling or destroying societies where inequality is found.

This is easy to see when you consider what happens when Progressive egalitarianism was practiced.

Imagine a society where everyone is completely equal in wealth, but where those individuals can still make independent choices regarding their own lives. If wealth were equal at 8:00 a.m., it would be unequal by 8:01. Almost immediately, some individuals would have spent, lost, or squandered their money. Still others would invest it, or use it to go to school, or use it as collateral for a loan. Every individual choice free people make as consumers, producers, and investors changes the distribution of national wealth, which by definition will progressively become more unequal.

Free choice and mandated equality are simply incompatible. Just as God gives us free will to behave sinfully or virtuously, the Constitution gives us the freedom—the right—to use our property and spend our money wisely or foolishly.

The only way to achieve true equality is by removing the consequences of decision-making or preventing individuals from making decisions for themselves in the first place. Equality of outcome—the kind Socialists want—is achievable only when freedom is destroyed.

Taking a policy of egalitarianism to its logical conclusion, anything that gives any individual a leg up must be verboten. Social justice warrior John Rawls, in his defense of egalitarianism, goes so far as to contemplate the destruction of the family because, as French radical Jean Jacques Rousseau put it, bringing up young people in perfect equality requires they be saved from "the intelligence and prejudices of fathers."[5] "Families dissolve," says Rousseau. "But the State remains."[6]

Until it doesn't.

The Siren Song of Socialism

Everywhere socialism has been tried throughout history, the promise is the same: Hand the provision of this good or that service over to the government and it will finally be affordable and available for all equally—forever and amen. Not only will the best schools or health care or jobs become merely free, but because government will cut out all those grubby, for-profit middlemen, we'll actually *save* money on them. Higher quality, lower prices, full equality—socialism sounds like a dream.

That's the allure. But that's all it is. Socialism always *sounds* good until you get around to actually trying it. And then you find, usually the hard way, it's all a lie.

Socialism is like the sirens in Greek mythology—the beautiful temptresses who lure smitten sailors into shallow water, rocky shoals, and their doom. The historical record of socialism is disastrous—one long, sad, violent, mess after another.

The first modern experiment in radical, government-mandated-and-enforced "equality" was the French Revolution, which began as a rebellion among poor and mistreated peasants and ended with daily, organized, and ritualistic murder in the streets. Most of the civilized world looked on (and still look back) in horror at the Reign of Terror in Paris, except for a handful of intellectuals, including G. W. F. Hegel and his disciple Karl Marx, who would a century later inspire revolutionary Communism and socialism.

Fast-forward to the Russian Revolution in 1917, which preached global solidarity with Socialists everywhere.

Then came the backlash to international socialism, *national* socialism—fascism—which combined state economic controls with frenzied, nationalistic fervor in Italy and Germany. The result was a war that embroiled pretty much the entire planet for five years.

After World War II put an end to the fascists, the Soviet Union's Communist satellite regimes took control of the nations of Eastern Europe, Soviet-supported revolutions cropped up from China to Latin America, and even post-colonial India embraced the Soviet model of economic planning. At its zenith, socialism and Communism governed large parts of the world's population—and won the hearts and minds of a much higher proportion of the world's elites.

How did all that socialism work out?

The best estimate is these various Communist and Socialist regimes were responsible for the deaths of about 100 million people in the 20th century—wars they started, death camps, and violent purges in places like Russia and Cambodia. (It doesn't count the millions of baby girls forcibly aborted during China's monstrous "one-child" policy.) But, as cruel and bloodthirsty as every Socialist regime has ever been, most of the body count was not due to violence, but simply disease, poverty, and starvation from state-directed economics.

Socialism is nothing less than moral, cultural, and physical ruin for any country who tries it. And you don't need to plumb the depths of Soviet or Nazi death camps to see the true face of socialism. Modern-day Venezuela will do just fine.

Until about two decades ago, Venezuela was the richest country in Latin America. It was not perfect—no country is—but it had a prosperous economy and flourishing society. Venezuela's vast oil reserves made it a hub of trade and investment, one of the economic engines of the western hemisphere. Now, just a few years into the Socialist revolution of Hugo Chávez—a protégé of Cuba's Fidel Castro—the nation is a social and economic basket case. Chávez was a thug and a criminal, as was his successor Nicolás Maduro.

However, as *National Review*'s Kevin Williamson (author of the *Politically Incorrect Guide to Socialism*) notes:

> Repression on the Venezuelan model is not extraneous to socialism—it is baked into the socialist cake. Lenin, Stalin, Mao, Castro (and Castro!), Chàvez [sic], Maduro, Honecker, Ho Chi Minh, Pol Pot, the Kim dynasty, Shining Path: No ideology is that unlucky. Violence and oppression is not something that just happens to accompany efforts to impose political regimentation on the economy—which is to say, on private life—but is an inescapable accompaniment to it.[7]

Even comparatively well-intended Socialists are perfectly capable of running great countries into the ground. In the late 1970s, after successive Progressive presidents of both parties, the United States found itself stymied with "stagflation," the simultaneous phenomena of low economic growth and high inflation, which economists previously thought was impossible.

In the same era, the United Kingdom was stuck in the mud of Western Socialistic consensus too. Ronald Reagan and Margaret Thatcher are remembered as heroes for reinvigorating their respective economies with market-based reforms. Indeed, every country to have embraced such reforms has seen positive results.

What is socialism? It's the imposition of political control over national economies. Thanks to the overheated and imprecise nature of modern political debate, it's easy to confuse almost *any* government action as "socialism." But that's not quite right. While Socialist countries usually have much higher taxes, spending levels, and regulations, these *fiscal* policies alone don't define the extent of a Socialist economic system. Socialism is *central planning and government control* of the economy. If you listen to Socialists speak, you will begin to understand what this means.

Recall this quote, from Bernie Sanders, which we mentioned in Part I:

You can't just continue growth for the sake of growth in a world in which we are struggling with climate change and all kinds of environmental problems. All right? You don't necessarily need a choice of 23 underarm spray deodorants or of 18 different pairs of sneakers when children are hungry in this country.[8]

Sanders raises an interesting point here. We probably *don't need* twenty-three brands of underarm spray deodorants. Mankind got along without any for thousands of years, after all. The reason we have them is the American people *want* them. And, while Sanders may have his preferred brand, that brand obviously isn't everyone else's favorite. And, in America, in the free enterprise system of Conservative individualism, everyone is supposed to get the same say over deodorant brands as senators and presidents. The same goes for shampoos and toothpastes and toothbrushes, kitchen utensils and appliances, pillows and pillowcases, sheets and comforters, and everything else you can buy at the store. Twenty-three brands of deodorant may seem to you or me like it's too many, but who are we to say which one or two or ten we should get rid of? Why should we be able to keep our favorite brands on the shelves but ban the rest?

In an open, free economy—like ours is supposed to be—there is no national political *plan* for deodorant. People are free to use it or not. Companies are free to manufacture it, test it, market it, advertise it, and sell it. Customers are free to pick and choose whichever brands they like based on price, effectiveness, scent, whatever. Because the United States is a huge country with millions of different people and preferences and plenty of money to buy what they want, our retailers stock a dizzying array deodorant brands, sizes, and scents.

You may have a favorite deodorant brand, or you may just get whatever is on sale. But, like most Americans, you probably don't give much thought to how many choices there are. If you like Speed Stick or Secret, you probably don't care or even notice the Degree or Dove brands next to them on the shelf.

Socialists? They care.

They think it's wasteful—even sinister—that there are dozens of deodorant brands, of varying sizes and shapes and scents and quality. After all, a few weeks of testing should be able to demonstrate which one or two brands may be "best," so the most efficient thing to do would be to ban all the others, so all the companies and workers trying to sell those other brands of deodorants could put their time and effort to better use.

What use? Ah, that's where the planners come in. In their dreams, Socialists are among a highly-educated elite of well-meaning geniuses who sit around conference tables directing businesses, workers, and consumers like pieces on a board game. *We don't need all those deodorants, you see; what we need instead is X (whatever X is). And so, all you people trying to sell those other deodorants now make and sell X instead. That way, our society will still have enough of the deodorant it needs but will also now have more people working on this other thing we obviously don't have enough of.*

Do you see the problem? It's in the word "we." Who is this "we" who decides what our economy has too much and too little of? When it comes to economic goods and services, the free market *is* "we." After all, why does America have dozens of brands of deodorant? The same reason we have dozens of different kinds of pizza and socks and ballpoint pens—because people spend money on them. These products add value to people's lives and people voluntarily spend their money to buy them. The real answer to Bernie Sander's question, "Why do we need 23 underarm spray options?" is "Because the American people have decided they don't want 22 or 24."

People are not pieces on a board game. Even seemingly simple decisions—like deciding what to make for dinner tonight—are extremely complex, factoring in literally thousands of considerations of price, nutrition, time of day, time to cook, who's eating, weekday or weekend, what you had for lunch, if you're on a diet, and on and on and on. Socialists believe having a handful of smart people make these kinds of decisions for everyone is efficient—but it never works out that way. Because human beings are not animals and not machines.

Two centuries ago, the United States began a worldwide revolution by building an economy around a seemingly obvious fact. Rather than trying to control how people spend their own money, respect them enough to decide for themselves and see what happens. We showed what happens in our chapter *Keeping Our Land of Opportunity* when people are left to make their own decisions. Free market capitalism is the best organizing principle for any economic system.

Prior to the founding of the United States, almost everyone who ever lived was mired not just in poverty, but extreme poverty. Then, beginning around 1776, slowly, we started getting rich. Then our trading partners got rich. Then our former adversaries, who became our allies and partners, became rich. And then, in a matter of a few years, China, India, and Eastern Europe liberalized their economies, and they started getting rich. Now, at long last, this trend is stretching into Africa and other parts of the world where extreme poverty still exists.

Communities will flourish when people are free to earn and spend money, to enter voluntary exchange with other free people, and when the integrity of all these exchanges are protected by a written rule of law, sound money, and overseen by a transparent, accountable political system. When powerful people—be they billionaires, bureaucrats, or anyone in between—gum up those works, the "golden goose" stops laying eggs.

Just as bad is when the powerful just steal the eggs to keep them for themselves.

Good for Thee, Not for Me

It's easy to chalk up socialism's catastrophic failures to especially bad men like Stalin, Hitler, Mao, or Pol Pot. But even benign Socialists are *human*, and, as we have seen, that is reason enough not to trust them with too much power.

What the Left never tells you about Socialistic "equality" was summarized nicely by author George Orwell in his dystopian classic, *Animal Farm*. What begins as a farm of animals living equally slowly transforms. The pigs begin to assert themselves, taking more and more power for themselves. One day, the rest of the animals find their food portions short-changed while the pigs are enjoying the excess harvest of apples and cow's milk.

When confronted by the rest of the animals, aghast at the gluttony and privilege in what was supposed to be a farm of equals, Napoleon, the leader of the pigs, craftily responds,

> Comrades! he cried. You do not imagine, I hope, that we pigs are doing this in a spirit of selfishness and privilege? Many of us actually dislike milk and apples. I dislike them myself. Our sole object in taking these things is to preserve our health. Milk and apples (this has been proved

by Science, comrades) contain substances absolutely necessary to the well-being of a pig. We pigs are brainworkers. The whole management and organization of this farm depend on us. Day and night we are watching over your welfare. It is for YOUR sake that we drink that milk and eat those apples.[9]

This is how "equal" policies always end. The same way *Animal Farm* does, incidentally, with one single commandment scrawled on the barn door: "*All Animals Are Equal / But Some Are More Equal Than Others.*"

That is more or less how Washington, D.C. sees itself and the rest of the country today. When the Feds tell you how to live, chances are they are exempting themselves. And, if they haven't done it in the law, they'll find another way to do it.

When Obamacare—which was supposed to make healthcare equal and affordable for all Americans—was written, it didn't apply to members of Congress. Only after Sen. Chuck Grassley (R-Iowa) shamed Democrats in a speech on the Senate floor were senators and representatives forced to give up their health plans for Obamacare. But, even then, congressional committee staff—that is, the invisible men and women who actually wrote the law—kept themselves exempt. A good portion of congressional staff are still exempt from the law and shielded from the decreasing quality and high expenses plaguing everyone forced to live under Obamacare.

Even more outrageous is how Congress ensured the cost of their own insurance wouldn't go up—knowing full well costs would increase for average Americans. Congress—an institution with approximately twelve thousand employees—labeled itself a "small business" to exempt itself from much of Obamacare's coverage requirements. (Under the law, a small business is an organization with under fifty employees.)

This ensured congressional staff and lawmakers could continue to receive their employer contribution to the cost of their plans, estimated at between $5,000 and $12,000 annually. The rest of America? Not quite so lucky.[10, 11]

As our friend and former coworker Christopher Jacobs has written extensively, the same people running the Obamacare exchanges in D.C. (where he is required to purchase health insurance), do not purchase Obamacare for themselves. They receive generous taxpayer-funded insurance subsidies to purchase their coverage through the District of Columbia's government rather than through D.C.'s Obamacare exchange.[12]

But, while shocking, this behavior is not surprising. Congress has exempted itself from a host of mandates it imposes on the rest of the country. The Occupational Safety and Health Act (OSHA) does not apply to Congress. Neither do protections for retaliation against whistleblowers.

In fact, after lecturing the rest of America about the stories coming out of the #MeToo movement, it took Congress until December of 2018 to finally agree on a set of standards for itself when handling workplace sexual harassment.[13]

The policies put forward by the Progressive Left reflect the same *Animal Farm* mentality.

Rep. Alexandria Ocasio-Cortez has called climate change her generation's "World War II," and proposed legislation which her own fact sheet speculates would require banning air travel, eliminating internal combustion engines (which power roughly 270 million automobiles in the United States), and retrofitting every building in America.[14] [15] Yet she does not appear to take many of the carbon-cutting measures she'd like to impose on the rest of us.

During her campaign, she expensed more than $29,000 for rides in emissions-spewing vehicles, despite her campaign headquarters being immediately next to a subway station. She also spent more than $25,000 on flights, though she now openly speculates air travel should be banned.[16]

It's not that we think climate-change Progressives should walk everywhere, but it's a little hard to take them seriously when they can't even make a small effort to live out their principles while finger-wagging at the rest of us.

The same goes for policies like single-payer health care or equal access to education. Like Orwell's pigs, people with means and connections will always find a way around policies they insist are good for the rest of us. In the United Kingdom, the National Health Service is the largest single-payer health care system in the world. Yet, after seventy years, the NHS still provides different levels of care to the rich and poor.[17]

The NHS and all single-payer plans, wherever they've been tried, tell us equal access to equal-quality care cannot be mandated. People with means will always find a way to game the system. The answer is not to punish people for future schemes but to create policies that disincentivize cheating. Access to quality, affordable healthcare can be addressed with policy reforms that incentivize doctors and hospitals to provide the best care to the most people. We'll get into those solutions in a later chapter.

Education, another area that's supposed to be equal access, also has a tilted playing field. In early 2019, it was revealed at supposedly "meritocratic" institutions of higher education like Harvard, Yale, Georgetown, and even the University of Southern California were enrolling students via a system of cheating on standardized exams or outright bribes.[18] These institutions take millions of dollars in federal grants each year on the promise they will provide equal educational opportunities to those who meet rigorous entrance requirements.

But, as the 2019 cheating scandal showed, those with means will always find a way around the requirements. In a related case, a group of Asian-American students is currently suing Harvard University for discrimination, alleging they have to meet a higher threshold for entrance as a result of the university's diversity policies elevating students with poorer grades.[19] One reason to suspect they may be right is Harvard and other elite colleges used to do the same thing to Jewish applicants.

This same mentality is at work with many Democrats who oppose school choice programs. Choice gives poorer students the ability to use a portion of public education money to pay for a private school of their choosing—moving them out of failing public schools. The beneficiaries of these choice programs are usually black families, 66 percent of whom support school choice programs across the country.[20] In reference to school choice, President Trump has called education "the civil rights issue of our time."[21] But many Democrats virulently oppose these policies, saying they remove critical resources from public schools.

These same Democrats, however, don't subject their children to the public schools they deem good enough for the rest of us.

A 2011 survey by The Heritage Foundation found 23 percent of the House of Representatives' Education, Labor, and Pensions Committee Members sent their children to private schools, while nearly 40 percent of the Senate Health, Education, Labor, and Pensions Committee members did—all while these same committees fought over whether or not their privilege should be extended to low-income students. 35 percent of Congressional Black Caucus Members and 31 percent of Congressional Hispanic Caucus Members sent their own kids to private schools despite routinely opposing school choice policies in Congress. Overall, 44 percent of senators and 36 percent of representatives in the 111th Congress had at one time sent their children to private schools. But federal school choice policies for the rest of America still remain an aspirational goal.[22]

The fullest expression of the *Animal Farm* mentality is the Left's attitude toward taxes. The caricature of Progressives is their desire to tax everyone, so they can turn around and spend all the money themselves. But that's not quite true. The Left likes high *baseline* tax rates—even in the United States, federal income tax rates have been as high as 70 percent or even 90 percent. But what the Left *really* likes is the power high baseline rates give them to do favors for the politically connected. Under a low tax regime, businesses all have a good opportunity to make profits, reinvest in new ideas and markets, while the customers pick the winners and losers. When taxes start out high, however, many businesses' profitability depends on policy favors from the government—and the winners and losers aren't picked by consumers but by politicians.

Even union membership, which the Left has, for years, told us is essential to treating employees fairly, crumbles when it doesn't have the cudgel of compulsion behind it. After the Supreme Court ruled against compulsory union dues for public sector unions—literally forcing public sector employees to pay into unions whether they wanted to or not—union membership dropped precipitously. The major public sector unions lost nearly 210,000 agency fee payers, representing an over 90 percent drop. It turns out that, when given a choice, most employees didn't actually find union services that valuable.[23]

There is an old Conservative joke that goes, "The only way to get rid of corruption in high places is to get rid of the high places." The more power given to government officials, the more these officials will help themselves and their big special interest sponsors. This cronyism and unfairness on behalf of the rich and powerful is often blamed on capitalism. And that helps explain why so many young people today are more open to the false egalitarian promises of socialism.

Millennial Socialism

In millennials' defense, they never lived through World War II or the Cold War to see the ravages of national socialism and Communism loose in the civilized world. The media and academia—many of whom spent the Cold War cheerleading for Moscow against the West—are only too happy to keep the past hidden. Millennials didn't grow up seeing the U.S. and UK accept then reject socialism at home and then conquer the "Evil Empire" abroad.

Rather, they have grown up in an era of Western decadence, corruption, and institutional failure defined by the debacles of the Iraq War, the Great Recession, and corporate bailouts.

The Great Bailout Scam

In 2008, a real estate bubble—inflated by foolish federal policies that lowered credit standards for mortgages and encouraged banks to lend more than borrowers could reasonably hope to pay back—crashed on the American economy. Asset values for homes and stock market prices plummeted. The Baby Boom generation, which was just starting to retire, watched as their wealth, built up over decades, started to evaporate—not by the millions or billions, but *trillions* of dollars.

In response, Washington stepped in to prop up asset prices. You probably remember the Troubled Asset Relief Program (TARP), which bailed out Wall Street banks whose bad bets in the mortgage market were driving them into insolvency. You might also remember the Federal Reserve Board's "quantitative easing" policy of cheap money that began in 2008 and ran to 2014. In effect, the Fed lowered interest rates so far below market levels it drew hesitant investment back into various asset markets—in effect reinflating the pre-crash bubble. TARP was, directly, a bailout of imprudent Wall Street banks and investors; indirectly, it was a bailout of Baby Boomers paid for by their children's and grandchildren's generations against their will.

The result is twofold. First, the artificial explosion in asset prices—especially real estate—has raised the cost of living and priced the millennial generation out of many of the cities and even whole regions where they might want to live. Artificially high costs and low wages have pushed millennials to stay in college for more and more higher education—and more and more corresponding debt—as they figure out how to afford this artificially expensive world the bailouts created. This financial pressure also leads to delayed marriage and childbearing. It's harder and more expensive for millennials to achieve the American Dream than for previous generations—in large part *because* of what those previous generations did to bail themselves out of their own financial mistakes.

As Irish economist David McWilliams put it:

> When asset prices rise much faster than wages, the average person falls further behind. Their stake in society weakens. The faster this new asset-fueled economy grows, the greater the gap between the insiders with a stake and outsiders without. This threatens a social contract based on the notion that the faster the economy grows, the better off everyone becomes. What then? Well, politics shifts.[24]

The generation that grew up cheering America's victory over socialism embraced socialism not to save the free market, but to insulate themselves from the consequences of their own poor decisions and irresponsibility. The only politics millennials know is the George W. Bush years that led to disaster and the politics of the Obama years that left millennials holding the bag. It's no wonder they are disillusioned.

The last thing we should do now is give the government that has failed millennials—and most Americans—even more power. Past generations tried the same thing and we're still paying the price for it.

CHAPTER 10

Policy Failures of the Left

In 1964, President Lyndon Baines Johnson initiated an ambitious effort, led by the federal government, to improve America. "The Great Society," Johnson declared, "[[...]] demands an end to poverty and racial injustice," is also "a place where every child can find knowledge to enrich his mind and enlarge his talent [...] where the city of man serves not only the needs of the body and the demands of commerce but the desire for beauty and the hunger for community."[1]

His speech and grand vision launched a constellation of federal agencies and programs over the next several decades, including the Department of Education, the Department of Housing and Urban Development, Medicare, Medicaid, and the National Endowment of the Arts, to name a few.

When government is the means, the ends seem limitless, at least if you're a Liberal. But how have these policies panned out? Millions of Americans still find healthcare unaffordable or unavailable, even after Democrats remade the economy with the passage of the Patient Protection and Affordable Care Act (colloquially known as Obamacare) in 2010. And education has fared even worse. After years of policies and trillions of dollars spent, the most recent comparison of test scores from thirty-five developed nations ranked the United States nineteenth in science, twentieth in reading, and thirty-first—fourth from the bottom—in math.[2]

And, despite pledges that our entitlement programs—Medicare and Social Security, in particular—would keep our elderly population sustained and our country secure, both programs are financially insolvent and a crisis of suicide and loneliness among the elderly continues to spread.

For Liberals, the answer to every nail is a massive, government-sponsored hammer. But decades of employing these policies have proven their approach simply doesn't work. Even worse, years of expanding government into every nook and cranny of our lives has had an even more insidious effect: it has stolen and replaced many of the things Conservatives know Americans must keep. Individual liberty, the "little platoons" keeping our communities strong and thriving, property rights, and even the free practice of religion have all diminished the more government has grown.

A growing government is simply incompatible with the preservation of ancient traditions upholding a strong civil society.

This is particularly true in four key policy areas: education, health care, climate change, and abortion. There are many more areas where the Left has instituted failed policies, but we've decided to focus in on these four, given how much attention both parties pay to these areas, and how clear the lines of distinction are between Liberals and Conservatives.

This chapter discusses how these Liberal policies have failed. In Chapter 11, we will provide some Conservative solutions.

Education

One of the greatest legacies of President Lyndon Johnson was the promise of education.

Yet the most recent data for math and reading achievement for twelfth graders on the National Assessment of Educational Progress (NAEP) demonstrate just how poorly most American students fare. According to the data, just 25 percent of twelfth graders were proficient in math, and only 37 percent were proficient in reading. These numbers are nearly unchanged from 2013. Or 2009. What is higher in 2015, however, is the percentage of twelfth graders performing *below* basic proficiency in math and reading—up 10 percent on both counts.[3]

In fact, the NAEP's long-term assessment finds today's high school seniors perform no better in reading than the high school seniors of the early 1970s. Moreover, disparities between white and black students continue to widen. Twelfth grade black students face a twenty-nine-point achievement gap in reading compared with their white counterparts—a gap that has increased over time.[4]

Current policy is failing despite spending per pupil which, even adjusting for inflation, has risen dramatically. In the 2018–2019 school year, government will collectively spend $640.3 billion on public schools. That's an average of $14,340 for every student enrolled in K-12 public education. Over the past thirty years, spending on a per-pupil basis has grown by 41.7 percent *after accounting for inflation*.[5] Have public schools gotten 41.7 percent better in the past thirty years to justify this additional spending? Hardly.

The Department of Education now funds more than one hundred federal education programs designed to enhance individual student learning, close the achievement gap between white and black students, and make American students globally competitive. The results speak for themselves.

What has increased over time? School staffing and administration. Since 1970, student bodies have increased by approximately 8 percent. The number of public-school teachers during this period increased by 60 percent. Non-teaching staff—meaning central office bureaucracy—increased by a stunning 138 percent over the same time period. Teachers now comprise only half of all public-school employees, but we have more teachers teaching fewer students than at any point in history. The ratio of students to full-time teachers in our schools has fallen to historic low levels.[6]

Perhaps because our school system places a greater emphasis on hiring bureaucrats than teachers, American students continue to lag behind their international peers. Regular comparisons from the Organization for Economic Cooperation and Development (OECD) attest to the United States' anemic performance. The OECD's 2012 rankings indicated students in the top performing area—Shanghai, China—achieved "a performance that is the equivalent of over two years of formal schooling ahead of those observed in Massachusetts," one of our best performing states.[7] The test results demonstrate how American education lags literally years behind the world's best performers—and our economic competitors. Since that time, America's test scores have fallen even further, dropping from twenty-seventh out of thirty-four countries in math in 2012 to thirty-first out of thirty-five in 2015.[8]

Even federal attempts to ensure every child begins their educational journey on equal footing have produced dubious results. Over forty-four years, the Head Start program has spent a whopping $180 billion but produced minimal gains in educational achievement. The Department of Health and Human Services' own research found Head Start participants performed lower than their peers in kindergarten math. "By third grade, Head Start had little to no effect on cognitive, social-emotional, health, or parenting outcomes of participating children."[9] A 2010 study by the Department of Health and Human Services found the Head Start program actually harmed participating children, with teachers reporting non-Head Start students were more prepared in math skills than those who participated in the program.[10]

By centralizing education in America, we have lost the role of the community, replaced teachers with bureaucrats, pushed parents to the margins, and forgotten about the kids altogether. Increased federal control has largely replaced parental responsibility and attempted to make schools the only source of education. But simply because we send our children to school does not mean we lose oversight of or responsibility for their education. Schools, as columnist George F. Will has pointed out, cannot supplant families as the transmitters of social capital—the habits, manners, and mores necessary for thriving.[11]

Moreover, as the last fifty years have shown us, Washington is simply incapable of transforming our educational system from above. The best reform ideas have come at the state and local level, where lawmakers are closest to the needs of those they serve.

Health Care

The American people know well the shortcomings of Obamacare. During his campaign for the presidency in 2008, candidate Barack Obama promised his health care plan would cut the average family's health insurance premiums by $2,500 per year.[12] His advisers claimed they could achieve such a reduction in premiums by the end of President Obama's first term in office.[13]

Yet, after Obamacare's became law, insurance premiums have continued to increase. Premiums for employer-sponsored coverage rose from $13,375

in 2009 to $18,764 in 2017—a more than 40 percent increase.[14] On the
Obamacare Exchanges, premiums more than doubled from 2013 to 2017
as all the law's new regulatory requirements took effect.[15] A March 2018
study concluded the law's pre-existing condition provisions "account[ed]
for the largest share of premium increases," by attracting sicker and costlier
patients to the exchanges.[16]

How about the promise President Obama made repeatedly: if you liked
your health care, you could keep it? Tell that to the many individuals—
at least 4.7 million, by one count—who received insurance cancellation
notices when Obamacare first went into effect.[17] Because their coverage did
not meet standards set by government bureaucrats, millions of people lost
the health coverage they liked.[18] *Politifact* dubbed Obama's broken promise
its Lie of the Year for 2013.[19]

Liberals always shout from the mountaintops about the people their
big-government plans help—but they rarely acknowledge the people they
hurt. For instance, the father of one if our Capitol Hill colleagues lost
his health coverage when Obamacare went into effect because it wasn't
"bureaucrat-approved." He and his wife tried finding a new plan but
couldn't afford the Obamacare-compliant alternatives. Shortly thereafter,
he was diagnosed with colon cancer and incurred tens of thousands of
dollars in debt to pay for his treatment.

Thanks to Obamacare, his "coverage" consisted largely of a GoFundMe
page, where generous family members, friends, and colleagues helped him
get back on his feet financially.[20] But the fact that he needed such assistance in the first place speaks to the way in which Liberals' solutions are
designed to foster dependence on government. Before Obamacare came
along, this man and his family (like millions of other responsible Americans) were minding their own business, having done the right thing by
purchasing health insurance to provide for themselves and their families.
After Obamacare, many families faced financial ruin because their insurance plans were cancelled by order of government bureaucrats.

The next time a Liberal tries to tell you about how Obamacare helped
people with pre-existing conditions, ask them about the millions of Americans who lost their insurance because of Obamacare. We don't know about
you, but we won't take lessons in generosity or compassion from people

who take away innocent families' health coverage and leave them wracked with tens of thousands of dollars in debt as a result.

The Answer Is Not More Government

Yet the same people who created this government-run health care monstrosity, which has failed on all of the levels explained above, think the answer lies in giving government even more power and control over people's lives through socialized medicine in the form of a single-payer, government-run health care system. Every time a government program like Obamacare fails, Liberals claim it didn't go far enough—just one more regulation, one more tax increase, and a little more central control will finally lead to the Socialist utopia the Left always promises is just around the corner. Their logic: government caused the problem; therefore, more government must obviously be the solution!

Obamacare illustrates this phenomenon perfectly. The law's regulations on insurers raised premiums, which necessitated new federal subsidies to make coverage "affordable." Those subsidies necessitated new federal spending, which necessitated new taxes to pay for the spending. And, when it failed, Liberals prescribed more government—in the form of price caps, regulations, and more centralized decision-making by Washington bureaucrats—to fix the problems the government created. Multiply this scenario by every other issue, product, and service under the sun, and you get the idea—actually, you get Cuba or Venezuela or North Korea.

Ironically, Barack Obama gave a speech summarizing Obamacare's major shortcomings. In 2010, he claimed Republicans drove the economy into a ditch, "and we got to tell them, you can't have the keys back because you don't know how to drive. You don't know!"[21]

He didn't mean it this way, but his metaphor aptly describes what the Left did to our health care system with Obamacare. Premiums increased; deductibles rose through the roof; people only signed up for "free" coverage because they didn't value the benefits Obamacare provided; the "free" coverage discouraged millions of people from working and rising out of poverty; many of its cost-control experiments have failed, and may have increased death rates rather than reducing them; and some of the law's own architects have admitted they didn't know what they were doing when crafting the legislation.

These are the people who want *more* power over health care—and ultimate government control over every doctor and every patient in America? Why should we let them have even more control, when, to borrow Obama's own phrase, they ran our health care system into the ditch?

The question answers itself. With Obamacare having wrecked our health care system—and, with it having failed on so many of its own measures of success—Conservatives can and should make the case not just against Obamacare, but against the intrusive and coercive philosophy that thinks government is the solution to just about every problem. In reality, as Ronald Reagan famously noted in his first inaugural address, government is more often the problem than the solution.

Climate Change

There is likely no issue that has done more to divide Progressives and Conservatives than climate change. Ever since the term "global warming" was loosed into the vernacular in 1975, the rift between Progressives and Conservatives has continued to widen.[22]

Particularly on the Progressive Left, climate change has become something of a religion. It is the highest good, to which all else—economic growth, technological development, and general human comfort—must be sacrificed.

This is evidenced by how they frame the Conservative viewpoint on the issue: anyone who doesn't agree with the Left's assessment of the issue is a "climate change denier." (The media has, predictably, adopted the same labels.) But this characterization is as dismissive as it is false. Many Conservatives—ourselves included—agree the climate is changing. What we disagree with the Left about is how much, what's causing it, and the ways we should go about addressing it.

Climate Alarmism

According to the Left, climate change should have killed us all years ago. In 1970, environmentalist Paul Ehrlich confidently proclaimed the "population will inevitably and completely outstrip whatever small increases in food supplies we make. The death rate will increase until at least 100-200 million people per year will be starving to death during the next ten years." Later that year, he projected between 1980 and 1989, some four billion people— including sixty-five million Americans—would perish in the "Great Die-Off."[23]

Life magazine echoed Ehrlich, claiming in January 1970: "scientists have solid experimental and theoretical evidence to support [...]the following predictions: In a decade, urban dwellers will have to wear gas masks to survive air pollution [...]by 1985, air pollution will have reduced the amount of sunlight reaching earth by one half... [...]"[24]

How sad these early climate alarmists must be to find out their predictions of human extinction failed to measure up.

The massive failure to predict global climate devastation did not stop the next generation of prognosticators, however.

In 1998, Philip Shabecoff warned if the "buildup" of greenhouse gasses was allowed to continue, "the effect is likely to be a warming of three to nine degrees Fahrenheit [between now and] the year 2025 to 2050 [...] The rise in global temperature is predicted to [...] [...] cause sea levels to rise by one to four feet by the middle of the next century."[25] Around the same time, the United Nations sounded the alarm that global warming would cause rising sea levels that would wash entire countries away by the year 2000.[26]

In 2006, former Vice President Al Gore warned sea levels could rise twenty feet.[27] In 2012, Peter Wadhams, a professor of ocean physics at the University of Cambridge, predicted "global disaster" from the demise of the Arctic Sea in just four years.[28] In 2009, then-British Prime Minister Gordon Brown predicted the world had only fifty days to save the planet from global warming.[29]

A decade later, the 2016 Democratic Party platform compared the fight against global warming to World War II (because, obviously, storming the beaches of Normandy is the same as buying an electric car). Those who dare to raise a question are compared to Nazis and Holocaust deniers.

All these climate-change paroxysms raise the question—how're we doing?

Well, contra Prime Minister Brown, ten years later, the earth is still spinning. And thirty years after the doomiest of doomsday predictions about global warming, they have failed to come true. Shabecoff predicted a warming of three to nine degrees Fahrenheit, but he's had to settle for a warming of less than one degree and a climate temperature largely holding steady.

A study by the National Oceanic and Atmospheric Administration looked at the historical record of hurricanes and sea surface temperatures and found "the U.S. landfalling hurricane record [...] shows no significant increase or decrease." The report went on to say: "the historical Atlantic hurricane record does not provide compelling evidence for a substantial greenhouse warming-induced long-term increase."

In other words, climate change isn't causing more hurricanes. In fact, NOAA's tracking model showed an approximate 25 percent decrease in the "overall number of Atlantic hurricanes and tropical storms with projected 21st century climate warming."[30] According to data from the Environmental Protection Agency, pollutants ranging from carbon monoxide to ozone are down 84 percent and 32 percent, respectively, since 1980. Particulate matter is down by about 40 percent since 2000.[31]

To be clear, there is a role for climatologists and environmentalists and groups advocating for the earth and its protection. But a problem arises when these groups become too busy searching for the next ecological doomsday to realize the fruits of their own success—or the role market forces and technological development have played in reducing carbon emissions.

Though the Left would rather scream "Denier!" at anyone who would be so bold as to raise an eyebrow at yet another prediction of impending death, scientific division about the scope and size of the global warming problem does exist.

The Nongovernmental International Panel on Climate Change (NIPCC) is a group of scientists who have been examining the climate change problem for years. They cite hundreds of peer-reviewed scientific papers that raise significant questions around the so-called climate consensus. (Interestingly, the Left—the self-professed party of peer-reviewed science—fails to acknowledge their conclusions.) Assessments by the NIPCC find sea levels have not been rising at an accelerated rate and global temperatures have stayed largely the same for the last twenty years.

The number and strength of hurricanes are decreasing, as are floods and forest fires.[32]

Scientific inquiry is by its nature intended to be skeptical. There's a reason many of the greatest scientific breakthroughs began by challenging, and then overturning, the prevailing consensus. (Just ask Galileo, who was thrown in jail for suggesting the sun, rather than the earth, inhabited the center of our solar system.) There's a reason many scientists live by the motto, *"nullius in verba"*—Latin for "take nobody's word for it."

But the Left—and a complicit media—have made skepticism and inquiry verboten when it comes to climate change. Given the decades of misplaced alarmism and flat-out error, the Left would do well to engage their critics in thoughtful scientific debate, rather than simply trying to silence those with whom they disagree.

The dedication to political outcomes over objectivity threatens to undermine the seriousness with which we view the entire debate.

Indeed, as scientist Judith Curry has written,

> The scientific establishment behind the global warming issue has been drawn into the trap of seriously understating the uncertainties associated with the climate problem [[...]] this behavior risks destroying science's reputation for honesty. It is this objectivity and honesty which gives science a privileged seat at the table. Without this objectivity and honesty, scientists become regarded as another lobbyist group.[33]

The Left's Answer to Climate Change? More Power to the Government

The Left's solutions to climate change have one thing in common: take power away from the American people and give it to Washington. The other thing they have in common is requiring a tremendous amount of sacrifice for negligible gains.

For the latest and greatest example of this, look no further than the Green New Deal proposed by Senator Ed Markey (D-Mass.) and Rep. Alexandria Ocasio-Cortez (D-N.Y.). Their proposal is light on details, but the accompanying "fact sheet" makes clear the pair intend a "massive transformation of our society."

Among the measures necessary are eliminating air travel, "retrofit[ing] every building in America," getting rid of cars with combustion engines, building "charging stations everywhere," banning air travel, and eradicating fossil fuels and nuclear energy sources entirely.[34]

But, for Markey and Ocasio-Cortez, addressing climate change doesn't stop there. Also prioritized in their proposal is a government-guaranteed job, free education, a house, a union, and a living wage even for those "unwilling to work."

The Left doesn't just want to address climate change. They want to remake your life—just like Socialists everywhere and in every era.

The Green New Deal may be the most overt example of this, but it's been happening for years. In 2016, President Obama made the United States a signatory to the Paris Climate Accords, an international agreement among nations to reduce global carbon emissions. The problem? It was largely unenforceable. That is, it would have required the U.S. to reduce our carbon emissions by nearly 30 percent below 2005 levels, even though most of the world's major polluters would continue to emit tons of greenhouse gases into the atmosphere. As previously discussed, the rate of carbon emissions in the United States has fallen over the last decade (while emissions have gone up in China and India).

Moreover, there is a serious economic cost for taking on the compliance burden of the agreement. Researchers have estimated that over ten years, the Paris Climate Accords would cost a family of four $30,000 per year in higher energy prices in addition to four hundred thousand lost jobs—two hundred thousand in manufacturing alone. Overall, the agreement amounted to a $2.5 trillion global tax on American production.[35]

There are some on the Left who would say (and have) this is worth it; that the climate is in crisis and we, as a global leader, must be the one to act. But even this justification is challenging because, if the United States eliminated all carbon emissions, it would only serve to reduce the earth's temperature by less than 0.02 degrees Celsius by 2100. If the entire world eliminated all carbon emissions, it would amp that up by just a hundredth, to 0.03 degrees of global warming averted by 2100.[36]

Former senator and Secretary of State John Kerry (D-Mass.) said it best when speaking at the United Nations Framework Convention on Climate Change:

The fact is that even if every American citizen biked to work, carpooled to school, used only solar panels to power their homes, if we each planted a dozen trees, if we somehow eliminated all of our domestic greenhouse gas emissions, guess what—that still wouldn't be enough to offset the carbon pollution coming from the rest of the world.

If all the industrial nations went down to zero emissions—it wouldn't be enough, not when more than 65 percent of the world's carbon pollution comes from the developing world.[37]

Consider the example of Germany, whose government committed to a growing share of their energy production coming from renewable sources. Energy prices there have risen 70 percent.[38] The country recently announced it will have to abandon its plan to cut greenhouse gas emissions to 40 percent below 1990 levels.[39]

In France, the "yellow vest" riots erupting in Paris in 2019 were a response to French President Emmanuel Macron's attempt to institute a fuel tax aimed at discouraging driving. Unfortunately, the rural families outside Paris rely on their cars to get back and forth to work. Macron has a motorcade (remember, "some are more equal than others") and Paris city dwellers have a large public transit system, but the plight of those in rural France never seemed to enter their minds. The episode illustrates another element of climate change policies seeking to change behavior—they hurt the middle class more than the rich, and the poor most of all. A Stanford study quantified the costs of climate change regulation, finding it is ultimately "the lowest income group" who "pays, as a percent of income, more than twice what households in the highest 10 percent of the income distribution pay."[40]

The Progressive Left, who herald themselves as advocates of the underprivileged, have no answer for the fact their policies hurt poor families the most. Under Progressive policies, it's always "the little guy" who is left holding the bag while the elite high-five themselves for their virtue and wisdom. It's poor kids who languish in rotten schools, poor mothers and families who suffer on the wrong side of welfare "poverty traps," and lower-income workers who are held back by expensive health care and energy regulations. And, as we've documented, the crown jewel of Progressive public policies—climate change—hurts the weakest and most vulnerable among us the most.

Abortion

Perhaps the most insidious application of "equality" promoted by the Left is the one-sided "choice" of terminating a pregnancy. Pro-choice politicians always refuse to recognize the other entity who never gets a choice when an abortion is carried out: the child.

This shouldn't be surprising considering the origins of the abortion movement, which began under Margaret Sanger, the founder of Planned Parenthood. Sanger, a noted racist, supported abortion of black babies and those she deemed "defective," e.g., those with mental retardation or other disabilities.[41]

The movement she founded has emerged in recent years as the moral core of the Democratic Party platform. For a while, Democrats supported abortion as a "safe, legal, and rare" option for women. But the Progressive Left has taken them from "safe, legal, and rare" to "unrestricted, unregulated and unlimited" abortion.

In 2015, undercover videos from pro-life activist David Daleiden and his team at the Center for Medical Progress showed Planned Parenthood executives trafficking in the body parts of aborted babies, casually discussing the market worth of a baby's body parts over lunch. Perhaps because they couldn't bear the horror, Planned Parenthood, Democrats, and the mainstream media feverishly denied the practice occurs, alleging instead the videos were "deceptively edited."

However, four years later, the Fifth Circuit Court of Appeals found the videos were not altered, and Planned Parenthood "at a minimum violated federal standards regarding fetal tissue research and standards of medical ethics."[42]

In 2019, Democrat Governor of Virginia Ralph Northam shocked the nation with his calm and clinical description of abortion-cum-infanticide.

In a national radio interview, Northam, a pediatric neurologist by training, described what would happen when a mother equivocated whether or not she wanted the baby she just delivered:

> If a mother is in labor [[...]] the infant would be delivered. The infant would be kept comfortable. The infant would be resuscitated if that's what the mother and the family desired, and then a discussion would ensue between the physicians and mother.[43]

Democrats shushed a horrified public by repeating the refrain of "women's health" (despite the fact Northam's comments were predicated on an already born baby), diverting to a straw-man argument, "late term abortions are incredibly rare" (according to data from the Centers for Disease Control, there were over five thousand late-term abortions in 2018; and again, the issue is about babies born alive), and babies born alive after botched abortions don't happen (another misrepresentation—twenty-four infants were born alive after botched abortions in 2017 alone), or this was for the health of the mother or fetal abnormality (a study from the abortion-friendly Guttmacher institute showed women don't primarily seek late-term abortions for their health or due to fetal abnormality).[44][45][46][47][48]

When confronted with legislation in the U.S. Senate to extend legal protections to babies who are born alive after an attempted abortion—that is, American citizens—forty-four Senate Democrats voted against it.[49]

As of this writing, Governor Ralph Northam is still in office, even after it was revealed he dressed in blackface on at least two occasions while a young man, on top of his comments promoting infanticide. Leading Democrats running for president have said we all need to "move on."[50]

Meanwhile, leading Democrats still promote abortion as a policy of equality toward women, routinely failing to acknowledge the presence of another human life in the equation.

Science tells us babies can now survive outside the womb twenty-two weeks after conception.[51] The point of viability—the age where babies can survive outside the womb, and the premise on which *Roe v. Wade* allowed abortions—continues to occur earlier in pregnancy. But the Left, the so-called party of science, continues to fight for legalizing abortions up to and after birth.

The Left also ignores the inequality of outcomes abortion has on the minority and disabled community. Black women make up 13 percent of the female population in the United States, according to census data. But they receive 40 percent of the abortions performed each year.[52] That is a virtual genocide against black babies.

Countries like Iceland brag about "eliminating" genetic conditions like Down Syndrome in their country. But they haven't eliminated a medical condition—just the babies diagnosed with it. That's not health care; it's the opposite of health care. Tragically, American women are not far behind. American women choose to abort 67 percent of babies with Down Syndrome, despite legions of examples of Down Syndrome babies growing into productive, successful, and most importantly, happy, adults.[53] Your coauthor's (Rachel's) younger brother, Jesse Bovard, is one of them.

Abortion is the great unequalizer. It sacrifices human life to the tyranny of convenience. It is an act of violence perpetrated by the powerful, against the weak. A society refusing to acknowledge this fact, that nods along to the glossy rhetoric about "women's health" or "reproductive rights" will never be truly equal. It will be burdened with the knowledge that unique and individual lives—future humans full of potential—are snuffed out every day without a voice and without a say, without the ability to live out their precious lives in this dream of a country our forefathers labored so intensely to give them.

On education, health care, the environment, and abortion, the Left is not the party of science, or equality, or freedom, or justice. They are the party of power—of taking it from you and using it, in your name, for themselves and against the weakest members of our society.

CHAPTER 11

Conservative Ideas and Policies

I regard the extension of the range of choice, that is, an increase in the range of effective alternatives open to the people, as the principle objective and criterion of economic development; and I judge a measure principally by its probable effects on the range of alternatives open to individuals.[1]

—PETER BAUER

We've identified the core of the Left's view of how the country should be run: mandated equality of outcomes foisted on us by government bureaucrats through Socialist policies.

But what about Conservatives? What do we think and how do we assess policy proposals presented to us?

Ultimately, Conservatism is far less rigid than the orthodoxy of the Progressive Left today, where the rules are constantly changing but always strictly enforced. Failing to live up to any one of them will get you publicly shunned and declared unfit (or, worse, "un-woke").

Conservatism is less demanding (and, it seems to us, less exhausting) on its adherents. As Russell Kirk described it, "conservatism is the negation of ideology: it is a state of mind, a type of character, a way of looking at the civil social order."[2]

He goes on:

The attitude we call conservatism is sustained by a body of sentiments, rather than by a system of ideological dogmata [...]. The Conservative movement or body of opinion can accommodate a considerable diversity of views on a good many subjects [...]. In essence, the Conservative person is simply one who finds the permanent things more pleasing than Chaos and Old Night [...]. A people's historic continuity of experience, says the Conservative, offers a guide to policy far better than the abstract designs of coffee-house philosophers.[3]

Though portrayed by the mainstream media as rigid and inflexible, Conservatism is actually quite broad. There are many ways to be a Conservative—and we speculate, if you are someone who wants to keep the things that matter in your own life, you are, at least personally (if not politically) a Conservative.

This is particularly true when you consider Conservatives are not at all opposed to social improvement and change. Change and social progress are necessary. "A body that has ceased to renew itself has begun to die," said Kirk. "But if that body is to be vigorous, the change must occur in a regular manner, harmonizing with the form and nature of that body; otherwise change produces a monstrous growth, a cancer, which devours its host."[4] Change, to be meaningful and lasting, must also be prudent, taking into account the values, consequences, and character of the people it will impact the most.

Russell Kirk's essay on ten Conservative principles provides a handy guide to those looking for a general definition of what it means to be a Conservative.[5] But how does it apply to the way Conservatives view policymaking?

Conservatives, first and foremost, support policies that enhance the ability of all Americans to make individual decisions apart from the government. This is based upon the idea every individual, every family, and every business knows the intricacies of their lives, budgets, and long-term goals better than the faraway state, and, thus, can make more informed decisions on their own behalf. (This is distinct from Liberalism or Progressivism, which starts from the assumption third-party experts know what is best for every individual).

Starting from this premise, Conservatives tend to analyze policy proposals through four key lenses.

Does This Policy Allow Civil Society to Flourish?

Civil society consists of our communities and institutions like schools, churches, volunteer organizations, unions, and the like. When Edmund Burke talked about living in "little platoons," he was referring to civil society. Same with Tocqueville's "individualism rightly understood," Robert Nisbet's "quest for community," and Russell Kirk's "voluntary communities."

We depend on our civil society, and the millions of individual decisions made at the local level, to raise healthy families and strong, independent individuals. Conservatives believe civil society is essential to human flourishing, and local institutions are key to carrying this out. So, when we examine policies, we want to ensure each one of them supports, rather than hampers, the ability of civil societies to grow and develop.

In education policy, for example, we might ask, "Does this policy allow the community to shape its system of schools more than the distant state?" Or, when considering the role of churches in caring for the community, "Does this tax or regulatory policy help or hurt churches in carrying out their mission?" Or, "Will this new law make it harder for American Heritage Girls and Trail Life troops to form and meet around the country?"

The more we collectivize decisions of individuals and communities, the more we diminish the role unique communities and local institutions have in engaging with and facilitating the development of those who live and work around them. Good policy will put in place guardrails to ensure the rule of law is followed and enforced while maximizing the ability of individuals and communities to freely choose a manner of living best for them.

Does This Policy Allow Religious Freedom to Flourish?

Religious freedom is a necessary function of civil society, but it is one that has been attacked on all sides lately. It is a central component to American freedom, and one Conservatives must fight to protect. Put simply, religious liberty promises individuals and communities are free to practice their beliefs publicly and privately, without interference from the state.

A strong society tolerates differences in opinions, worldviews, and lifestyles. And we celebrate policies comporting with our mutual freedom to think and speak and worship for ourselves, in accordance with our individual faiths, rather than be bound to one standard defined for us by the government.

What Are the Long-Term Consequences?

The economist Frédéric Bastiat referred to two types of policy consequences: the seen and the unseen. Unfortunately, we tend to focus more on the "seen," as opposed to the long-term effects of what is coming down the pike. Rather, policy-makers should be doing as economist Henry Hazlitt advised: "The art of economics consists in looking not merely at the immediate but at the longer effects of any act or policy; it consists in tracing the consequences of that policy not merely for one group but for all groups."[6]

Many policies are swept into effect by the tyranny of now because they are suddenly popular, or there is an urgent feeling someone ought to "do something." But Conservatives aren't just interested in fixing an immediate problem. We must always try to project how the ripple effects of rapidly constructed policies will impact the future.

Policy has short-term and long-term outcomes; Conservatives are concerned with both.

Does This Policy Centralize Power Within the State, or Disperse It Among the People?

It is very easy for the state to gather power unto itself—by creating dependence of corporations through complex tax breaks, controlling the religious choices of individuals, or even by dictating the standards for the cars and appliances Americans are allowed to buy. But Conservatism fundamentally believes, as Kirk put it, "a central administration, or a corps of select managers and civil servants, however well-intentioned and well-trained, cannot confer justice and prosperity and tranquility upon a mass of men and women deprived of their old responsibilities."[7]

Good policy must support individuals in making free choices—not make choices for them.

So what specific policies do Conservatives support? What follows is not intended to be a detailed or exhaustive platform of Conservative legislative proposals. It instead offers a general discussion of how the Conservative perspectives and approaches from the previous chapter can be applied to several important issue areas.

Education as the Foundation of Freedom

A free and prosperous country depends on citizens able to succeed in such a society. This requires the availability of quality education, skills training, and character development for every child in America—goals accomplished only through a partnership among parents, churches, community, and the government. These goals cannot be achieved by sending children to schools controlled by a government monopoly with curriculum designed by Leftist ideologues. Yet this is the design of the American education system.

As we've discussed, elitists on the Left demand most children in America attend a government-run school selected by bureaucrats while sending their own children to private schools and universities where they don't have to mix with the unwashed masses. The Left rails at favoritism for the rich while they spend thousands—sometimes millions—in tuition and even bribes to send their children to the finest private schools. (Recall the scandal we referenced before, where wealthy parents in business and Hollywood were found to be bribing and cheating their children into supposedly meritocratic ivy league universities).

Since a well-educated citizenry is essential to a free society, public funding of education is a legitimate function of government. But government funding of education should not be synonymous with government-run schools. Public funds for education should be used to empower parents with the right to choose where and how their children are educated.

Many states have actively developed more education choices for parents. The popularity of charter schools is growing. The National Alliance for Public Charter Schools reports there are over 6,900 charter schools in the U.S. educating over three million students. Demand from parents is increasing and most charter schools maintain waiting lists of parents hoping for better education opportunities for their children.

The appeal of these schools is easy to understand. Charter schools retain taxpayer funding but receive greater freedom from many of the onerous regulations that bog down traditional neighborhood schools. Instead, the schools' charters hold administrators accountable to both parents and regulators for their educational outcomes. Regulators can even shut down consistently underperforming charter schools—something that rarely happens in traditional public education. Parents have seen how this accountability leads to better results, allowing charter schools to grow by leaps and bounds. A total of forty-three states and the District of Columbia have authorized charter schools.[8]

In addition to creating charter schools, the Midwest also helped spawn a movement for parents to choose the school that best meets their child's needs, whether public or private. In 1990, the Wisconsin legislature authorized an opportunity scholarship program for low-income students in the city of Milwaukee, a program which slowly grew over time. What began with a few hundred students in its first year has grown to serve nearly thirty thousand students as of this writing.[9]

In time, the success of the Milwaukee program sparked other school choice initiatives in many other states. Hundreds of thousands of students now participate in various school choice programs—tuition deductions, tuition credits or opportunity scholarship programs—every year.[10]

School choice works because it empowers parents, not government bureaucrats. Just as no two snowflakes are alike, every child has unique talents, gifts, interests, and learning styles. No one can recognize and understand those talents better than a child's parents—and no bureaucrat, however well-meaning, can ever replicate the love and concern parents show for their sons and daughters. By placing parents in control of their children's education, school choice gives them the ultimate form of accountability: the power to hire their child's teachers and school and the power to fire them too.

Unsurprisingly, parents like having this form of accountability over something as important as their children's education—and they don't much like it when Liberals try to snatch it away.

Upon taking office, Barack Obama and Democrats in Congress set their sights on ending a school choice program Congress established for poor children in the District of Columbia. They closed it to new students and wanted to shut it down completely. But parents like Virginia Walden Ford—a single mother who pushed Congress to create the opportunity scholarship program in 2004—mobilized to block Democrats' actions.[11] With the help of Republicans in Congress, these engaged, committed parents saw the D.C. Opportunity Scholarship program reauthorized. As a result, some students in the nation's capital will continue to have more options beyond Washington's trouble-plagued public school system.

Critics of private school choice, including President Obama, claim the programs do not increase student performance. But the results suggest otherwise. Of a total of eighteen randomized control studies analyzing the performance of students who use opportunity scholarships to study in private schools compared to students who remain in public education, fourteen found school choice opportunities improved student outcomes.[12]

Believe it or not, the benefits of school choice are not confined to students attending private schools. Of thirty-three studies examining the effects of school choice on public school students, thirty-one—all but two—found *private* school choice improves the educational outcomes for students who remain in *public* education.[13] The competition school choice generates—breaking up the monopoly of the national teachers' union and government bureaucrats—ultimately benefits private and public school students alike.

> One of the most alarming myths about school choice is that choice opportunities hurt local public schools. Research has consistently shown that this could not be further from the truth and that public schools actually improve when power is given back to the parents.[14]

School choice also gives financial benefits to taxpayers, above and beyond its improvements in the educational system. Because most private schools spend money more efficiently than government-run institutions, and because some opportunity scholarship programs limit the amount of the scholarship to a percentage of public-school spending, school choice generates sizable savings. Two recent studies analyzed twenty-six different scholarship programs and found they saved taxpayers a total of between $4.9 billion and $6.6 billion, or an average of more than $3,100 for every scholarship awarded.[15]

Thankfully, school choice continues to grow and expand, bringing benefits to more states and more families. In 2011, Arizona created a new school choice model—Educational Savings Accounts (ESAs).[16] These accounts give parents a percentage of a school district's per-pupil spending and allow them to send their children to public, private, religious, special needs, home schools, or whatever options best meet their children's needs. ESAs take the promise of school choice to its highest level by allowing parents to select from multiple options—including extra one-on-one tutoring, supplemental courses, computers and the purchase of online education courses—to customize their children's education.

Since Arizona first created ESAs, another five states have followed with similar programs, and they have proven very popular, particularly for families with special needs children. And with ESAs, whatever funds are not spent in one school year can be rolled over and saved for future education opportunities—even to pay for college.

Under current laws, states have some latitude to implement school choice programs, but federal laws and regulations restrict federal funds from following students, and federal mandates encumber education innovation. One proposal by Conservatives in Congress called Straight A's would loosen the federal hold on education by allowing states to opt out of the federal education straitjacket in return for commitments to achieve certain measurable outcomes for students. This proposal does not force any changes for states that don't want to change. It simply gives states the opportunity to try something different. Given the poor performance of public schools in America, this opportunity for change is only common sense.

Quality Health Care for Everyone

The federal government has a long history of meddling in health care and we have written extensively in previous chapters explaining the unintended consequences of these laws and regulations. Suffice it to say, government actions have reduced health care provider competition and patient choices—almost completely eliminating market pressure to lower prices, expand choices, and improve quality.

Conservatives have proposed many ideas to solve the current problems with our health care system:

- Allow individuals to deduct the cost of their health insurance, just like businesses;

- Allow small businesses, groups, and associations to pool their members or employees to buy insurance less expensively;

- Allow people to buy less expensive, high deductible health plans to cover unforeseen "catastrophic" expenses and put more tax-free money into Health Savings Accounts to pay for more routine health care, as well as the cost of their health insurance;

- Encourage insurance companies to offer "whole life, permanent health insurance" plans people can buy and keep throughout their lives; and

- Create an option for seniors allowing Medicare to pay a part of the cost of private health plans so people can keep their personal insurance when they retire.

The solutions, again, are common sense—once you correctly diagnose the problem. Current government policies have raised health costs; undoing these policies will reduce them.

Tax Treatment of Health Insurance

Federal tax law makes it difficult for insurance companies to offer affordable plans individuals can buy when they are young and keep from job to job and into retirement. Because the federal government offers a generous tax subsidy to employer-provided plans—but *not* to health insurance plans individuals buy for themselves—most people get their health coverage from their employer.

This unequal tax treatment causes several problems. First, most people change their health coverage when they change their job—and they lose their health coverage when they lose their job. Most businesses also don't give their employees much choice when it comes to their coverage options, meaning workers can't pick the plan that best meets their needs. And employer subsidies can encourage employees to choose expensive health insurance and overuse health care because they think their employer "pays for their health care," when those generous subsidies actually reduce workers' paychecks.

Equalizing the tax treatment of health insurance would help resolve these problems by giving people choices and empowering them to pick the plans. Allowing people to buy and keep health plans when they are young and healthy would largely resolve the issue of pre-existing conditions later in life. As it is, most people get their health insurance from their employer and lose it every time they change jobs. This creates numerous windows of potential jeopardy for people who develop serious health conditions as they grow older.

Fee-for-Service Medicine

Most private insurers base their reimbursement models upon those used by the government-run Medicare program. Until very recently, Medicare paid doctors and hospitals on the basis of fee-for-service medicine. This arrangement meant doctors were paid more for performing more services on patients—even when those services resulted from errors the doctors made!

Well before Obamacare, however, private sector innovators came up with solutions to the problems presented by government reimbursement. For instance, in 2007 Geisinger Health System in Pennsylvania started offering patients a "warranty" on heart bypass and other operations.[17] If patients suffered any complications or needed rehospitalization following their operation, Geisinger would absorb those charges. The program proved so successful Medicare and other private sector innovators like Walmart have adopted it more broadly.

Freeing patients from the restrictions imposed by government programs like Medicare would allow doctors to innovate more freely. For instance, direct primary care arrangements—in which patients pay a small amount of $50-100 per month for regular care by a physician group—have recently grown in popularity. Expanding access to Health Savings Accounts would allow more patients to use their own (tax-free) money to pay for the care they want, outside of any government-imposed restrictions.

Access to Care

Liberals don't like to admit it, but they have one main way to contain health care costs: limiting the supply of care. In government-run systems like those in Britain, fewer hospital beds and MRI machines mean patients wait to access care.

In the United States, these types of restrictions include two regulations. Certificate-of-need laws in most states require groups wishing to open a new hospital or medical facility to first receive a certificate from a government board—a "Mother, may I?" approach to health care. Likewise, scope of practice restrictions in many states prevent professionals like nurse practitioners from using all the elements of their medical training.

As you might imagine, special interests have a strong incentive to keep these restrictions in place because they block out competition in health care. Well-connected hospitals and doctor groups lobby state legislatures constantly to preserve these restrictions and prevent other groups from invading "their turf."

But, if states repealed their certificate-of-need and scope-of-practice restrictions, patients would have more options—and often at lower prices too. Families wouldn't need to wait for hours at the doctor's office when their child gets a cold or sprains an ankle—they could be treated faster, and more affordably, by a nurse practitioner at a MinuteClinic.

Prescription Drugs

Any discussion about health care should include Conservative solutions for the high price of prescription drugs. Drugs are many Americans' largest health care expense. Americans spend more than $400 billion a year on prescription drugs.[18]

Government regulation helps lead to high prescription prices. New drugs often take decades to develop, with research and development, testing, and clinical trials required by the Food and Drug Administration (FDA) costing an average of $2.6 billion for each new prescription drug.[19]

Reforming the FDA can help slow the skyrocketing cost of prescription drugs. Streamlining the approval process would help to address the high cost of research and development for new drugs. Fast-tracking drugs already approved in other countries and approving generic drugs more quickly would encourage competition that can bring down prices. Other similar reforms could reduce the cost and time required to get drugs to market.

Medicaid

Medicaid, a state-federal health insurance plan for the poor, contains several structural shortcomings. Many doctors do not accept Medicaid patients because the system reimburses doctors for services at extremely low levels. The generous federal match rate also creates an incentive for waste, fraud, and abuse by states. Obamacare's 90 percent federal match rate encouraged states to expand Medicaid coverage beyond the poor to cover able-bodied, working people who could buy other insurance, which exploded budgets for many states and crowded out spending for other services such as transportation infrastructure and education.[20]

A Conservative solution would focus on requiring states to bear at least half the costs of Medicaid (to discourage overuse) and giving states block grants in exchange for added flexibility—that is, Washington would cut each state a check and let state policymakers decide how to spend it on specific categories of patients or services. Most importantly, Conservatives should help people transition from Medicaid to private health insurance plans. Currently, people can lose Medicaid coverage if their income increases, which discourages work and traps people in welfare dependency. States should develop transitional sliding-scale policies that allow Medicaid to pay a portion of the cost of private insurance as people move from dependency to independence.

Medicare

Of all its health care programs, the federal government spends the most on Medicare, a program for people sixty-five and older and individuals with disabilities. Medicare is largely paid for by payroll taxes, but these taxes no longer cover costs, meaning the program will soon become insolvent. Fewer and fewer doctors are accepting new Medicare patients because, like Medicaid, Medicare often pays doctors and hospitals less than the actual cost of the services they provide.

Common sense suggests, if Medicare is near insolvency while serving only people sixty-five and older and if fewer doctors are accepting new Medicare patients, then the federal government has little business expanding coverage still further. But the Left remains insistent on its utopian dream of eliminating private insurance and putting all Americans on a government-run health plan.

A Conservative solution for the current one-size-fits-all, insolvent Medicare program would offer a voluntary choice for seniors. The idea, called "premium support," would allow people who turn sixty-five to keep their private health insurance, with Medicare paying part of the cost of their plan. Depending on the details of the proposal, competition between private plans and traditional Medicare could reduce costs for both seniors and the federal government, sustaining the current program for those who want to keep it while giving others the option of keeping their private plans and their doctors.[21] Everyone wins! But the Left bitterly opposes giving people this kind of health care freedom.

Summary of Health Care Problems and Solutions

Health care has become mind-bogglingly complex because of government's role. Our tax system makes it prohibitively expensive for most people to buy individual health insurance plans they can own and keep throughout their lives. Most people get their health plans through their employers and lose their insurance every time they change jobs. Those who develop pre-existing health conditions during their lives often find it difficult to find insurance plans they can afford.

State and federal regulations make it difficult for new and innovative insurance companies to create a wide variety of plans to meet the needs of people at all ages and with different health conditions. Consumers still can't buy insurance plans offered in other states, which locks them into one state's set of regulations. Large insurance companies with virtual monopolies in many states have powerful lobbying groups in Washington to make sure they are protected from lower pricing and innovative competitors. And physicians and hospitals are forced to design their services around a convoluted system and bureaucratic third-party payers that cause inefficiencies, waste, higher costs, and lower quality care. Still wonder why health care remains so expensive?

Conservative health care solutions would transform America's health care system from a bureaucratic, largely government-controlled industry to a consumer-friendly service offering people more affordable choices and more freedom. To achieve this goal, consumers must have more control and ownership of their health insurance, more control of their physician choices and health care decisions, more choices of inpatient and outpatient care providers, and more knowledge on the costs and choices of health care services.

Social Security

All the taxes collected for Social Security each year are spent on current retirees, but these taxes no longer cover the annual costs of the program. Social Security has had a cash flow deficit since 2010. This means the U.S. Treasury must find funds from other sources each year to pay Social Security benefits.

Before 2010, Social Security had a cash flow surplus each year. These surpluses accumulated (on paper) to nearly $3 trillion in the Social Security Trust Fund. But this money was not actually saved. The federal government spent it on other government programs and left only Treasury bonds (essentially IOUs) in the Trust Fund. So, the $2.8 trillion currently in the "Trust Fund" is simply government debt. This would be like a corporation using pension funds to cover the monthly payroll and then leaving nothing in the fund to pay retirees. In the private sector, this is called an unfunded pension plan (which is illegal).

The annual deficit for Social Security will continue to increase by hundreds of billions of dollars as more Baby Boomers retire. This will pressure policymakers in Washington to reform the program. Reforms currently being discussed include raising payroll taxes on younger workers, increasing the retirement age, reducing benefits and "means testing" to reduce or eliminate benefits for wealthy retirees. None of these ideas are fair because had current payroll taxes been saved and invested in individual accounts for workers, today's retirees would be independent of government and have significant retirement income.

In addition to its unsustainable financial situation, another serious problem with the current Social Security system—because every American is at least partially dependent on it for their retirement income—is that it has become the means of political manipulation and fear-mongering. Every politician in Washington knows Social Security needs to be fixed, but most will campaign on maintaining the status quo or even increasing benefits while accusing their opponent of planning to cut benefits. American voters should not be subjected to political threats to take what is rightfully their own money.

The Conservative goal for Social Security is to transform it into a fully funded pension plan to give future retirees security and independence from government. This goal is more difficult today than when Conservatives first proposed the idea of personal Social Security accounts because the program no longer has annual surpluses to fund these accounts. Nevertheless, it should be an American priority to transition Social Security from an unfunded pension plan to a fully funded 401K-style retirement savings plan.

This transition could begin by investing a part of every workers' payroll taxes in personal investment accounts. These accounts would be combined with traditional Social Security to fund retirement benefits for the next several decades. But future generations of American workers could retire with safe and secure pension benefits wholly funded from their own Social Security accounts that could not be threatened or manipulated by politicians.

We offer one additional idea to reduce the long-term deficits of the current Social Security system without reducing current benefits. Offer buyouts to current and near-retirees who have alternative assets to fund their retirement income. While most Americans do not have adequate savings for retirement and will require all their Social Security benefits, there are millions of Americans who do not need their Social Security benefits. If these financially independent Americans were offered lump sum payments that represented a portion of their lifetime actuarial payout, many would likely take the money to pay off mortgages or purchase retirement homes. This would reduce the long-term deficit of the Social Security program.

Welfare

Government charity programs in America—various welfare income programs, government housing, food stamps, and Medicaid health insurance—are mostly funded and regulated by the federal government but managed by the states. This has encouraged states to overuse these programs because it brings more federal "matching" dollars to their states.

And leftist politicians in Washington are continuously working to expand the number of voters who are dependent on government benefits.

Total welfare benefits in America now exceed $1 trillion with the federal government paying about 75 percent of this total.[22] Medicaid alone represents almost 30 percent of the average state's budget[23] with other Welfare benefits averaging another 20 percent.[24] This spending crowds out other state priorities, such as education, infrastructure, and economic development.

Conservative solutions to government charity programs are focused on getting people off these programs and making them more independent. First, there should not be encouragement or perverse incentives for people to become dependent on government charity in the first place unless it is absolutely necessary. Currently, leftist bureaucrats and political activists continuously seek to expand the number of people who are dependent on federal and state charity.

Welfare programs should be means-tested to identify those who are truly needy. Able-bodied recipients should be required to work or actively seek work. All government charity programs should have transitional mechanisms that encourage and assist recipients to move toward independence and private sector solutions. States should be required to fund over half of all Medicaid and Welfare programs and have the flexibility to manage these programs without federal obstacles to innovation. This would reduce or eliminate the current incentives for states to expand charitable spending.

National Transportation Infrastructure

The federal government collects 18.4 cents for every gallon of gasoline sold in the U.S.; states add their own fuel taxes. On average, consumers pay combined federal and state fuel taxes of about fifty cents per gallon. These taxes are supposed to be used to maintain local, state, and federal roads and bridges.

> While gas taxes tend to be politically unpopular, they are a relatively good embodiment of the "benefit principle," or the idea in public finance that the taxes a person pays should relate to the benefits received.[25]

As with many federal programs, the federal government pays only a portion of the costs of transportation infrastructure while largely controlling programs through mandates and regulations. The federal government collects approximately $35 billion in fuel taxes and the states, collectively, raise about $40 billion.[26]

The condition of America's infrastructure suggests the federal Department of Transportation is not doing its job. Currently, fuel tax dollars are diverted to local mass transit and politically directed earmarks while federal regulations requiring union "prevailing wages," beautification, bike paths, and other non-essential requirements create waste and inefficiencies. States need more flexibility to maximize the efficient use of fuel tax dollars.

Conservatives have proposed legislation to devolve federal control and fuel tax revenue back to the states. Research has found that federal roads could be maintained with only three cents per gallon. The rest of the fuel tax dollars should be collected and controlled by the states.

> "Wasteful, inequitable, and bristling with burdensome regulations, the Federal Highway Program is in dire need of reform. Although members of Congress have attempted to enact changes in the past, the influence of many lobbyists and influential constituencies continues to thwart the process. By maintaining this predictable money morass, Congress and the president are ignoring the needs of the motorists who pay the taxes to fund the program—as well as the needs of an economy that depends on cost-effective mobility. Yet some legislators remain committed to reform and have proposed Congress 'turn back' some or all of the federal highway program to the states, where it once was lodged."[27]

Tax Reform

The current federal tax system exempts nearly half of Americans from federal income taxes.[28] All workers pay for Social Security and Medicare through payroll taxes, but every voter should have some stake in the cost of the federal government—even if it is a very nominal amount. Leftist proposals such as Medicare for All and the New Green Deal should have some cost considerations for all voters.

Taxing personal and business income, capital gains, death, fuel, alcohol, and a wide array of other trade and excise taxes—along with all the exemptions, deductions, and credits allowed by the tax system—creates an incomprehensible, unenforceable, and expensive collection process fraught with waste and fraud. Collecting taxes from over 300 million Americans, twenty-eight million small businesses, twenty-two million self-employed workers, and numerous other sources of revenue creates a system that is impossible to manage efficiently.

Conservatives have proposed many ideas to simplify the federal tax system. Most of these ideas advocate for a lower, flatter tax rate that includes more people—all with generous standard deductions for lower income workers and credits for children. Perhaps the simplest tax reform would eliminate the collection of taxes from individuals altogether. Proposals such as the Fair Tax eliminate direct taxes on individuals and shift all tax collections to businesses. This would greatly simplify tax collections.

The Fair Tax has been criticized for transferring all federal income taxes to a retail sales tax. This could add up to 30 percent to the cost of retail products and create incentives for "black market" sales. But this criticism can be overcome by balancing retail sales taxes with other business taxes based on their purchases. Businesses have more sophisticated accounting systems than individuals and could easily collect retail sales taxes and payroll taxes, and pay taxes on purchases of raw materials, component parts, or other inputs.

There are many ways to reduce the costs, improve efficiencies, and increase the fairness of the current tax system. But the Left is focused only on increasing taxes on the "rich" who already pay most of the taxes in America. The top 1 percent of income earners now pay more taxes than the bottom 90 percent combined.[29] Taxes, like many other issues for the Left, are just another means of political manipulation and electioneering.

Energy and Environmental Policy

A clean and healthy environment is something Conservatives want to keep. The covenants we make with God and each other are inextricably linked with *place*. As the English writer G. K. Chesterton put it: "I think God has given us the love of special places, of a hearth and of a native land, for a good reason [...] [...]. God bade me love one spot and serve it."[30]

Love and service include patriotism and community bonds, but they also extend to our physical environment. We may differ about the urgency of the density of the ozone layer or the quantity of glacial ice in the arctic, but we are all passionate about our neighborhoods, local parks, streams, and air quality. And we all jealously guard our own backyards, our favorite hiking trails, scenic overlooks, and our own gardens and family water supplies.

Many environmental activists and political Progressives believe Conservatives simply don't care about the environment as much as they do because we disagree with them about their environmental *policies*. But caring doesn't justify ineffective policies, especially if the motivation of policies is simply to gain more control of economic activities. We should set aside political goals and agree on what we want our policies to accomplish.

Why not start from a less accusatory position and assume Conservatives and Progressives both want clean air and water; to reduce harmful pollutants and emissions; to facilitate the development and competitiveness of renewable fuels; and to generally protect our environment from danger and degradation? What are the best ways, the best policies and strategies, to bring about these shared goals?

The Left's ambition always seems to be for government to take more control and to "protect" the environment by using its taxing, spending, and regulatory powers to coerce businesses and consumers to become more "green." They use exaggerated threats from climate change to justify even the most irrational policy ideas (e.g., the Green New Deal). But there is overwhelming evidence that government control of energy and economic activities does not result in a cleaner environment.

History provides some good case studies of how Socialist economic controls have seriously degraded the environment. The Soviet Union and its satellite countries in Eastern Europe, Communist China, Cuba, and North Korea were all Socialist economies that created environmental disasters.

In the 1980s, the United Nations found East Germany was the most polluted country in the world.[31] Water in Soviet Russia was notoriously foul. In 1990, a report in the journal *Multinational Monitor* found, "In

Leningrad, nearly half of the children have intestinal disorders caused by drinking contaminated water from what was once Europe's most pristine supply."[32]

Ill-conceived Soviet-built canals in Central Asia dried up the Aral Sea, exposing the surrounding region to pesticide-infested dust storms. In the 1950s, the Chinese government's careless schemes of deforestation, irrigation, and pest extermination resulted in famines that killed tens of millions of innocent people.

The Kim regime in North Korea and Castro brothers in Cuba did no better. Since the 1990s, North Korea has lost upwards of 40 percent of its forests for energy production because the Socialist government could not provide enough fossil fuels to produce electricity. The air quality in the capital of Pyongyang is toxic because they are still burning coal like Dickensian London. Meanwhile, the major harbors and rivers in Castro's Cuba are among the most contaminated in the Western Hemisphere.

Leftists ignore how government-centric environmental policies have failed, and they often accuse capitalism of raping the environment. But again, the facts dispute leftist claims and support Conservative solutions.

The data confirm the freer an economy, the cleaner its environment.[33] Research has found, "Economically freer countries throughout the world continue to outperform their repressed counterparts on environmental protection."[34]

Leftists miss the point when they focus on our environmental laws as not being enough. Rather, it's our property rights and civic responsibility we should be focusing on. Property owners' have strong personal incentives to *take care of and be responsible for their property*. There is no market or profit incentive to pollute the air or water, especially not in the United States—it poisons one's neighbors, invites lawsuits, and can cost a business owner customers or even his entire livelihood.

Protecting private property is a primary motivator to protect the environment. Environmental costs to businesses are like any other costs, and so competitive businesses are constantly reducing waste and pollution to lower those costs. Even as our population and our economy grow, the United States, per capita, is getting greener all the time.

Conservatives view the environmentally friendly tendencies of free people and free markets as something to celebrate. We championed the fracking boom, which has helped transition more and more of our energy market from coal to cleaner-burning natural gas. And, as the natural gas revolution continues to reshape the energy industry, we are confident there will continue to be new innovations to reduce emissions even more—just as we did when we moved from coal to oil in the last century.

There is no reason that, in the near future, combustion engines for cars and trucks shouldn't transition from gasoline to abundant, domestically produced compressed natural gas. The technology is already available. Natural gas vehicles (NGVs) have significantly less emissions than gas or diesel.

Meanwhile, fully renewable energy technologies like solar and wind are becoming more efficient and competitive and will become a more significant part of America's energy grid in the future. But, for the next several decades, America must use the energy God has given us to create better lives for ourselves and our allies who could benefit from our energy exports.

Despite demonstrable progress in the development and use of cleaner, greener technologies, the Left is impatient for action. They demand massive government intervention into the economy with the impossible goal of producing a carbon-free paradise right now.

But what logical, thinking person really believes ivory tower politicians and bureaucrats will take better care of our environment than citizens or businesses living and working in the environment? Inevitably, government is driven more by powerful special interests than a real desire to serve the public. We see examples of poor government management all around us. Well-intentioned forestry policies in Liberal California have led to overgrowth, which is now leading to massive, uncontrollable forest fires. Government attempts to pick winners in the renewable fuels market has led to the loss of hundreds of millions of dollars in the Solyndra and Tesla debacles.[35] If politicians had a special talent for picking good investments, you can bet they would be on Wall Street, not Capitol Hill.

There are obvious roles for government to protect our environment. Establishing reasonable standards and supporting the sharing of best practices is a reasonable role of government. Prohibiting and prosecuting polluters is essential. But classifying harmless gases such as CO_2 as pollutants to achieve political objectives discredits the whole environmental movement.

Sometime in the future, human ingenuity will likely replace our dependence on fossil fuels or, at least, render those fuels harmless to our environment. This is a goal Conservatives support. But we believe the ingenuity to accomplish our environmental goals will come from the competitive cooperation of thousands of scientists and engineers, operating interdependently with billions of consumers around the world—not a handful of politicians and bureaucrats creating environmental bogeymen to frighten people into giving up more control of our lives.

Foreign Policy

Conservatives believe a strong military and modern defense system will deter wars. A weak America invites aggression all around the world. This was evidenced during the tenure of President Barack Obama when Russia invaded Ukraine, North Korea tested nuclear weapons, Iran developed nuclear weapons, Iran and Russia took control of Syria, and China expanded its territory into the South China Sea.

A Conservative foreign policy insists America should act in the best interest of our country and our allies. American borders must be secure. The protection of American citizens should always be government's top priority. America must play a leadership role in the world to encourage human rights, commerce, and peace. But we should avoid foreign entanglements, nation building, and unwinnable wars.

Congress, too, should play more of a role in asserting their Article I leadership over America's foreign adventuring. "Undeclared wars" – or, conflicts engaged in by the executive without a vote in Congress – are now the norm. This lack of transparency and accountability has led to America being at war in at least seven places around the world, sometimes for decades at a time.[36] The more the people's representatives are involved in these decisions, which result in the life or death of American military members, the better for everyone.

Summary of Conservative Ideas and Policies

The ideas in this section represent only a small sample of the Conservative perspective on public policy. Most of the solutions for America's problems will be found in the states and among the people. Few problems will be solved by more laws or federal government programs. "We the People" are the best source for solutions. The following chapter discusses how citizens can make a difference.

CHAPTER 12

Winning:
How We Keep What Works

It is now the moment when by common consent we pause to become conscious of our national life and to rejoice in it, to recall what our country has done for each of us, and to ask ourselves what we can do for our country in return.[1]

—OLIVER WENDELL HOLMES

As we travel around America speaking to Conservatives, we often hear the same question from those who are concerned about the direction of the country: "What can I do?" Most Americans genuinely want to do their part to create a better future, but many aren't sure what direction to go. Others don't know what they can do as individuals to help. How do Conservatives win? How do we build a movement of citizens who know what to keep and know how to keep the things that matter?

Winning for Conservatives means everyone wins. The whole idea of Conservatism is finding and keeping the things that make life better for everyone. We want a country that raises up citizens who are healthy, educated, capable, God-fearing, moral, independent, self-sufficient, charitable, service-oriented, responsible, community-minded, and patriotic. A country with citizens like this will be a shining city on a hill and a beacon for the entire world.

But this kind of country cannot be built by government bureaucrats. It can only be built by people who understand the nature of mankind and the principles that bring out the best in all of us. Most of this is accomplished outside of government by individuals and the institutions of civil society. We looked to Russell Kirk, along with the thinkers he spotlights in *The Conservative Mind*, to provide the principles and philosophical framework to build a successful society. These are the ideas—even as our times and society constantly change—we are asking Americans to keep.

Kirk begins his framework of Conservative thought with "a belief in a transcendent order, or body of natural law, which rules society as well as conscience."[2] In a later work, Kirk referred to this idea as "a belief in a fixed moral order." This submission by citizens to an eternal spiritual order—that is, direction by a community of souls from the bottom up, not top-down from the government—is the foundation of Conservatism and the prerequisite for the rule of law, civilized behavior and a free society.

The contemporary Left rejects both the existence and role of a transcendent order by driving religious principles and morality to the margins of public life. But the refuse from their Progressive theories is piling up all around America. The human and fiscal toll of forgetting what has worked in the past is inestimable.

As Kirk writes, "True politics is the art of apprehending and applying the Justice which ought to prevail in a community of souls."[3]

If our belief in a transcendent order is essential to conserve the things that made America great, then *keeping our faith* is essential to *keeping our covenants* and keeping all the other things that make life better for Americans.

This brings us to one of the most important things Conservatives must do to win: bring religious faith back into American life.

Re-engaging Churches to Restore America

A recent Pew Research Center study found while belief in God, religious affiliation, and church attendance has decreased slightly over the past decade, America stands alone among the nations of the world in their adherence to religious faith.

The Pew study goes on,

The share of U.S. adults who say they believe in God, while still remarkably high by comparison with other advanced industrial countries, has declined modestly, from approximately 92% to 89% (in 2015), since Pew Research Center conducted its first Landscape Study in 2007 [...]. And the percentages who say they pray every day, attend religious services regularly and consider religion to be very important in their lives also have ticked down by small but statistically significant margins.

The falloff in traditional religious beliefs and practices coincides with changes in the religious composition of the U.S. public. A growing share of Americans are religiously unaffiliated, including some who self-identify as atheists or agnostics as well as many who describe their religion as "nothing in particular." Altogether, the religiously unaffiliated now account for 23% of the adult population, up from 16% in 2007.[4]

What does this tell us about keeping our faith and how we as Conservatives can support this effort? One key is not repeating the two major mistakes Christian Conservatives made in the past.

Before the federal government began its massive intervention into civic life, local pastors, rabbis, priests, and other religious leaders were often communities' most visible leaders. Churches led many of the charity programs for the poor and sick, and children's parents were the predominate influence in local public schools. Prayer and religious morality were an integral part of America's education system.

But when Washington started to stake its claim to more and more of the space once filled by "We the People"—with Great Society legislation, court rulings, and regulations—government bureaucracy began to crowd out citizen volunteerism. Churches began a slow retreat from the public square—and without much of a fight. Admittedly, it may have been difficult for religious leaders to anticipate all the negative consequences of the secularization of America. At the time, most Americans assumed all these full-time, professional experts would be able to run things better than ordinary citizens had been running them as amateurs and volunteers.

But now we know better. Our society is fracturing around us, and it is well past time for religious leaders to step in from the sidelines and back into the arena for the fight to save America.

But religious leaders must join the fight in a way that succeeds, not repeat the second major mistake by Conservative Christians.

In the 1970s and '80s, religious activists began political movements to use the government to restore a Christian order in America. The so-called religious Right—organizations like Moral Majority and the Christian Coalition—tried to reinstate Christian principles through government edict (at least that was the perception by the opponents of those organizations, as well as many leftist donors and supporters). But, for Conservatives, government-directed morality—especially at the federal level—is the antithesis of what we believe.

The Left responded to Christian political activism by using the power of the federal courts, along with state and federal legislative action, to squash many of the remnants of religious traditions in public life. They prohibited recognition of religious holidays on public property. They succeeded in throwing prayer and moral teachings out of public schools. They legalized abortion on demand, often paid for with taxpayer dollars. They expanded incentivized dependency and disincentivized marriage. They eventually redefined the institution of marriage to include same-sex couples. They have even tried to blur the reality of separate sexes and promoted the use of taxpayer funds to pay for sex change surgeries—even for children.[5]

Conservatives and Christians may be outraged at how the Left has used the government to advance their agenda, but we cannot respond by trying to advance our own agenda using the force of government—unless we define our agenda in the context of freedom. Instead of attempting to advance a religious or moral agenda through government, Conservatives must demand the freedom of all Americans to believe, speak, and live in accordance with their beliefs. And we must insist our government not promote behaviors destructive to individuals and society as a whole. In other words, Conservatives should support government policies allowing differences to flourish—even differences we don't like.

But, as we seek to restore the things that make America work, Conservatives should always bear in mind the warning of poet T. S. Eliot—a poet rather than politician, yet one of the thinkers Russell Kirk cites in *The Conservative Mind*. Eliot once wrote, "The last temptation is the greatest treason: to do the right thing for the wrong reason."[6]

Politics isn't about religion and religion isn't about politics. Religious and political issues often run parallel and sometimes intersect, but they are not the same thing. Old Screwtape's temptation of making a god out of politics is as dangerous to Conservatives as it is to Progressives. God doesn't belong to a party and His kingdom doesn't have election campaigns. Politics is something citizens in a republic are obliged to do, as James Madison said, specifically because "men are not angels." We are not supposed to put our trust in princes, let alone politicians.

Of course, there is nothing wrong with one's religion informing one's political beliefs—how could it be otherwise? But when we start to confuse—or worse, conflate—the goals of politics and religion, we can corrupt the former and betray the latter.

As C. S. Lewis said, "Aim for Heaven, and you will get earth 'thrown in;' aim for earth and you will get neither."[7] And so, aim for Heaven every day—not just in private worship, but in public acts of friendship, fellowship, neighborliness, citizenship, and even commerce. Your public and even your political life should very much be a part of your religious life, but not the other way around. A Conservative never forgets politics was made for this world, but we were not.

Conservatives Must Fight for the Freedom to be Different

Kirk's second principle of Conservative thought is the "Affection for the proliferating variety and mystery of human existence, as opposed to the narrowing uniformity, egalitarianism, and utilitarian aims of the most radical systems."[8] This can be a hard concept for committed partisans on both Left and the Right to embrace. But Conservatives must insist on the freedom of others to believe and live differently. The Left, by its very nature, will fight us every step of the way and will try to use government to win. It is not freedom they want, but the power to force people to believe and live as they prescribe.

If you really want to know "what you can do," the first thing you need to know is you will have to stand firm for what you believe, push back against those who try to intimidate you, speak up for what you believe is right and wrong, and demand the right to associate with those who share your beliefs. In short, you need to be willing to fight. The Left will not willingly give you the freedom to be different, so, if you want to live free, you will have to fight. If you're not willing to fight, you will lose. And so will America.

The Fight Is in the States

We will not review again all of Kirk's principles of Conservatism or many of the issues and policies we've covered in previous chapters. It is important, however, for Conservatives to understand *where* to fight the battle to save America. We must continue to fight the Left at the federal level, but the real opportunities for change are at the state level. This is how we keep our republic.

Governors and state legislatures are closer to the people and more likely than Congress to listen to voter demands. Our Constitution intended for states to take the lead on most issues, and it is essential for states to reassert their role as the leaders of our republic. There are many issues where states can take the lead despite federal interference: healthcare; transportation; infrastructure; environment; tax and pension reform; protection of unborn life; and many others. But perhaps the most decisive and impactful issue for states is education choice.

States implementing Education Savings Accounts (a concept we described earlier) will open the doors of freedom for America. This is the only way we can expand education opportunities for children to learn about the things that make America work and the things we must keep to make life better for everyone. With ESAs, public schools will improve, and faith organizations can get back involved with education. Children can learn about the "transcendent order" and the importance of an "affection for the proliferating variety and mystery of human existence." They can learn about American history, the miracle of capitalism, the rule of law, and the uniqueness of our Constitution. Education choice is the only way we can raise up a generation of Americans who know what we must keep to be successful.

States must push back against the federal government in many other issue areas. Without the collective pressure from states, politicians and bureaucrats in Washington will continue to expand their power and take power away from the states and the people. Unless states reassert their constitutional role, we will lose our republican form of government and our freedom.

In addition to states pushing their own reforms in areas such as education choice, another way for states to reign in our out-of-control federal government is to use Article V of the Constitution to restore the original limits on federal power. Article V allows two-thirds of the states (thirty-four) to call a convention to propose amendments to limit the jurisdiction of the federal government, require a balanced budget, and other amendments such as term limits on federal officials. Amendments agreed to by this convention of states would then be subject to the traditional ratification process requiring the approval of three-fourths (thirty-eight) of the states. This is the process being promoted by the Convention of States (conventionofstates.com). At this writing, fifteen states have already agreed to a convention to propose amendments to limit federal power. We encourage Conservatives to get involved with this effort in their states.

If we can win back our schools and our Constitution, we can win back our future.

Electing the Right People

Conservatives have become frustrated after working to elect many self-professed Conservatives to public office only to have them join the swamp in Washington or in their state capitals. People often ask, "What happens to good people after they are elected?" It's a good question and the answer is twofold. First, we must do a better job of vetting candidates to make sure they are real Conservatives with the courage to fight. And second, we must do a better job of supporting them once they are elected.

We cannot count on the Republican Party to recruit and elect true Conservatives. Their priority is to win elections, and many of their consultants have convinced party leaders Conservatives cannot win in many parts of the country. We have proved them wrong repeatedly, but with much of the campaign money for the Republican Party at the state and federal level coming from big corporations and Wall Street, Conservatives will always have to fight to keep the Republicans from following the Democrats to the Left (we should note that corporate America and Wall Street give as much campaign money to Democrats as Republicans, depending on which party is in control).[9]

We cannot give advice about the best way to select candidates in every state, but we do recommend a few trustworthy organizations that help elect strong Conservatives to Congress. First, the House Freedom Fund is the political arm of the House Freedom Caucus (HFC), a group of Conservatives in the U.S. House that agree to stand together on key issues and votes. HFC members are often attacked by the Washington establishment and their media puppets but, for Conservative Americans, they are the members of the House most committed to work together to advance Conservative policies.

The House Freedom Fund (housefreedomfund.com) interviews, endorses, and provides campaign funds for real Conservatives. The Senate Conservatives Fund (senateconservatives.com) does the same thing for Senate candidates. Both organizations have a proven record of supporting the strongest Conservatives in the House and Senate. There are a few other credible political groups at the national level such as the Club for Growth that is focused on free market policies. We highly recommend Conservatives support these organizations and the candidates they endorse.

Support Conservatives in Congress

Over many years trying to advance the Conservative cause in Washington, we have seen a lot of good people beaten down by the swamp. Some call it "drinking the Kool-Aid," but the truth is; there has been no support system in Washington for Conservatives—at least, not until recently. Your authors, DeMint and Bovard, were part of a team of veteran Conservative fighters who founded the Conservative Partnership Institute (conservativepartnership.org).

The Conservative Partnership Institute is a service organization for members of Congress and their staff. We educate, train and place staff in Congressional offices. We convene and facilitate consensus among members of Congress. We help unify Conservative groups to "have the backs" of members of Congress who are fighting the good fight in the arena. And our Conservative Partnership Center offers a place for leaders of the Conservative movement to meet, share ideas, and unify around common causes. Our goal is to keep Conservatives in Congress strong and help them be more effective.

Stay Informed

One of the greatest threats to our freedom and our republic is the decline of objective and honest media sources. The "mainstream media" is no longer mainstream because it advocates leftist ideology and disdains traditional American values. Democracies depend on informed voters but, in America, it is increasingly difficult for voters to find the truth about candidates, political parties and issues.

Media companies that depend on advertising revenue are subject to coercion by leftist corporate interests. Most broadcast and cable networks have yielded to pressure from advertisers and eliminated Conservative content. Fox News may be the one exception, but increasingly Conservative champions on Fox News like Tucker Carlson and Sean Hannity are under pressure to abandon "fair and balanced" reporting. Conservatives need to stand with these courageous media hosts.

Conservative radio talk shows around the country continue to be the mainstay of relevant political commentary even though they depend on advertising revenue. They will continue to be pressured to "moderate" their views and content, so Conservatives need to thank the advertisers that continue to support local, regional, and national radio talk show hosts.

Conservatives are increasingly finding more objective and honest news from subscription-based media organizations such as Blaze Media (the merger of The Blaze and CRTV). Media receiving the majority of their revenue from Conservative subscribers are more accountable to the people who watch and listen to their shows and less likely to cave to pressure from advertisers. Podcasts and blogs from proven Conservative hosts are also good sources of honest information. In addition to The Blaze and CRTV, we work with folks at Fox News, *The Federalist*, Breitbart, the *Washington Examiner*, *The Washington Times*, American Greatness, CNS News, the *Daily Caller*, One America News, *The American Conservative*, *National Review*, and EWTN.

Because of dramatic changes in media technology, traditional media sources are likely to go the way of dinosaurs. This is good news if

Conservative investors and entrepreneurs use this opportunity to gain a larger share of the media market. In the future, Conservative audiences will need to be even more vigilant and resourceful to make sure they are getting credible information.

Stay Involved

There are a host of Conservative organizations working to keep you informed of issues you care about. Here is a partial list of some groups we work with regularly.

- American Association of Christian Schools
- American Civil Rights Union
- American Conservative Union
- Americans for Prosperity
- American Legislative Exchange Council
- Alliance Defending Freedom
- American Ideas Institute
- Americans for Tax Reform
- American Principles Project
- Americans United for Life
- Center for Immigration Studies
- Center for Security Policy
- Citizens United
- Christians United for Israel
- Club for Growth
- Competitive Enterprise Institute
- Concerned Women for America
- Concerned Veterans for America
- Conservative HQ
- Convention of States
- Defense Priorities
- Eagle Forum

- Family Research Council
- The Federalist Society
- First Liberty
- Foundation for Individual Rights in Education
- FreedomWorks
- ForAmerica
- Foundation for Government Accountability
- Gun Owners of America
- The Heartland Institute
- The Heritage Foundation
- Home School Legal Defense Association
- Independent Women's Forum
- Intercollegiate Studies Institute
- Judicial Watch
- Leadership Institute
- March for Life
- Media Research Center
- National Association of Gun Rights
- National Right to Work
- National Taxpayers Union
- Numbers USA
- Open the Books
- State Policy Network
- Students for Liberty
- Susan B. Anthony List
- The Tax Foundation
- Taxpayers for Common Sense
- Tea Party Patriots
- Texas Public Policy Foundation
- True the Vote
- Young Americans for Liberty
- Young America's Foundation

Conservatives Must Lead by Example

If there is a trademark of the professional Left, it is hypocrisy. They will take a person's property to save an endangered rodent but demand human babies be lawfully killed up until the moment of delivery—and even after. They will decry the "carbon footprint" of those living in mobile homes while casting their judgements from twenty thousand square-foot mansions in Beverly Hills. They will decry unequal education for the poor while stealing their places in universities with large bribes to admission officials. They will demand special rights for those with politically correct views while silencing the speech of those with traditional beliefs. And they will demand government control of our lives until someone controls the government who they don't control. Then it's time to investigate.

Conservatives must set a better example. We should make it our goal to know what ideas have created the most positive outcomes for the most people throughout American history. We need to know our mistakes, so we don't repeat them. And we need to know how to apply the best ideas from the past to create a better future for everyone—whether they agree with us or not.

Americans face a lot of complex challenges and we need to lower the temperature and raise the level of our civic and political debates. Sometimes the solutions involve complex government policies, but more often, the solutions should be kept in the hands of the people. Senator Mike Lee, while poking fun at the absurdities included in the Democrats Green New Deal in early 2019, reminded his colleagues in a speech in the Senate chambers that regular people are the real heroes in the American story:

> The courage needed to solve climate change is nothing compared with the courage needed to start a family. The true heroes of this story aren't politicians or social media activists. They are moms and dads and the little boys and girls that they are, at this moment, putting down for naps, helping with their homework, building tree houses with, and teaching how to tie their shoes. The planet does not need us to "think globally and act locally" so much as it needs us to think *family* and act personally. The solution to climate change is not this unserious resolution, but the serious business of human flourishing—the solution to so many of our problems at all times and in all places: fall in love, get married, and have some kids.[10]

The Left may bristle at the thought of more children in the world, but the solutions to our problems will always come from a new generation of citizens who build on the successes of the past to create a better future. This is the real meaning of "Conservative"—the continuous pursuit of what to keep and the willingness to work—even fight—to keep those things that make life worth living.

Acknowledgments

We are grateful for Russell Kirk and all the courageous patriots who laid the foundations for today's Conservative Movement. We stand proudly on their shoulders.

This book could not have been written without the support and encouragement from our colleagues at the Conservative Partnership Institute. We hope this book will become the cornerstone of our work educating, equipping, and unifying the Conservative Movement.

We are extremely appreciative and proud of the writing and editorial support of Michael Connolly, a staff leader in the office of Senator Mike Lee. Michael's name should be on the cover of this book with ours.

And this book could not have been published without the professional support of our friend and associate publisher, Gary Terashita of Fidelis Books, an imprint of Post Hill Press.

—*Jim DeMint*

Conservatism is, first and foremost, a philosophy of gratefulness. And for this project, I have gratefulness in abundance.

First and foremost, this project would not have been possible without the opportunity and encouragement of Senator Jim DeMint, and his wife, Debbie. I'll probably never stop pinching myself that I've written a book with one of the heroes of the Conservative movement. From the bottom of my heart, Senator and Mrs. DeMint, thank you for believing in this country, and for believing in me.

This project would also not be complete without Michael Connolly, whose invaluable assistance, wisdom, encouragement, and friendship quite literally made this process possible. Same goes for our intrepid publisher, Gary Terashita. Thank you for your insights and encouragement.

I also couldn't have done any of this without my friends and coworkers at the Conservative Partnership Institute: Ed Corrigan, Wesley Denton, Cameron Seward, Matt Buckham, Sean McMahon, Drew Mueller, and Kimberly Wallner, Richard McAdams, and Doug Stamps. CPI has been the adventure of a lifetime, and none of it would have been possible without the dedication, hard work, and friendship of each of you. My deepest thanks.

Thank you, also, to Chris Jacobs, for sharing your brilliant health care mind with me, and thank you as well to CPI interns Noelle McMahon and David Grogan for their research help.

Finally, to my own little platoon: Mom, Dad, Amy, Ryan, Landon, Jesse, Sam, Julie, Emma, and Lawrence. (And, of course, my dog Chloe, who spent many a late evening sleeping on my feet while I typed away.) Thank you for being my tribe, and my encouragement in all things. My light shines bright because of you all.

—*Rachel Bovard*

ENDNOTES

INTRODUCTION

1   Kirk, Russell. *The Conservative Mind: From Burke to Eliot*, iii. Washington, DC: Regnery Publishing, Inc., 1985.

2   Ingraham, Christopher. "Not Only Are Americans Becoming Less Happy – We're Experiencing More Pain Too," *The Washington Post*. December 06, 2017. Accessed June 8, 2018. https://www.washingtonpost.com/news/wonk/wp/2017/12/06/not-only-are-americans-becoming-less-happy-were-experiencing-more-pain-too/?noredirect=on&utm_term=.7df6716267e4.

3   Shorter, Edward. "The Increasing Suicide Rate." *Psychology Today*. May 03, 2013. Accessed June 8, 2018. https://www.psychologytoday.com/us/blog/how-everyone-became-depressed/201305/the-increasing-suicide-rate.

4   Brooks, David. "The Sharp Decline in American Patriotism." *The Seattle Times*. September 16, 2016. Accessed June 8, 2018. https://www.seattletimes.com/opinion/the-sharp-decline-in-american-patriotism/.

5   Lang, Nico. "Why Teens Are Leaving Facebook: It's 'meaningless'." *The Washington Post*. February 21, 2015. Accessed June 8, 2018. https://www.washingtonpost.com/news/the-intersect/wp/2015/02/21/why-teens-are-leaving-facebook-its-meaningless/?noredirect=on&utm_term=.49b544c82201.

6   "New Survey Says for Most Americans, Family Is the Main Source They Look to for Meaning and Fulfillment." BCNN1 - Black Christian News Network. November 21, 2018. Accessed June 9, 2018. http://blackchristiannews.com/2018/11/new-survey-says-for-most-americans-family-is-the-main-source-they-look-to-for-meaning-and-fulfillment/.

7   King, Martin Luther. "Letter from a Birmingham Jail." Letter from a Birmingham Jail [King, Jr.], www.africa.upenn.edu/Articles_Gen/Letter_Birmingham.html.

8   Ibid.

9   Neuhaus, Richard John. *American Babylon: Notes of a Christian Exile*, 252. New York: Basic Books, 2010.

OVERVIEW TO CHAPTERS 1–6

1   Kirk, Russell. *The Conservative Mind: From Burke to Eliot*, xx. Washington, DC: Regnery Publishing, Inc., 1985.

2   "Conservatism." Wikipedia. May 08, 2019. Accessed December 30, 2018. https://en.wikipedia.org/wiki/Conservatism.

3 Milikh, Arthur. "Civility and Rebarbarization." National Affairs. 2018. Accessed June 21, 2018. https://www.nationalaffairs.com/publications/detail/civility-and-rebarbarization.

4 Kirk, Russell. *The Conservative Mind: From Burke to Eliot*, 9. Washington, DC: Regnery Publishing, Inc., 1985.

5 Ibid., pp 438.

6 "Progressivism." Wikipedia. May 12, 2019. Accessed May 18, 2019. https://en.wikipedia.org/wiki/Progressivism.

7 Kirk, Russell. *The Conservative Mind: From Burke to Eliot*. Washington, DC: Regnery Publishing, Inc., 1985.

8 Krayden, David. "Eric Holder: 'When Did You Think America Was Great?'" *The Daily Caller*. March 29, 2019. Accessed April 3, 2019. https://dailycaller.com/2019/03/29/eric-holder-america-never-great-maga/.

CHAPTER 1

1 Guinness, Os. *The Forgotten Key to American Freedom*, 38. Place of Publication Not Identified: Richard King Brown, 2017.

2 Brooks, David. "How Covenants Make Us." *The New York Times*. April 05, 2016. Accessed August 15, 2018. https://www.nytimes.com/2016/04/05/opinion/how-covenants-make-us.html.

3 Pally, Marcia. *Commonwealth and Covenant: Economics, Politics, and Theologies of Relationality*. Grand Rapids, MI: William B. Eerdmans Publishing Company, 2016.

4 Ibid., pp 155-57.

5 Brinig, Margaret F., and Steven L. Nock. "What Does Covenant Mean for Relationships." *Notre Dame Journal of Law, Ethics & Public Policy* 18, no. 1 (2004).

6 Guinness, Os. The Forgotten Key to American Freedom, 1. *Last Call for Liberty: How America's Genius for Freedom Has Become Its Greatest Threat*. Downers Grove, IL: IVP Books, an Imprint of InterVarsity Press, 2018.

7 Ibid.

8 Alexis de Toqueville, *Democracy in America*, Vol 1, Part 1, Chapter 5, translated by Arthur Goldhammer.

9 Robinson, Marilynne, Rowan Moore Gerety, Alexander Chee, T. Cooper, Garth Greenwell, Eileen Myles, Darryl Pinckney, Brontez Purnell, Michelle Tea, Kira Madden, Adam O'Fallon, and Marilynne Robinson. "[Essay] | Save Our Public Universities, by Marilynne Robinson | Harper's Magazine Part 3." *Harper's Magazine*. February 11, 2016. Accessed August 15, 2018. https://harpers.org/archive/2016/03/save-our-public-universities/3/.

10 Nisbet, Robert A. *The Quest for Community: A Study in the Ethics of Order and Freedom*, 22. Wilmington, DE: ISI Books, 2014.

11 Murray, Charles A. *In Pursuit: Of Happiness and Good Government*. Indianapolis: Liberty Fund, 2013.

12 Madison, James. "The Federalist #10." Constitution Society. Accessed August 20, 2018. http://www.constitution.org/fed/federa10.htm.

13 "I've Been to the Mountain Top," April 3, 1968, http://www.americanrhetoric.com/speeches/mlkivebeentothemountaintop.htm, Accessed May 18, 2019.

ENDNOTES

14 "Where Do We Go From Here?" Address delivered at the 11th Annual SCLC Convention, August 16, 1967. https://kinginstitute.stanford.edu/where-do-we-go-here, Accessed May 18, 2019.

15 "The Meaning of the King Holiday," Coretta Scott King, Remarks at The King Center http://www.brha.com/2018/01/03/the-meaning-of-the-king-holiday/, Accessed May 18, 2019.

16 King, Jr., Martin Luther, "Letter from a Birmingham Jail," April 16, 1963, Accessed on May 21, 2019, https://www.africa.upenn.edu/Articles_Gen/Letter_Birmingham.html.

17 Kazin, Michael. "The Best Dissent Has Never Been Anti-American." *The Washington Post*. February 09, 2003. Accessed June 20, 2018. https://www.washingtonpost.com/archive/opinions/2003/02/09/the-best-dissent-has-never-been-anti-american/310c7952-f8fe-40dd-945f-fbe5af46ad65/?utm_term=.941dba7a4ed7.

18 Kirk, Russell. *The Conservative Mind: From Burke to Eliot*, 274. Washington, DC: Regnery Publishing, Inc., 1985.

19 Abraham Lincoln, Speech on the Dred Scott Decision, June 26, 1857, https://www.virginia.edu/woodson/courses/aas-hius366a/lincoln.html, Accessed May 18, 2019.

20 Interview with Cory Booker, "Real Time With Bill Maher." Season 14, episode 10. Aired March 25, 2016. Sourced in this *NYT* column by David Brooks: https://www.nytimes.com/2016/04/05/opinion/how-covenants-make-us.html, Accessed June 20, 2018.

CHAPTER 2

1 de Tocqueville, Alexis. *Tocqueville, Democracy of America*, transl. Arthur Goldhammer. New York: Library of America, 2004.

2 Madison, James, "Memorial and Remonstrance Against Religious Assessments (1785)," December 24, 1784, Antonin Scalia Law School–George Mason University, https://www.law.gmu.edu/assets/files/academics/founders/Madison%27sMemorial.pdf.

3 Kirk, Russell. *The Conservative Mind: From Burke to Eliot*, 218. Washington, DC: Regnery Publishing, Inc., 1985.

4 "Founders Online: To George Washington from William White, 3 March 1797." National Archives and Records Administration, National Archives and Records Administration, founders.archives.gov/documents/Washington/99-01-02-00389.

5 "Founders Online: From John Adams to Massachusetts Militia, 11 October 1798." National Archives and Records Administration, National Archives and Records Administration, founders.archives.gov/documents/Adams/99-02-02-3102.

6 Stark, Rodney. *The Victory of Reason: How Christianity Led to Freedom, Capitalism, and Western Success*, 18. Random House Trade Paperbacks, 2006.

7 Eidenmuller, Michael E. American Rhetoric: "Ronald Reagan: Remarks at a Dallas Ecumenical Prayer Breakfast," www.americanrhetoric.com/speeches/ronaldreaganecumenicalprayer.htm.

8 Zimmerman, Mark. "A July 4 Remembrance of America's Catholic Founding Father." Crux, 5 July 2016, Accessed April 6, 2019. cruxnow.com/church-in-the-usa/2016/07/04/july-4-remembrance-americas-catholic-founding-father/.

9 "Persecution of Catholics." The Pluralism Project. pluralism.org/document/persecution-of-catholics/.

10 Will, George F. *The Morning after: American Successes and Excesses*, 223-24. 1981-1986. Free Press, 1986.

11 Murray, John Courtney. "Religious Freedom." Georgetown University Library, Accessed April 6, 2019. www.library.georgetown.edu/woodstock/murray/1965ib.

12 "Nomination Of Russell T. Vought, Of Virginia, To Be Deputy Director Of The Office Of Management And Budget." U.S. Government Publishing Office, 2017. www.congress.gov/115/chrg/shrg26919/CHRG-115shrg26919.pdf.

13 Ibid.

14 Ibid.

15 Blake, Aaron. "Did Dianne Feinstein Accuse a Judicial Nominee of Being Too Christian?" *The Washington Post*, 7 Sept. 2017. Accessed April 5, 2019. www.washingtonpost.com/news/the-fix/wp/2017/09/07/did-a-democratic-senator-just-accuse-a-judicial-nominee-of-being-too-christian/?utm_term=.a92281190354.

16 "Founders Online: From John Adams to Hezekiah Niles, 13 February 1818." National Archives and Records Administration, National Archives and Records Administration, founders.archives.gov/documents/Adams/99-02-02-6854.

17 King, Martin Luther. "Letter from a Birmingham Jail." Letter from a Birmingham Jail [King, Jr.], Accessed November 2, 2018. www.africa.upenn.edu/Articles_Gen/Letter_Birmingham.html.

18 Neuhaus, Richard John. *The Naked Public Square: Religion and Democracy in America*, 82. 2nd ed., William B. Eerdmans, 1997.

19 Ibid., pp ix.

20 Neuhaus, Richard John. *The Naked Public Square: Religion and Democracy in America*, 84. 2nd ed., William B. Eerdmans, 1997.

CHAPTER 3

1 FoxNews. "De Blasio, Citing 'socialistic Impulse,' Wants More Government Control of NYC Property." Fox News. Accessed November 24, 2018. http://www.foxnews.com/politics/nycs-de-blasio-would-love-to-see-city-control-rents-and-housing-development.

2 "Study Conducted for CNN Via SSRS." SSRS.http://cdn.cnn.com/cnn/2019/images/04/29/rel6a.-.2020.democrats.pdf. This distance between the white elites promoting identity politics and those who would supposedly benefit from them—African Americans—was on display recently in a Gallup poll, which showed that it was primarily white Americans who supported African American Democratic primary candidates. The African-American community overwhelmingly supported the candidacy of former Vice President Joe Biden, who is white.

3 King, Martin Luther. "I Have a Dream." *Martin Luther King I Have a Dream Speech - American Rhetoric*, www.americanrhetoric.com/speeches/mlkihaveadream.htm.

4 Krantz, Laura. "'Bell Curve' Author Attacked by Protesters at Middlebury College." BostonGlobe.com. March 05, 2017. Accessed January 3, 2019. https://www.bostonglobe.com/metro/2017/03/04/middlebury/hAfpA1Hquh7DIS1doiKbhJ/story.html.

5 Holcombe, Madeline, and Joe Sutton. "Kevin Hart Says He Won't Host Oscars after Furor over Homophobic Tweets." CNN. December 07, 2018. Accessed January 3, 2019 . https://www.cnn.com/2018/12/07/entertainment/kevin-hart-oscars-step-down/index.html.

6 Frum, David. "Every Culture Appropriates." *The Atlantic*. September 04, 2018. Accessed January 3, 2019. https://www.theatlantic.com/ideas/archive/2018/05/cultural-appropriation/559802/.

CHAPTER 4

1 Kirk, Russell. *The Conservative Mind: From Burke to Eliot*, 164. Washington, DC: Regnery Publishing, Inc., 1985.

2 Kirk, Russell. *The Conservative Mind: From Burke to Eliot*, 165. Washington, DC: Regnery Publishing, Inc., 1985.

3 Ibid., pp 164.

4 Ibid., pp 165.

CHAPTER 5

1 "Founders Online: From Thomas Jefferson to Edward Carrington, 27 May 1788." National Archives and Records Administration. Accessed December 30, 2018. https://founders.archives.gov/documents/Jefferson/01-13-02-0120.

2 Klimon, William M. "Mediating Institutions." Acton Institute. Accessed December 30, 2018. https://acton.org/pub/religion-liberty/volume-2-number-3/mediating-institutions.

3 Burke, Edmund. *Reflections on the Revolution in France*, 51, https://socialsciences.mcmaster.ca/econ/ugcm/3ll3/burke/revfrance.pdf, Accessed May 18, 2019.

4 Ibid., pp 68.

5 Kirk, *The Conservative Mind: From Burke to Eliot*, p. 9.

6 Ibid., p. 8.

7 Kirk, Russell. "Ten Conservative Principles." Kirk Center. https://kirkcenter.org/conservatism/ten-conservative-principles/, Accessed May 18, 2019.

8 "Introduction to the Work of Edmund Burke." Edmund Burke. Accessed January 9, 2019. https://thegreatthinkers.org/burke/introduction/.

9 "Jobs: 'Follow Your Heart.'" *HuffPost*. December 05, 2011. Accessed January 9, 2019. https://www.huffpost.com/entry/steve-jobs-stanford-commencement-address_n_997301.

10 Kirk, Russell. *The Conservative Mind: From Burke to Eliot*, 35. Washington, DC: Regnery Publishing, Inc., 1985.

11 Ibid., pp 35.

12 Ibid., pp 29.

13 Dickrell, Stephanie. "More than 1 in 2 Americans Will Get STD in Lifetime." *St. Cloud Times*. August 22, 2015. Accessed January 9, 2019. https://www.sctimes.com/story/life/wellness/2015/08/21/americans--get-std-lifetime/32123427/.

14 Burke, *Reflections on the Revolution in France*,18. Accessed May 19, 2019. https://socialsciences.mcmaster.ca/econ/ugcm/3ll3/burke/revfrance.pdf.

15 Kirk, Russell, *Prospects for Conservatives: A Compass for Rediscovering Permanent Things,* Chicago, Henry Regnery Company, 1956, 263.

16 Santayana, George. The Life of Reason. United States: Echo Library, 2006. (Italic added for emphasis.)

17 Kirk, Russell. *The Conservative Mind: From Burke to Eliot*, 45. Washington, DC: Regnery Publishing, Inc., 1985.

18 Scotchie, Joseph, *The PaleoConservatives: New Voices of the Old Right*, Transaction Publishers, 1st Edtn, 1999. 73.

19 Ibid.

20 Ibid.

21 Ibid.

22 Kirk, Russell. *The Conservative Mind: From Burke to Eliot*, 29. Washington, DC: Regnery Publishing, Inc., 1985.

23 Burke, *Reflections*, 65. Accessed May 19, 2019. https://socialsciences.mcmaster.ca/econ/ugcm/3ll3/burke/revfrance.pdf.

24 Birzer, Bradley. *Russell Kirk: American Conservative*. University Press of Kentucky, 2015, pp, 101.

CHAPTER 6

1 Smith, Adam. *The Wealth of Nations*, 443. London: Penguin Books, 1986.

2 Ibid., pp 17.

3 Bacevich, Andrew J. *The Limits of Power: The End of American Exceptionalism*, 24-25. New York: Metropolitan Books/Henry Holt and Company, 2009.

4 "Capitalism." Merriam-Webster. Accessed January 11, 2019. http://www.merriam-webster.com/dictionary/capitalism.

5 Hayek, Friedrich A. Von. *The Road to Serfdom*, 80. Chicago: University of Chicago Press, 2014.

6 Bastiat, Frederic. *The Law*, 9. New York: The Foundation for Economic Education, 1996.

7 Feuerherd, Ben, "Ocasio-Cortez: System that Allows Billionaires is 'Immoral,'" *New York Post*, January 22, 2019, Accessed May 19, 2019, https://nypost.com/2019/01/22/ocasio-cortez-system-that-allows-billionaires-is-immoral/.

8 Marcotte, Amanda, "As Usual, Alexandria Ocasio-Cortez is Right: There Should be No Billionaires," Salon.com, January 22, 2019. Accessed May 19, 2019, https://www.salon.com/2019/01/22/as-usual-alexandria-ocasio-cortez-is-right-there-should-be-no-billionaires/.

9 Bastiat, Frederic. *The Law*, 9. New York: The Foundation for Economic Education, 1996

OVERVIEW OF CHAPTERS 7–12

1 Kirk, Russell. *The Politics of Prudence*. Wilmington, DE: ISI Books, 2004.

2 Arciga, Julia. "Kamala Harris: 'I Am a Gun Owner… for Personal Safety.'" *The Daily Beast*. April 12, 2019. Accessed April 14, 2019. https://www.thedailybeast.com/kamala-harris-i-am-a-gun-owner-for-personal-safety.

3 Kirk, Russell. *Ten Conservative Principles*. Washington, D.C.: Heritage Foundation, 1987.

4 Haidt, Jonathan. *The Righteous Mind: Why Good People Are Divided by Politics and Religion*. New York: Vintage Books, 2013.

5 Burke, "Reflections on the Revolution in France," 18. Accessed May 19 2019. https://socialsciences.mcmaster.ca/econ/ugcm/3ll3/burke/revfrance.pdf.

6 "Marist Poll Finds 3 in 4 Americans Support Substantial Abortion Restrictions." Knights of Columbus. Accessed April 9, 2019. http://www.kofc.org/en/news/polls/abortion-restrictions-supported.html.

7 Sowell, Thomas, *A Conflict of Visions: Ideological Origins of Political Struggles*, June 5, 2007, Basic Books.

CHAPTER 7

1 Kirk, Russell. *The Conservative Mind: From Burke to Eliot*, 162. Washington, DC: Regnery Publishing, Inc., 1985.

2   "Top 20 Political Songs: Imagine | John Lennon | 1971." *America's Current Affairs & Politics Magazine*. Accessed May 13, 2019. https://www.newstatesman.com/music/2010/03/lennon-imagine-political.

3   Diaz, Daniella. "These Democrats Want to Abolish ICE." CNN. July 03, 2018. Accessed April 2, 2019. https://www.cnn.com/2018/07/02/politics/abolish-ice-democrats-list/index.html.

4   Samuels, Brett. "O'Rourke Says He'd 'absolutely' Take down Border Wall near El Paso If He Could." The Hill. February 15, 2019. Accessed April 2, 2019. https://thehill.com/latino/430134-orourke-says-hed-absolutely-take-down-border-wall-near-el-paso-if-he-could.

5   Dinan, Stephen. "House Votes in Favor of Illegal Immigrant Voting." *The Washington Times*. March 08, 2019. Accessed April 2, 2019. https://www.washingtontimes.com/news/2019/mar/8/house-votes-favor-illegal-immigrant-voting/.

6   Fagan, Patrick. "How U.N. Conventions On Women's and Children's Rights Undermine Family, Religion, and Sovereignty." The Heritage Foundation. Accessed April 2, 2019. https://www.heritage.org/civil-rights/report/how-un-conventions-womens-and-childrens-rights-underminefamily-religion-and.

7   "Obama's Quiet Mission to Export Gay Rights Overseas." NBCNews.com. Accessed April 2, 2019. https://www.nbcnews.com/feature/nbc-out/obama-legacy-quiet-mission-export-gay-rights-overseas-n673861.

8   Schlesinger, Stephen. "Obama: Every Country Is Exceptional." *HuffPost*. November 23, 2013. Accessed April 20, 2019. https://www.huffpost.com/entry/obama-every-country-is-ex_b_3975284.

9   Bovard, Rachel. "Religious Bigotry from Senate Democrats Shouldn't Hold up the Confirmation Process." The Hill. October 12, 2017. Accessed May 13, 2019. https://thehill.com/opinion/campaign/355078-religious-bigotry-from-senate-democrats-shouldnt-hold-up-the-confirmation.

10 Brufke, Juliegrace. "Dem Lawmaker: Why Can't Resolution 'singularly Condemn' Anti-Semitism?" The Hill. March 07, 2019. Accessed May 13, 2019. https://thehill.com/homenews/house/433049-dem-lawmaker-why-cant-resolution-singularly-condemn-anti-semitism.

11 McArdle, John. "WETLANDS: EPA's 22-year Battle with Cranberry Farmer Ends, but Questions and Anger Linger." March 19, 2012. Accessed April 2, 2019. https://www.eenews.net/stories/1059961629.

12 McCormack, John. "Obama to Latinos: 'Punish' Your 'Enemies' in the Voting Booth." *The Weekly Standard*. October 25, 2010. Accessed February 20, 2019. https://www.weeklystandard.com/john-mccormack/obama-to-latinos-punish-your-enemies-in-the-voting-booth.

13 Skocpol, Theda. *Protecting Soldiers and Mothers: The Political Origins of Social Policy in the United States*, 131. Cambridge, MA: Belknap Press of Harvard Univ. Press, 1996.

14 Rubinow, Isaac Max. *Social Insurance*, 11. Harvard University, 1916.

15 Skocpol, Theda. Protecting Soldiers and Mothers: The Political Origins of Social Policy in the United States, 174. Cambridge, MA: Belknap Press of Harvard Univ. Press, 1996.

16 Bacevich, Andrew J. *The Limits of Power: The End of American Exceptionalism*, 67. New York: Metropolitan Books, Henry Holt and Company, 2009.

17 Masterpiece Cakeshop, Ltd., Et Al. *V.* Colorado Civil Rights Commission. 543 U.S. (2018).

CHAPTER 8

1 Schrager, Adam and Rob Witwer, *The Blueprint: How the Democrats Won Colorado and Why Republicans Everywhere Should Care*, Fulcrum Publishing, 2010, pp. 7.

2 "21,995,000 to 12,329,000: Government Employees Outnumber Manufacturing Employees 1.8 to 1." CNS News. September 08, 2015. Accessed April 9, 2019. https://www.cnsnews.com/news/article/terence-p-jeffrey/21955000-12329000-government-employees-outnumber-manufacturing.

3 Congressional Research Service, U.S. Postal Service Workforce Size and Employment Categories, FY1995-FY2014. https://fas.org/sgp/crs/misc/RS22864.pdf Accessed May 19, 2019.

4 "Union Members Summary." U.S. Bureau of Labor Statistics. January 18, 2019. Accessed April 9, 2019. https://www.bls.gov/news.release/union2.nr0.htm.

5 Sherk, James. "Majority of Union Members Now Work for the Government." The Heritage Foundation. January 22, 2010. Accessed April 9, 2019. https://www.heritage.org/jobs-and-labor/report/majority-union-members-now-work-the-government.

6 "CDC - Health Care Workers - NIOSH Workplace Safety and Health Topic." Centers for Disease Control and Prevention. Accessed May 2019. https://www.cdc.gov/niosh/topics/healthcare/default.html.

7 Greenleaf, Robert K. *Servant Leadership: A Journey into the Nature of Legitimate Power and Greatness.* New Jersey: Paulist Press, 1977.

8 Chaitin, Daniel. "AOC to Critics of Green New Deal: 'I'm the Boss' until You Try." *Washington Examiner.* February 25, 2019. Accessed April 5, 2019. https://www.washingtonexaminer.com/news/aoc-to-critics-of-green-new-deal-im-the-boss-until-you-try.

9 Reilly, Katie. "Hillary Clinton Transcript: 'Basket of Deplorables' Comment." *Time.* September 10, 2016. Accessed April 5, 2019. http://time.com/4486502/hillary-clinton-basket-of-deplorables-transcript/.

10 Pilkington, Ed. "Obama Angers Midwest Voters with Guns and Religion Remark." *The Guardian.* April 14, 2008. Accessed April 5, 2019. https://www.theguardian.com/world/2008/apr/14/barackobama.uselections2008.

11 Nolan, Hamilton. "Dumb Hicks Are America's Greatest Threat." *Gawker.* November 19, 2015. Accessed April 5, 2019. https://gawker.com/dumb-hicks-are-americas-greatest-threat-1743373893.

12 Tylecote, Radomir. "The EU Is Quietly Seizing Control of Its Members' Finances." *The Telegraph.* February 28, 2019. Accessed March 3, 2019. https://www.telegraph.co.uk/politics/2019/02/28/eu-quietly-seizing-control-members-finances/.

13 Camarota, Steven A. "The Impact of Non-Citizens on Congressional Apportionment." CIS.org. December 6, 2005. Accessed March 3, 2019. https://cis.org/Impact-NonCitizens-Congressional-Apportionment.

14 Scott Walter, *Presentation on the Left*, Capital Research Center, 7 August 2013.

15 Ibid, Walter

16 Ibid, Walter

17 Ibid, Walter

18 Ibid, Walter

19 Ibid, Walter

20 John Loeffler, from Steel on Steel News Radio, https://www.steelonsteel.com/saul-alinsky-rules-for-radicals/, Accessed May 20, 2019.

21 McLeod, Judi. "Saul Alinsky's Son: 'Obama Learned His Lesson Well.'" Canada Free Press. September 2, 2008. Accessed February 16, 2019. https://canadafreepress.com/article/saul-alinskys-son-obama-learned-his-lesson-well.

22 Shah, Anup. "Media Conglomerates, Mergers, Concentration of Ownership." January 2, 2009. Accessed February 16, 2019. http://www.globalissues.org/print/article/159.

CHAPTER 9

1 Haltiwanger, John. "A Large Percentage of Millennials Are Embracing Socialism and a Majority Disapprove of Trump, a New Poll Indicates." *Business Insider*. October 04, 2018. Accessed March 24, 2019. https://www.businessinsider.com/millennials-are-embracing-socialism-poll-indicates-2018-10.

2 De Tocqueville, Alexis. *Democracy in America*. London, England: Penguin Books, 2003.

3 Lewis, C.S. "Screwtape Proposes a Toast." *The Saturday Evening Post*. 1959. Accessed March 20, 2019. http://www.saturdayeveningpost.com/wp-content/uploads/satevepost/screwtape-proposes-a-toast-SEP.pdf.

4 Rockwell, Lew. "Rockwell: The Menace of Egalitarianism." Mises Institute. October 08, 2015. Accessed March 20, 2019. https://mises.org/wire/rockwell-menace-egalitarianism.

5 Rousseau, Jean Jacques. "A Discourse on Political Economy: Understanding the Economic Basis of Liberty." Oxford: Oxford University Press, 2008.

6 Ibid.

7 Williamson, Kevin. *The Politically Incorrect Guide to Socialism*. Washington, D.C.: Regnery Pub., 2011.

8 Zanotti, Emily. "Bernie Sanders Says Spray Deodorant Is Starving America's Kids." *The American Spectator*. May 27, 2015. Accessed March 20, 2019. https://spectator.org/bernie-sanders-says-spray-deodorant-is-starving-americas-kids/.

9 Orwell, George. *Animal Farm*, London: Secker and Warburg, 1945.

10 Bresnahan, John. "Boehner's Fight for Hill Subsidies." POLITICO. October 02, 2013. Accessed March 26, 2019. https://www.politico.com/story/2013/10/john-boehner-hill-obamacare-subsidies-097634.

11 Bordelon, Brendan. "How Five Republicans Let Congress Keep Its Fraudulent Obamacare Subsidies." *National Review*. May 09, 2015. Accessed March 26, 2019. https://www.nationalreview.com/2015/05/how-five-republicans-let-congress-keep-its-fraudulent-obamacare-subsidies-brendan/.

12 Jacobs, Christopher. "DC Council Bills Taxpayers Half A Million To Avoid Enrolling In Obamacare." *The Federalist*. December 7, 2018. Accessed March 26, 2019. http://thefederalist.com/2018/12/07/dc-council-bills-taxpayers-half-million-avoid-enrolling-obamacare/.

13 Viebeck, Elise. "House, Senate Agree on Bill to Establish New Sexual Harassment Policy for Congress." *The Washington Post*. December 12, 2018. Accessed March 26, 2019. https://www.washingtonpost.com/powerpost/house-senate-agree-on-bill-to-establish-new-sexual-harassment-policy-for-congress/2018/12/12/da4e8db0-fe46-11e8-ad40-cdfd0e0dd65a_story.html?utm_term=.8ec8294d14d2.

14 Mayersohn, Norman. "The Internal Combustion Engine Is Not Dead Yet." *The New York Times*. August 17, 2017. Accessed March 26, 2019. https://www.nytimes.com/2017/08/17/automobiles/wheels/internal-combustion-engine.html.

15 Kurtzleben, Danielle. "Green New Deal FAQ." NPR. Accessed March 26, 2019. https://apps.npr.org/documents/document.html?id=5729035-Green-New-Deal-FAQ.

16 Vincent, Isabel, and Melissa Klein. "Gas-guzzling Car Rides Expose AOC's Hypocrisy amid Green New Deal Pledge." *New York Post.* March 04, 2019. Accessed March 26, 2019. https://nypost.com/2019/03/02/gas-guzzling-car-rides-expose-aocs-hypocrisy-amid-green-new-deal-pledge/.

17 Neville, Sarah. "England's Poor Have Worse Access to GP Services than the Rich." *Financial Times.* December 30, 2018. Accessed March 26, 2019. https://www.ft.com/content/628b25ca-06d1-11e9-9fe8-acdb36967cfc.

18 Medina, Jennifer, Katie Benner, and Kate Taylor. "Actresses, Business Leaders and Other Wealthy Parents Charged in U.S. College Entry Fraud." *The New York Times.* March 12, 2019. Accessed March 26, 2019. https://www.nytimes.com/2019/03/12/us/college-admissions-cheating-scandal.html.

19 Hartocollis, Anemona. "Asian-Americans Suing Harvard Say Admissions Files Show Discrimination." *The New York Times.* April 04, 2018. Accessed March 26, 2019. https://www.nytimes.com/2018/04/04/us/harvard-asian-admission.html.

20 DeSanctis, Alexandra. "New Survey: Nearly Two-Thirds of Americans Support School Choice." *National Review.* January 18, 2018. Accessed March 26, 2019. https://www.nationalreview.com/corner/school-choice-poll-two-thirds-americans-support-education-reform/.

21 Klein, Alyson. "Trump Calls Education 'Civil Rights Issue of Our Time,' Pushes Choice." Education Week - Politics K-12. July 05, 2017. Accessed April 5, 2019. http://blogs.edweek.org/edweek/campaign-k-12/2017/02/trump_education_choice_child_c.html.

22 Burke, Lindsey. "How Members of the 111th Congress Practice Private School Choice." The Heritage Foundation. April 20, 2009. Accessed April 5, 2019. https://www.heritage.org/education/report/how-members-the-111th-congress-practice-private-school-choice.

23 Iafolla, Robert. "Mass Exodus of Public Union Fee Payers After High Court Ruling." Bloomberg BNA News. April 5, 2019. Accessed April 6, 2019. https://news.bloomberglaw.com/daily-labor-report/mass-exodus-of-public-union-fee-payers-after-high-court-ruling.

24 McWilliams, David. "Quantitative Easing Was the Father of Millennial Socialism." *Financial Times.* March 01, 2019. Accessed March 6, 2019. https://www.ft.com/content/cbed81fc-3b56-11e9-9988-28303f70fcff.

CHAPTER 10

1 Johnson, Lyndon B. "Great Society Speech." Teaching American History. May 22, 1964. Accessed February 12, 2019. https://teachingamericanhistory.org/library/document/great-society-speech/.

2 "Key Findings From PISA 2015 for the United States." OECD. 2016. http://www.oecd.org/pisa/pisa-2015-United-States.pdf.

3 "NAEP - 2015 Mathematics & Reading Assessments." The Nation's Report Card. Accessed April 1, 2019. https://www.nationsreportcard.gov/reading_math_g12_2015/.

4 "NAEP Dashboards - Achievement_gaps." The Nation's Report Card. Accessed April 1, 2019. https://www.nationsreportcard.gov/dashboards/achievement_gaps.aspx.

5 "Digest of Education Statistics, 2017." National Center for Education Statistics (NCES) Home Page, a Part of the U.S. Department of Education. Accessed April 1, 2019.

ENDNOTES

https://nces.ed.gov/programs/digest/d17/tables/dt17_236.15.asp. Calculation based on $13,480 spending per pupil in 2019-20 based on average daily attendance (in constant dollars), and $9,516 spending per pupil in 1989-90 based on average daily attendance (in constant dollars).

6 Burke, Lindsey. "How Escalating Education Spending Is Killing Crucial Reform." The Heritage Foundation. October 15, 2012. Accessed March 30, 2019. https://www.heritage.org/education/report/how-escalating-education-spending-killing-crucial-reform.

7 "Programme for International Student Assessment (PISA) Results from PISA 2012." OECD. http://www.oecd.org/unitedstates/PISA-2012-results-US.pdf.

8 "Key Findings From PISA 2015 for the United States." OECD. 2016. http://www.oecd.org/pisa/pisa-2015-United-States.pdf.

9 Burke, Lindsey. "Head Start Impact Evaluation Report Finally Released." The Heritage Foundation. January 10, 2013. Accessed March 30, 2019. https://www.heritage.org/education/report/head-start-impact-evaluation-report-finally-released.

10 Ibid.

11 Will, George F. "Education Is the Business of the States." The Washington Post. February 06, 2015. Accessed March 30, 2019. https://www.washingtonpost.com/opinions/education-is-the-business-of-the-states/2015/02/06/3ea1b6a0-ad6c-11e4-abe8-e1ef-60ca26de_story.html?utm_term=.e5fb28c77748.

12 BlackAndRight. "Flashback: Obama's Healthcare Cost Promises...." YouTube. October 06, 2013. Accessed April 1, 2019. https://www.youtube.com/watch?v=LW9tPdpu2jY.

13 Sack, Kevin. "Health Plan From Obama Spurs Debate." The New York Times. July 23, 2008. Accessed April 1, 2019. https://www.nytimes.com/2008/07/23/us/23health.html.

14 "Employer Health Benefits – Annual Survey." The Kaiser Family Foundation. 2018. Accessed April 1, 2019. http://files.kff.org/attachment/Report-Employer-Health-Benefits-Annual-Survey-2018.

15 "Individual Market Premium Changes: 2013 – 2017." ASPE. May 24, 2017. Accessed March 30, 2019. https://aspe.hhs.gov/pdf-report/individual-market-premium-changes-2013-2017.

16 Badger, Doug and Edmund F. Haislmaier. "How Obamacare Raised Premiums." Backgrounder. March 5, 2018. Accessed March 30, 2019. https://www.heritage.org/sites/default/files/2018-03/BG3291.pdf.

17 "Policy Notifications and Current Status, by State." Yahoo! Finance. December 26, 2013. Accessed April 1, 2019. https://finance.yahoo.com/news/policy-notifications-current-status-state-204701399.html.

18 Washington Free Beacon. "36 Times Obama Said You Could Keep Your Health Care Plan | SuperCuts #18." YouTube. November 05, 2013. Accessed April 1, 2019. https://www.youtube.com/watch?v=qpa-5JdCnmo.

19 Holan, Angie Drobnic. "Lie of the Year: 'If You like Your Health Care Plan, You Can Keep It.'" PolitiFact. December 12, 2013. Accessed April 1, 2019. https://www.politifact.com/truth-o-meter/article/2013/dec/12/lie-year-if-you-like-your-health-care-plan-keep-it/.

20 "Click Here to Support Help Coach White Crush Cancer Organized by Jim White." Gofundme.com. Accessed April 1, 2019. https://www.gofundme.com/coachwhite.

21 York, Byron. "Obama Stump Speech: Car Still in Ditch, No Slurpees." Washington Examiner. March 16, 2012. Accessed April 1, 2019. https://www.washingtonexaminer.com/obama-stump-speech-car-still-in-ditch-no-slurpees.

22 "What Is in a Name? Global Warming vs. Climate Change." NASA. Accessed March 5, 2019. https://pmm.nasa.gov/education/articles/whats-name-global-warming-vs-climate-change.

23 Perry, Mark J. "18 Spectacularly Wrong Predictions Made around the Time of First Earth Day in 1970, Expect More This Year." AEI. April 21, 2018. Accessed March 5, 2019. http://www.aei.org/publication/18-spectacularly-wrong-predictions-made-around-the-time-of-first-earth-day-in-1970-expect-more-this-year-2/.

24 Perry, Mark J. "18 Spectacularly Wrong Predictions Made around the Time of First Earth Day in 1970, Expect More This Year." AEI. April 21, 2018. Accessed March 5, 2019. http://www.aei.org/publication/18-spectacularly-wrong-predictions-made-around-the-time-of-first-earth-day-in-1970-expect-more-this-year-2/.

25 Shabecoff, Philip. "Global Warming Has Begun, Expert Tells Senate." *The New York Times*. June 24, 1988. Accessed March 5, 2019. https://www.nytimes.com/1988/06/24/us/global-warming-has-begun-expert-tells-senate.html?pagewanted=all.

26 Bastasch, Michael. "Let's Look Back On 25 Years Of Doomsday Global Warming Predictions." May 06, 2015. Accessed March 5 2019. https://dailycaller.com/2015/05/04/25-years-of-predicting-the-global-warming-tipping-point/.

27 Rettner, Rachael. "Al Gore's Movie 'An Inconvenient Truth' Says Sea Levels Could Rise up to 20 Feet. Is This True?" Scienceline. December 1, 2008. Accessed March 5, 2019. https://scienceline.org/2008/12/ask-rettner-sea-level-rise-al-gore-an-inconvenient-truth/.

28 Vidal, John. "Arctic Expert Predicts Final Collapse of Sea Ice within Four Years." *The Guardian*. September 17, 2012. Accessed March 5, 2019. https://www.theguardian.com/environment/2012/sep/17/arctic-collapse-sea-ice.

29 "PM Warns of Climate 'catastrophe'." BBC News. October 19, 2009. Accessed March 5, 2019. http://news.bbc.co.uk/2/hi/uk_news/8313672.stm.

30 Loris, Nicolas. "Setting the Record Straight on Climate Change and Hurricanes." The Heritage Foundation. September 19, 2018. Accessed March 9, 2019. https://www.heritage.org/environment/commentary/setting-the-record-straight-climate-change-and-hurricanes.

31 "Air Quality - National Summary." EPA. July 25, 2018. Accessed March 9, 2019. https://www.epa.gov/air-trends/air-quality-national-summary.

32 Newman, Alex. "Scientists Ridicule Latest Round of Federal 'Climate Change' Hysteria." The New American. November 26, 2018. Accessed March 9, 2019. https://www.thenewamerican.com/tech/environment/item/30735-scientists-ridicule-latest-round-of-federal-climate-change-hysteria.

33 Curry, Judith. "Science, Uncertainty and Advocacy." Climate Etc. June 22, 2015. Accessed March 9, 2019. https://judithcurry.com/2015/06/22/science-uncertainty-and-advocacy/.

34 Kurtzleben, Danielle. "Green New Deal FAQ." NPR. Accessed March 26, 2019. https://apps.npr.org/documents/document.html?id=5729035-Green-New-Deal-FAQ.

35 Groves, Steven. "The U.S. Should Withdraw from the United Nations Framework Convention on Climate Change." The Heritage Foundation. June 9, 2016. Accessed March 28, 2019. https://www.heritage.org/environment/report/the-us-should-withdraw-the-united-nations-framework-convention-climate-change#_blank.

36 Loris, Nicolas. "Setting the Record Straight on Climate Change and Hurricanes." The Heritage Foundation. September 19, 2018. Accessed March 28, 2019. https://

www.heritage.org/environment/commentary/setting-the-record-straight-climate-change-and-hurricanes.

37 Kerry, John. "Remarks on COP21 and Action Beyond Paris." U.S. Department of State. December 09, 2015. Accessed March 28, 2019. https://2009-2017.state.gov/secretary/remarks/2015/12/250502.htm.

38 Green, Kenneth P. "The Myth of Green Energy Jobs: The European Experience." February 15, 2011. Accessed March 28, 2019. https://www.aei.org/publication/the-myth-of-green-energy-jobs-the-european-experience/

39 Loris, Nicolas. "Germany Becomes the New Poster Child for Climate Change Hypocrisy." The Heritage Foundation. January 11, 2018. Accessed March 28, 2019. https://www.heritage.org/energy-economics/commentary/germany-becomes-the-new-poster-child-climate-change-hypocrisy.

40 Parker, Clifton B., and Clifton B. Parker. "Stanford Research Finds Carbon Regulation Burden Heaviest on Poor." Stanford University. February 28, 2014. Accessed March 28, 2019. https://news.stanford.edu/news/2014/february/kolstad-carbon-tax-022814.html.

41 Grossu, Arina. "Margaret Sanger, Racist Eugenicist Extraordinaire." FRC. May 5, 2014. Accessed March 31, 2019. https://www.frc.org/op-eds/margaret-sanger-racist-eugenicist-extraordinaire.

42 *Planned Parenthood of Greater Texas Family Planning and Preventative Health Services v. Smith*, No. 17-50282 (5th Cir. 2019)

43 Jennings, Scott. "Ralph Northam Should Be Remembered for Advocating the Slaughtering of Deformed Babies." USA Today. February 05, 2019. Accessed March 30, 2019. https://www.usatoday.com/story/opinion/2019/02/05/ralph-northam-advocating-abortion-infanticide-worse-than-blackface-column/2776498002/.

44 "Abortion Surveillance - United States, 2015 | MMWR." Centers for Disease Control and Prevention. November 23, 2018. Accessed March 30, 2019. https://www.cdc.gov/mmwr/volumes/67/ss/ss6713a1.htm#T7_down.

45 Foster, Diana Greene, and Katrina Kimport. "Who Seeks Abortions at or After 20 Weeks?" Perspectives on Sexual and Reproductive Health. November 04, 2013. Accessed March 31, 2019. https://onlinelibrary.wiley.com/doi/full/10.1363/4521013.

46 "ITOP Report of Infants Born Alive." Agency for Health Care Administration. 2017. Accessed March 31, 2019. http://ahca.myflorida.com/MCHQ/Central_Services/Training_Support/docs/ITOPLiveBirthsByCounty2017.pdf.

47 "Abortions in Arizona – 2017 Abortion Report." Arizona Department of Health Services. September 11, 2018. Accessed March 30, 2019. https://azdhs.gov/documents/preparedness/public-health-statistics/abortions/2017-arizona-abortion-report.pdf.

48 "Induced Abortions in Minnesota – January – December 2017." Minnesota Legislative Reference Library. July 01, 2018. Accessed March 31, 2019. https://www.leg.state.mn.us/docs/2018/mandated/180714.pdf

49 "Roll Call Vote 116th Congress - 1st Session." U.S. Senate: U.S. Senate Roll Call Votes 116th Congress - 1st Session. April 25, 2017. Accessed March 31, 2019. https://www.senate.gov/legislative/LIS/roll_call_lists/roll_call_vote_cfm.cfm?congress=116&session=1&vote=00027.

50 Richardson, Valerie. "Sen. Amy Klobuchar: 'We Have to Move On' from Virginia Gov. Ralph Northam Blackface Scandal." The Washington Times. March 18, 2019.

Accessed March 31, 2019. https://www.washingtontimes.com/news/2019/mar/18/amy-klobuchar-we-have-move-virginia-gov-ralph-nort/.

51 "Between-Hospital Variation in Treatment and Outcomes in Extremely Preterm Infants | NEJM." *New England Journal of Medicine*. May 7, 2015. Accessed March 31, 2019. https://www.nejm.org/doi/full/10.1056/NEJMoa1410689.

52 "Reported Legal Abortions by Race of Woman Who Obtained Abortion by the State of Occurrence." The Henry J. Kaiser Family Association. February 06, 2019. Accessed March 31, 2019. https://www.kff.org/womens-health-policy/state-indicator/abortions-by-race/?currentTimeframe=0&sortModel=%7B%22colId%22:%22Location%22,%22sort%22:%22asc%22%7D.

53 Griffin, Beth. "Eliminating Children with Down Syndrome Diagnosis Called Genocide." Grandin Media. April 27, 2018. Accessed March 31, 2019. https://grandinmedia.ca/eliminated-down-syndrome-kids-called-genocide/.

CHAPTER 11

1 Bauer, Peter. *Economic Analysis and Policy in Underdeveloped* Countries. Durham, NC: Duke University Press, 1957.

2 Kirk, Russell. *The Politics of Prudence*. Wilmington, DE: ISI Books, 2004.

3 Ibid.

4 Kirk, Russell. "Ten Conservative Principles." The Russell Kirk Center. November 05, 2018. Accessed April 5, 2019. https://kirkcenter.org/conservatism/ten-conservative-principles/.

5 Ibid.

6 Hazlitt, Henry. *Economics in One Lesson*. New York: Foundation for Economic Education, 1952.

7 Kirk, Russell. *The Politics of Prudence*. Wilmington, DE: ISI Books, 2004.

8 "About Charter Schools." National Alliance for Public Charter Schools. Accessed April 1, 2019. https://www.publiccharters.org/about-charter-schools.

9 "Wisconsin - Milwaukee Parental Choice Program." EdChoice. Accessed April 1, 2019. https://www.edchoice.org/school-choice/programs/wisconsin-milwaukee-parental-choice-program/.

10 "School Choice in America Dashboard." EdChoice. Accessed April 1, 2019. https://www.edchoice.org/school-choice/school-choice-in-america/.

11 Pershing, Ben. "House Likely to Approve D.C. School Choice Bill, but Future in Limbo." *The Washington Post*. March 30, 2011. Accessed April 1, 2019. https://www.washingtonpost.com/blogs/dc-wire/post/house-likely-to-approve-dc-school-choice-bill-but-future-in-limbo/2011/03/30/AFe2lH3B_blog.html?noredirect=on&utm_term=.4a298d385115.

12 Forster, Greg. "A Win-Win Solution – The Empirical Evidence of School Choice." Friedman Foundation. May 2016. Accessed April 1, 2019. http://www.edchoice.org/wp-content/uploads/2016/05/A-Win-Win-Solution-The-Empirical-Evidence-on-School-Choice.pdf.

13 Ibid.

14 "What Impact Does School Choice Have On Public Schools?" Empower Mississippi. September 27, 2017. Accessed April 1, 2019. http://empowerms.org/impact-school-choice-public-schools/.

15 Lueken, Martin. "Fiscal Effects of School Vouchers." EdChoice. September 2018. Accessed April 1, 2019. https://www.edchoice.org/wp-content/uploads/2018/09/

Fiscal-Effects-of-School-Vouchers-by-Martin-Lueken.pdf; Lueken, Martin. "The Fiscal Effects of Tax-credit Scholarship Programs in the United States." Taylor & Francis. April 5, 2018. Accessed April 1, 2019. https://www.tandfonline.com/doi/full/10.1080/155821 59.2018.1447725.

16 "Arizona-Empowerment Scholarship Accounts." EdChoice. Accessed April 1, 2019. https://www.edchoice.org/school-choice/programs/arizona-empowerment-scholarship-accounts/.

17 Abelson, Reed. "In Bid for Better Care, Surgery with a Warranty," *New York Times*. May 17, 2007. Accessed March 30, 2019. https://www.nytimes.com/2007/05/17/business/17quality.html.

18 Joseph, DiMasi A., Henry G. Gabrowski, and Ronald W. Hansen. "Innovation in the Pharmaceutical Industry: New Estimates of R&D Costs." Journal of Health Economics. February 12, 2016. Accessed March 30, 2019. https://www.sciencedirect.com/science/article/abs/pii/S0167629616000291?via=ihub.

19 Ibid.

20 Horton, Nic and Jonathan Ingram, "A Budget Crisis in Three Parts: How Obamacare Is Bankrupting Taxpayers," Foundation for Government Accountability. February 6, 2018. Accessed March 30, 2019. https://thefga.org/wp-content/uploads/2018/02/A-Budget-Crisis-In-Three-Parts-2-6-18.pdf.

21 "A Premium Support System for Medicare: Updated Analysis of Illustrative Options," Congressional Budget Office. October 5, 2017. Accessed March 30, 2019. https://www.cbo.gov/publication/53077.

22 NRO Staff. "Total Welfare Spending Now at $1 Trillion." *National Review*. October 10, 2017. Accessed April 1, 2019. https://www.nationalreview.com/corner/total-welfare-spending-now-1-trillion-nro-staff/.

23 "Medicaid's Share of State Budgets." MACPAC. 2017. Accessed April 1, 2019. https://www.macpac.gov/subtopic/medicaids-share-of-state-budgets/.

24 Russell, Jason. "How Much Does Your State Spend on Welfare?" *Washington Examiner*. February 12, 2015. Accessed April 1, 2019. https://www.washingtonexaminer.com/how-much-does-your-state-spend-on-welfare.

25 Loughead, Katherine. "Gas Tax Rates, July 2018 | State Gas Tax Rankings." Tax Foundation. May 02, 2019. Accessed March 30, 2019. https://taxfoundation.org/state-gas-tax-rates-july-2018/.

26 Vock, Daniel C. "States, Not Just Feds, Struggle to Keep Gas Tax Revenue Flowing." Governing. May 18, 2015. Accessed March 30, 2019. https://www.governing.com/topics/transportation-infrastructure/gov-gas-tax-revenue-states-inflation.html.

27 Utt, Ronald. "'Turn Back' Transportation to the States." The Heritage Foundation. February 7, 2012. Accessed March 30, 2019. https://www.heritage.org/transportation/report/turn-back-transportation-the-states.

28 Fottrell, Quentin. "More than 44% of Americans Pay No Federal Income Tax." Market-Watch. February 26, 2019. Accessed March 30, 2019. https://www.marketwatch.com/story/81-million-americans-wont-pay-any-federal-income-taxes-this-year-heres-why-2018-04-16.

29 Lundeen, Andrew. "The Top 1 Percent Pays More in Taxes than the Bottom 90 Percent." Tax Foundation. January 16, 2017. Accessed March 30, 2019. https://taxfoundation.org/top-1-percent-pays-more-taxes-bottom-90-percent/.

30 Hatchen, Matthew (ed.), *The Chestertonian Library: An Anthology of Chesterton's Works from 1891-1922*, vol 1, *Fiction: The Hill of Humor*, pp. 288, Hagios Books, 2017.

31 DePrisco, Adrienne. "Is Communism Good for the Environment?" Victims of Communism Memorial Foundation. April 20, 2018. Accessed March 31, 2019. https://www.victimsofcommunism.org/witnessblog/2018/4/20/is-communism-good-for-the-environment.

32 Ridgeway, James. "Environmental Devastation in the Soviet Union." U.S.S.R. In Crisis. September 1990. Accessed March 31, 2019. https://www.multinationalmonitor.org/hyper/issues/1990/09/ridgeway.html.

33 Méndez, Daniel Fernández. "The Real Relationship Between Capitalism and the Environment | Daniel Fernández Méndez." Mises Institute. January 12, 2018. Accessed April 1, 2019. https://mises.org/wire/real-relationship-between-capitalism-and-environment.

34 Roberts, James M., and Ryan Olson. "How Economic Freedom Promotes Better Health Care, Education, and Environmental Quality." The Heritage Foundation. September 11, 2013. Accessed April 1, 2019. https://www.heritage.org/international-economies/report/how-economic-freedom-promotes-better-health-care-education-and.

35 Woolley, Scott. "Tesla Is Worse Than Solyndra - How the U.S. Government's Bungled Investment in the Car Company Cost Taxpayers at Least $1 Billion." *Slate Magazine*. May 29, 2013. Accessed April 1, 2019. https://slate.com/business/2013/05/tesla-is-worse-than-solyndra-how-the-u-s-government-bungled-its-investment-in-the-car-company-and-cost-taxpayers-at-least-1-billion.html.

36 Liautaud, Alexa. "White House Acknowledges the U.S. Is at War in Seven Countries." VICE News. March 15, 2018. Accessed April 5, 2019. https://news.vice.com/en_us/article/a3ywd5/white-house-acknowledges-the-us-is-at-war-in-seven-countries.

CHAPTER 12

1 Billington, James and Library of Congress, *Respectfully Quoted: A Dictionary of Quotations*, pp. 149, 2010.

2 Kirk, Russell. *The Conservative Mind: From Burke to Eliot*, 8. Washington, DC: Regnery Publishing, Inc., 1985.

3 Ibid., 8.

4 Wormald, Benjamin. "U.S. Public Becoming Less Religious." Pew Research Center's Religion & Public Life Project. April 25, 2018. Accessed April 2, 2019. https://www.pewforum.org/2015/11/03/u-s-public-becoming-less-religious/.

5 AP. "Sex-change Treatment for Kids on the Rise." CBS News. February 20, 2012. Accessed April 5, 2019. https://www.cbsnews.com/news/sex-change-treatment-for-kids-on-the-rise/.

6 Eliot, T. S. *Murder in the Cathedral*. San Diego, CA: Harcourt, 1964.

7 Lewis, C.S. *The Joyful Christian*. B&H Publishing Group. April 1, 2000.

8 Kirk, Russell. *The Conservative Mind: From Burke to Eliot*, 8. Washington, DC: Regnery Publishing, Inc., 1985.

9 Durden, Tyler. "Which Political Party Does Corporate America Love The Most: Here's The Visual Answer." Zero Hedge. April 7, 2018. https://www.zerohedge.com/news/2018-04-05/visualizing-which-political-party-corporate-america-loves-most.

10 Senator Mike Lee, Speech on the Senate floor, March 29, 2019. Accessed May 20, 2019. https://www.lee.senate.gov/public/index.cfm/2019/3/remarks-on-the-green-new-deal.